*System Design for
Computer Applications*

System Design for

Computer Applications

H. N. LADEN, PH.D.

Chief, New Systems Development
Chesapeake and Ohio Railway Company
also
Director and Chief Staff Consultant
National Computer Analysts, Inc.

T. R. GILDERSLEEVE

Manager of Programming
and Technical Services
for the UNIVAC III
Sperry Rand Corporation

John Wiley & Sons, Inc.   New York · London · Sydney

18 17 16 15 14 13 12 11 10 9

Library of Congress Catalog Card Number: 63-17363

Printed in the United States of America

CONTENTS

PART ONE

The Computer

1

INTRODUCTION

TERMS

TERMS OF REFERENCE — BUSINESS DATA PROCESSING

The general business organization can be conceived of as a system of channels connecting the organization's parts with each other and with the organization's environment—its customers; vendors and stockholders; the government; service organizations, such as Blue Cross, insurance companies, and banks; employee unions and numerous other facets of the external world. Money, material, and other resources flow through these channels to create the conditions necessary for the organization's survival in its environment. Business data processing is the part of the organization's operation that is concerned with the attempt to record, measure, and control the flow of money, materials, and other resources through the channels making up the organization's "circulation system".

SYSTEM DESIGN

Systems and procedures activity within the business organization is concerned with the critical analysis of the data processing operations and their redesign. The entire business may be made the subject of a system study in some far-reaching efforts. The philosophy for such an approach has come to be known as the Total System Concept. More commonly, but possibly less profitably, the business is segmented into subsystems on the basis of function, organization, region, product line, or other integral characteristics. The data processing operations are then studied for subsystems or for specific units or procedures within the subsystems.

Regardless of the specific devices that may be incorporated into a system in the course of redesign, the systems activity follows a well-defined course—a period of fact-finding and analysis followed by a period of creative synthesis of a new system, first in broad design and

3

then in detailed design. Since our concern is primarily with computer-oriented systems, this course will now be run for such a system design project. Hopefully, this should clarify the terms of reference—system and procedures activity, computer system design, and programming.

SYSTEM ANALYSIS

The first phase of any system project is devoted to the analysis of the existing business data system. Facts are gathered about the old or existing operations within the system. Close attention must be paid to exceptions as well as to routine procedures. Almost invariably probing into function or purpose of the system leads to an early concentration within fact finding on the definition of system objective and on the collection and description of the existing output. This helps define the boundaries of the system.

In the determination of output requirements, one is concerned with the contents, format, timing of delivery, and frequency of updating of information supplied by the system. The data may be intermediate reports requiring later completion, finished reports, vouchers, checks, punched cards for further processing, incidental tabulations, phone calls, and so on. One needs to list all those to whom the output is distributed and needs to examine the use to which each puts his copy of the output. External distribution is especially noted, and legal or other uncontrollable restrictions imposed thereby are documented. Again, the broadness of definition of output is emphasized. It includes incidental summarizations which are fed backward rather than forward in the chain, such as work-in-progress reports, error listings, and so forth.

When the purposes and outputs of a system are established, one needs to establish how these are achieved in the system. What is the raw material for the data process? In answering this question, all inputs, their origins, and initiators are determined. Who outside the system also gets this same data? What is the phenomenon of the business being recorded and in what medium? What is the nature and format of the existing source documents? What in the input is fixed or predictable and what is variable and relatively unpredictable? What problems of accuracy (precision) and completeness (missing data) exist? What are the volumes of input data to be ingested? What legal or other restrictions exist? A comprehensive view of what constitutes input must be taken. For example, one must include various directories and reference files, changes thereto, standard rules and regulations presently used to make decisions in the handling of exceptional cases, telephoned reports, and other such data sources.

The analysis of facts gathered utilizes a variety of criteria and techniques. Output can be screened for relevance and purposefulness, redundancy, cost of a particular medium and format, and the convenience to the user of the output. In particular, many an output may be marked for disestablishment. Many intermediate outputs may well be disestablished in a redesigned system that produces a new output to more completely satisfy the ultimate purposes of the system. Similar considerations govern the analysis of input. Inevitably, there will occur frequently during this analysis ideas and notions for revision of the system under study. Hence, the creation of a new system is not truly distinct in time from the fact-finding and analysis phase.

SYSTEM SYNTHESIS

Synthesis of a new system begins with a statement of new or validated old objectives and purposes. This tends to provide at least broad direction and constraint to output. With this preliminary vision of output and its general content, one re-examines input possibilities. Often one is confronted with numerous outputs stemming from a multiplicity of overlapping source data. A major portion of the system synthesis is the study of inputs used in a variety of related sections and the provision for coordination of their collection. This can be the source of improvement in completeness of the input. It makes each input record more generally available to all potential outputs and users. It is also the source of major economies in processing. Elimination of partial or total overlap in reporting, pooling of related information fed in from a variety of sources, and mechanization of data recording as close to a source as possible, so that further extraction and transcription can be handled automatically, are among the principles used. If part or all of a body of source data is really fixed, then procedures are established to avoid reporting these data anew as if they are unknown. If the source data are predictable, *exception reporting* or other techniques exploiting statistical bias may be used. In these, only changes from prediction are reported *in extenso*. Unchanged source data are assumed present or reported in abbreviated form. Numerous document design tricks and machine devices exist for supplementing fixed and predictable data with unpredicted and variable data at substantially lower cost than that of full reporting of source data.

Input redesign includes considerations of the control of quality, timing, field procedures for the recording of source data, standardization of format, and so forth. The subsequent problems and costs of encoding, converting from one medium to another, and the multiple uses of the document are considered in the redesign. For example, it may include introduction of prepunched and preprinted forms for reporting fixed or predictable information. Recording, communications, and data conversion procedures for delivering input must be economically provided consistent with volume, quality, and timing factors.

Of course, the same concerns exist in the delivery of output to users. In the core of the new system, one provides for coordinating the production of all those outputs which relate to or are dependent upon the same reservoir of basic input information. Intermediate products are eliminated and outputs are tailored to the specific needs of the ultimate user. This causes the core of the new system to provide for bridging gaps between sections engaged in sequential activity rather than independent activities. The medium and format of ultimate output may be revised to make it more economical to produce by a particular mechanism. New methods and procedures may be designed for the production and distribution of output. Extension, discard, and redesign of previous output is almost a certain consequence of intensive system study in an area if one takes advantage of the opportunity to make numerous incidental methods improvements, fundamental changes in accounting and management control systems, desirable organizational changes, or similar revisions.

A major step in the synthesis of the new system is the derivation of an overall, logical block diagram representing the gross steps for going from inputs to outputs. These steps are themselves complexes of operations such as file maintenance, computing, editing, and so forth. The steps must be feasible in the light of the machinery and techniques envisioned for incorporation into the system. The designation of the steps is often defended by analogy or experience. Actually, attempts at this diagram begin almost with the initial analysis, since it represents one way in which the system analyst expresses, from time to time, his success at correlating the facts he has gathered. When the block diagram is finished it represents a gross logical description of the application.

With this logical structure in mind, the input and output requirements can be re-examined for compatibility, not only with the machinery and techniques to be incorporated into the system, but also with the organizational problems peculiar to the company. Decentralized or centralized input; source document creation—supervised or not; communications needs; central reports distribution or regional autonomy and review—all these problems and many more of an equipment, organizational, or procedural nature need to be resolved.

Wherever reference is made here to the design of new procedures, there is implied an important task of training personnel of the revised organization in the new procedures, preliminary to their test and installation, as well as the task of conducting the test and installation.

Up to this point, the description of systems activity applies quite generally without regard to machinery and techniques to be used within the system. It is only when the designer of the system is confronted with the problem of optimum employment of the specific machinery that the activity becomes specialized.

Computer system design begins with the consideration of a computer as an alternative solution to the problems presented by the operational requirements of a proposed system. Prototype system designs may be prepared using a variety of approaches—hardware and procedural. The probable costs of each of these should be estimated and due weight given to the differences in degree of fulfillment of requirements. In any event, once a computer solution is selected for installation, computer system design may proceed further.

In the design of the prototype system that incorporates a computer, computer orientation is necessary for meaningful results. It is extremely important, for instance, that the synthesis of the new system not be only the speeding up of the procedures of the old system. The new system must reflect a reorganization of the entire operation so that pieces are related to each other in much more direct, although more complex, logical patterns. That is, we must exploit not only the speed, but also the tremendous versatility and capacity of the computer to effect real economy. Thus, the synthesis of the new system is likely to be satisfactory only if the system and procedures personnel have been properly oriented to computer thinking. Even the analysis of the old system proceeds more satisfactorily with people who have the computer constantly in mind. Without this, the system analyst tends to get lost in detailed flow diagrams of the internal procedures in an area. These internal procedures reflect the limitations of precomputer tools and are largely irrelevant to the computer system design.

Within the framework of a system design which includes a computer, the system design activity has not yet been completely described. The next phase begins with the logical block diagram of complex operations. This must be broken down into acceptable steps, called runs, involving as input specific reels of tape, bundles of machine interpretable documents, decks of punched cards, and keyboard insertions, and producing as output still other specific reels of tape, printed copy, punched cards with or without imprinting, and so forth.

In a run, one generally tries to include the maximum amount of processing of each item of data one can accomplish within the existing limitation of input and output facilities. The number of these holds down the variety of input items and output product. The memory size and speed of the computer may limit the complexity of the run, as will the availability of output facilities. In some computers, minor print-outs can be produced on the Supervisory Control or Console Printer to make available an additional product. All the instructions may sometimes be dumped into memory to clear external facilities for additional output or input use.

More often, however, one cannot make the run more complex without bringing in some supplementary input from still other input media; there are not, however, enough input handling facilities available. Exploiting the full capability of the computer has as yet not been completely reduced to a science. There is room for substantial virtuosity!

When the block diagram has been refined into a run structure, the individual input and output streams are assigned names and numbers and assigned to specific external facilities. Estimates of number of items to be handled in each input and output stream and on each facility are made. The item itself is designed; an *item layout* is the counterpart of a card format in punched card technology. If files are to be stored internally, as on drums or discs, speed and capacity requirements are checked for conformity to equipment limitations. The number of reels of tape in each data variety which uses tape can then be estimated. This should be completed for all tapes associated with a run. Also, the number of tape handlers should be prescribed for each tape set (tape-swap or no, and so on). When this assignment of facilities and identification with corresponding input and output streams has been completed, one can turn to the run itself.

Each run is assigned a name and number. A detailed verbal description of the processing to be accomplished in the run is prepared and filed in a Run Book with the item layouts for both input and output items as well as for perpetually stored files such as exist in random access computer applications.

PROGRAMMING

Beyond this, the narrower technical functions of programming begin. With a rough conception of the way in which the available memory will be used, and sometimes with a specific memory-allocation chart developed early in the run programming, a detailed flow chart is developed. The distinction in a flow chart is that it bridges the gap between a verbal run description and the actual step-by-step instruction coding, by grouping standard complexes of computer code steps. It is essential that such a flow chart show all branchings of the manipulative streams, all logical decision points, and alternative choices.

With a flow chart in hand, the programmer proceeds to write precise sequences of instructions in a rigidly prescribed *source language* vocabulary on code sheets. The lines of coding are supplemented with reference data and informative annotations. These instructions are prepared in such a way that they can be entered readily into the computer. All the material related to the run—code sheets, print-outs of instruction tapes properly annotated, item layouts, memory allocations, operator instructions, flow charts, and so on, are filed in the Run Book. Of course, if the processing involves external input or output conversion, there is another variety of activity in some computers. The programmer must prepare card layouts for direct card input/output or for the tape-to-card conversion, plugboard wiring diagrams for the converter, and operator instructions; for card-to-tape conversion, one needs a plugboard wiring diagram, operator instructions, and test cards. Similar material must be provided for other auxiliary equipment such as the High Speed Printer, document readers, and perforated tape readers and punches.

In order to make tests of our coded programs, we are obliged to have sample data and even to handle actual data for a period of time. This implies that certain nonprogramming tasks are underway or completed and that sufficient progress has been made in the installation of new procedures and in the training of the line clerical organization so that such data can be made available. Also, the computer center must be staffed and the staff familiarized with the new instructions provided by the programmer.

The programmer must know what constitutes an adequate sample of data with which to test the coded program. Certainly, such a sample must provide for the occurrence of all the exceptions whose treatment the programmer proposes to mechanize.

The practice is to *debug* individual runs using synthetic test data in small volume. Beyond this, sequences of related runs are integrated into subsystems using samples of data. Finally, the entire system can be tested with sample data. The next step is to try the computer system in competition with the existing one. This is called parallel operation. The computer is obliged to handle typical volumes of actual data and the results of computer and existing system are compared. Hopefully, few errors crop up and last-minute patching is then effected. Also, timing trials presumably indicate the computer can meet its commitments. The computer system is then ready to assume the responsibility for production.

Meanwhile, of course, preparation elsewhere in the business for a rapid reshaping of the existing data processing system in the organization, and possibly even of the entire organization, has been in process. This is rough going, because initially there must be expansion to provide such services as test data and checking to the computer group; expansion to release personnel from normal production activity in order that the training and installation of new procedures be planned for and effected; and expansion to provide for planning and effecting the inevitable post-computer reorganization and cost reductions. These points are emphasized because it is only too easy to obscure the fact that computerization calls for intense, organization-wide involvement and the closest team work. Credit for its success seldom attaches to any one or any few individuals.

COMPUTER PERSONNEL

Thus, many classes of people and types of skills are involved in a major project involving the study and reshaping of the data processing operations of a business system; the study may possibly involve a revision of the fundamental aspects of management's approach to the problems of the business. Various activities have been described in a general system and procedures framework as well as unique activity that is specifically oriented toward application of a computer within data processing operations. The work of programmers and computer-oriented system designers has been described. Of course, there are machine operators both for the computer, its peripheral equipment, and for other supporting equipment in the office machinery field.

The emphasis here is on delineating the tasks of both programmer and computer system designer. The programmer is the man who prepares the instructions telling the computer what operations to perform and in what sequence to perform them. The system designer is the man who studies the company data processing operation proposed to be handled by the computer, determines what has to be done to implement the operation, decides how it is to be done on the computer, and directs the programmer in the programming of the computer to effect the implementation of the operation.

OBJECTIVES AND SCOPE

Briefly stated, this book is a text for computer system designers. To understand the problems faced by the computer system designer and to appreciate the tools available for his use, one must be conversant with programming. This programming knowledge, on the reader's part, is assumed here. If the reader does not have experience in the programming field, it is recommended that he initiate his study of this book with the perusal of a programming text such as *Programming Business Computers* by Daniel D. McCracken, Harold Weiss, and Tsai-Hwa Lee, John Wiley and Sons, New York, 1959.

More specifically, the objective of this book is to instruct in the principles of computer system design and their application. It is assumed that general system activity has resulted in an agreed on definition of the scope of the system. Within this definition, our objective is to produce efficient computer systems. It is assumed that the reader not only has some familiarity with programming, but also has some background in general system and procedures activity without particular orientation toward any type of hardware. In the bibliography of this book several texts about systems work are included for those who feel inadequately conversant with the terms of reference reviewed. However, many of the matters discussed in this book are as completely pertinent viewed in the context of general systems activity as they are within computer system design. Further, the increasing incorporation of computer devices within new designs for business data processing systems makes the principles enunciated here of relevance virtually to every systems and procedures staff.

Similarly, this is not a programmer's handbook; however, it does concentrate on the principles underlying computer system design. These principles and their application result in designs which must be implemented by the programmer. One can expect many programmers to have a curiosity about the rationale for the design and to seek an understanding of the basis for the constraints and directions provided in the run descriptions furnished to them by the system designer. In some systems organizations, design activity may not be clearly delineated from programming. In short, there is much in this book which should be of distinct interest to the programmer although it is primarily addressed to the computer system designer.

There are computers and there are other computers, even when one is restricted to digital computers as is the case here. Considering the fundamentally different characteristics among some of the varieties, it is difficult to evoke principles fully applicable to all types. A less awkward solution has been adopted here. It is to place emphasis on (magnetic) tape-handling, batch-processing computers. This emphasis is not an exclusion of other types of systems, since the material presented often applies to several types and the text generally states and identifies each one. Also, an alternative version or corresponding principle for the remaining types of computers is frequently provided. If this is not done invariably, it is sometimes because no corresponding situation exists for the types other than the one covered.

The reader should have no illusion that this work is encyclopedic enough to cover all the principles applicable to each computer. Certainly other books will be forthcoming specializing in each variety of computer. There is, however, much in this volume applicable to punched card systems, random-access serial processors, real-time on-line systems, so-called satellite computers, computers with off-line peripherals, computers with on-line peripherals, word-addressable and character-addressable computers, computers with serial or parallel arithmetic, conventional and concurrent-processing (multiprogramming) computers, and so forth. This is the era of modularity, the custom-tailored hardware configuration, and the time-shared multiplexing of applications. The type labels listed here are no longer so neatly differentiating as they once were. For example, the multiprogrammed tape computer, in which the main high-speed memory (generally magnetic core storage) has been supplemented by intermediate speed memories (drums or discs) of longer access times but much higher capacity, becomes a real-time on-line system for random access processing as well as a batch processor. Why, it even becomes an automatic message switching and relay center in the hub of a multistation intercommunication system, as well as a computer in the more traditional sense! Thus, there is no need to be excessively apologetic about not exhausting the principles of computer system design peculiarly dependent upon the equipment characteristics of each variety of computer installation. It is a comfort that many of the principles cited are so firmly based on fundamentals in information theory and on the essential nature of data processing that they are indeed pertinent directly or with minor modification to virtually every variety of computer mentioned.

STRUCTURE OF THE TEXT

This book is divided into three parts. Part one deals with system design considerations which result from the fact that a computer is being used as a data processor.

Part two is concerned with documents: the source documents in which the data to be processed by the computer are gathered, and the reports which are generated by the computer. Although much of the information in this part is general to the subject of form design, its emphasis is on those form-design considerations that are taken into account because the documents represent part of a computer system.

Part three deals with the broader aspects of the system designer's responsibility: how he conducts a study of a company operation, and how he implements the computer system he has designed.

ACKNOWLEDGMENT

In 1954–1955, The Chesapeake and Ohio Railway Company accelerated its pioneering efforts in business applications of electronic computers. There was then manifest a complete lack of formal training courses for personnel newly oriented to systems and procedures activity in general, and a lack of training with computer orientation in particular. Computer manufacturers provided limited customer training in programming techniques only.

To fill the training gap, C & O personnel began preparation of a textbook on systems and procedures and another on principles of computer system design. The former was never completed, but the draft was used to influence the Finance Division of the American Management Association to establish its now well-known courses in Systems and Procedures.

Repeated efforts were made over the next several years through various groups of computer users to interest manufacturers in the design of training courses transcending the coding aspects of computer activity. Although these efforts were not successful, the wide circulation of proposed course material was beneficial. Within Sperry Rand, experienced training officials were aware that the scope of the new training proposed would have a greater influence on the efficiency of computer applications than would coding dexterity. Some of the proposed material found its way into UNIVAC training and especially into technical literature directed to the experienced computer user.

With the onset of "second-generation" and even "third-generation" computers, there is manifest elaborate prefabricated programming libraries, English language programming, and a host of automatic programming schemes. The dependence on individual coding ingenuity as a method of achieving computer application efficiency has become reduced even more. Given the scope of a defined system, computer application efficiency has more and more come to be achieved through broader design aspects rather than through coding tricks.

It has become increasingly more common in organizing data processing activity to distinguish between system analysis, design and coding, and programming. With this demarcation, a clarification of training needs is provided. Training requirements for programmer responsibilities in such an organization have been met readily by computer manufacturers, schools, self-study, and so forth. Suitable programmer manuals are available. Courses in business systems are widely offered by numerous universities. However, none of these courses is specifically oriented toward efficient exploitation of a computer within the design of a business system. Most design know-how continues to be handed down as technical gossip or to be rediscovered.

This book draws together training material developed over the years by Dr. Laden and Mr. Gildersleeve. It incorporates the fruits of numerous intellectual exchanges among various members of Dr. Laden's staff, between them and other computer users, and among employees of Sperry Rand UNIVAC. Indeed, many of the principles cited and illustrative examples provided in this book stem from these exchanges. The present documentation stems from a system design course given by Sperry Rand UNIVAC for The Chesapeake and Ohio Railway Company during 1960 and 1961. Much of the material has been circulated in a series of internal memoranda within C & O and Sperry Rand. The authors express their gratitude to Sperry Rand for free access to the information in these publications. Significant results have also been selected from the literature which already exists on the subject of system design. In such an agglomeration, the ability to reference and acknowledge specific contributions is often lost. It is hoped that none is slighted thereby. Any shortcomings in this book should be attributed to the authors whose gratitude is extended to both the UNIVAC Division of the Sperry Rand Corporation and to The Chesapeake and Ohio Railway Company for providing access to information in company publications and files and for indulgence during the period of final preparation of this book.

2

INTRODUCTION TO COMPUTER
SYSTEM DESIGN

COMPUTERS IN SYSTEM DESIGN

Systems activity has been defined as a period of fact finding and analysis followed by a period of creative synthesis of a new system, first in broad design and then in detail. Fact finding is documentation. Analysis consists of a critical evaluation of the existing business data system, its objectives, outputs, and inputs. System synthesis consist broadly of a restatement of objectives, a definition of output in terms of these objectives, and a reorganization of the input data gathering and processing required to produce this output. There is literature covering these subjects. References are included in the bibliography at the end of the book.

As indicated in the previous chapter, when computing hardware is to be used in the implementation of the system, there comes a point in system synthesis at which consideration must be given to the computer, its characteristics, and the opportunities these characteristics offer for increased data processing efficiency. It is in this area of interaction between data processing goals to be achieved and the computer hardware to be used in reaching these goals that the knowledge referred to here as computer system design is applicable.

Computer system design is almost totally unformalized and undocumented. Knowledge in this area consists of principles, maxims and rules of thumb existing in overlapping but not congruent sets in the minds of people whose work is computer system design. These rules generally take the form of lessons distilled from the experiences of some project in which each person has engaged. They lack any statement in general form. A purpose of this book is to document many of these rules so that the novice computer system designer no longer will be dependent upon having them transmitted to him informally and unpredictably by word of mouth. Another purpose is to bring some of these principles, case histories, and examples together and group them into categories.

Computer system design begins with the block diagram of the data

15

processing system prepared as a result of system synthesis. This chart must be broken down into computer runs. In doing this job, the system designer's basic tool is the process chart.

THE PROCESS CHART

A process chart is a set of symbols representing computer *center* operations. The symbols are connected by arrows to indicate the sequence of operations. The process chart is the master plan of a computer system. It shows the inputs to the system, the outputs from the system, and the runs which take place to produce the various outputs from the one or numerous inputs. The process chart is a graphic representation of the coarse flow of data through the entire computer system.

A process chart may be contrasted with a flow chart. A flow chart is a set of symbols representing *internal* computer operations. The symbols are connected by arrows to indicate sequence. A flow chart and process chart differ in the operations symbolized.

On a process chart, the operations are computer center equipment processing operations that accept external input and produce external output. On a flow chart, the operations are small logical steps taken internally within a computer process to effect the process. The steps in a flow chart may be as small as individual order codes of the computer and as large as substantial clusters of such codes, called macroinstructions or subroutines. For each operation on a process chart, usually called a run, there is a flow chart to show how the processing operation within the run is achieved internally by the computer. A flow chart depicts the logical detail of a run; and a process chart, a related set of runs constituting the gross logical structure of a computer application or an integral subsection of such an application.

Because the process chart is a master plan, there are details it does not show. It does not show the format of input or output documents, the internal details of individual runs, the item design of files, or the programming techniques used. Sometimes it is concerned only with the computer system. In such cases it does not show manual, punched card, and other noncomputer operations required before and after computer operations. However, it can be, and often is, extended to show data flow for the entire application system, computer and otherwise.

Because the process chart is concerned only with the logical structure of a final system, it does not show the schemes for transition from existing to replacement systems. However, a plan for this transition may result in a transition system with a corresponding process chart of its own. The process chart does not show how a computer system is to be installed, what file creation schemes are to be used in implementing the system, or how the computer is to be scheduled for the system. It may, however, provide data on the frequency or other scheduling constraints on the processing. For example, the process chart may indicate that weekly paychecks are due Friday.

PROCESS CHART SYMBOLS

There is considerable agreement on the symbols used to represent the more common operations on a process chart. At present, process chart symbols and their content are established by convention at each computer installation. There is some variation from installation to installation. Standardization in this area is under active discussion by standards groups, but as yet no industrywide conventions have been established.

A run is symbolized by a rectangle as shown in Figure 2-1a. A gross

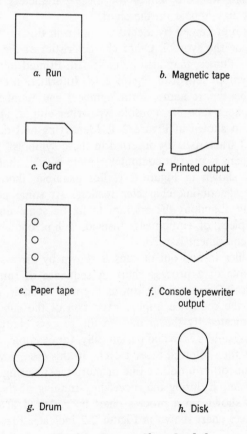

a. Run   b. Magnetic tape

c. Card   d. Printed output

e. Paper tape   f. Console typewriter output

g. Drum   h. Disk

Fig. 2-1 Process Chart Symbols

description of the processing done in the run is written in the rectangle or alongside it. If the run has several phases, the description of each is provided in sequence of performance.

A magnetic tape file is represented by a circle as shown in Figure 2-1b. Usually, the identification of the file is shown in the circle. Other characteristics of the file may be indicated also. Among these characteristics might be the following:

1. Item size or record length
2. Tape blocking, if optional
3. File size in items or blocks
4. Recording density, if optional
5. Reel size, if optional
6. Number of reels

In cases where standard values for these parameters are adopted, only exceptions may appear on the chart.

A card file is represented by a card as shown in Figure 2-1c. The file is identified inside the symbol. Other characteristics of the file, such as card types and volumes, may also be indicated. Printed output is represented by the symbol shown in Figure 2-1d. Information entered in the symbol might be report name, form number, and number of copies. Symbols for a paper tape file, console typewriter output, and drum and disk files are also shown in Figure 2-1. Identifying and descriptive information are characteristically inserted in these symbols.

Other equipment is used in computer centers besides that represented by the symbols shown in Figure 2-1. For example, there are optical scanners and magnetic-ink character readers. At some point, the installation usually abandons the attempt to fix on some unique symbol for each such piece of equipment. Instead, a box containing a label identifying the equipment is used.

The flow of files in and out of runs is shown by arrows. Figure 2-2 shows an example of a process chart. A sequence of runs such as is shown in Figure 2-2 is generally run as a group. That is, execution of the first run in the sequence implies execution of the subsequent runs in the order indicated by the arrows on the process chart. Such a sequence of runs is usually executed periodically, for example, once a week. The sequence is then referred to as a cycle, in this case, a weekly cycle.

A cycle of runs often produces one or more tapes during one running that are used as input during the succeeding running of the cycle. Such an operation is shown on a process chart by a dotted arrow. For example, the process chart shown in Figure 2-2 indicates that the updated master file produced during one cycle becomes the input master file on the succeeding cycle.

Conformity in the use of symbols on process charts is an aid to communication, since it allows others familiar with the symbols to read the system designer's process chart.

In succeeding chapters, we discuss characteristic process charts and the computer-system design considerations underlying them for a large number of prototype business data processing operations.

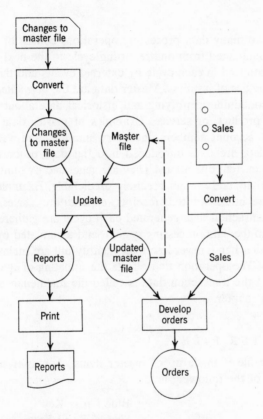

Fig. 2-2 Example of a Process Chart

3

FILE MAINTENANCE

The inputs to many data processing operations consist of two types: master data maintained from one reporting cycle to the next, and transaction data produced in each cycle by external events and the variations in internal activities of business. Master data are the *permanent information records* containing identifying and historical data about an individual, account, product, or service. Examples of master data are names and addresses, account numbers, inventory amounts, and wearout rates. Transaction data are data introduced into the data processing system in response to current operations. They are generated by human or other behavioral activity and are not precisely predictable. Examples of transaction data are hours worked, receipts, expenditures, sales, and shipments. The transaction data generated each cycle are gathered together, introduced into the data processing system, and assimilated by it. Master data, on the other hand, never lose their identity but are maintained from cycle to cycle. The operation that effects the updating of the master file on the basis of the transaction data is called file maintenance and is the subject of this chapter.

THE MASTER FILE

The master file is made up of master items. A master payroll item might consist of the following fields.

Badge Number
Name
Address
Social Security Number
Hourly Rate
Days Absence Allowed per Year
Number of Income Tax Exemptions
Union Dues Key

Blue Cross Key
Size of Bond Key
Weekly Bond Deduction Amount
Cumulative Total of Bond Deductions
Number of Days Classified Absence
Number of Days Personal Absence
Number of Days Medical Absence

Number of Days Laid Off	Year-to-date FICA Taxable Earnings
Total Hours Worked	
Quarter to date FICA Taxable Earnings	Year-to-date FICA Tax
	Year-to-date Gross Earnings
Quarter to date FICA Tax	Year-to-date Withholding Tax

A master inventory item might consist of the following fields.

Stock Number	Emergency Lead Time
Material Description	Vendors Name and Address
Issuing Unit of Measure	Vendor Code
Ordering Unit of Measure	Storage Location
Onhand Quantity	Shipping Point
Onorder Quantity	Class
Maximum Quantity	Average Cost Price
Minimum Quantity	Month-to-date Issued Amount
Emergency Quantity	Month-to-date Issued Quantity
Reorder Quantity	Reconciliatory Factor
Lead Time	

MASTER FILE ORDER

To post transactions to the master file, the master file must be in some order. There are two fundamental considerations in choosing master file order. One is how much sorting the order chosen forces on the system. The other is the susceptibility of the order to change. These considerations apply in full force to tape computers processing batch data in serial fashion. Another consideration often encountered in random access computers is the ease of generating the location of the master file item from the contents of the transaction to be posted. For example, master file items may be assigned locations addressed directly by a key in the transaction item. This consideration is sometimes also present in tape computer processing, especially where all or a substantial part of a file manages to fit into memory at one time—table look-up, for example.

For efficient computer utilization, the input files to a run generally must have the data on them recorded in some compatible order. Some sorting of input files must be done to achieve this compatibility. Thus, sorting is inevitable. Even for random access processing, sorting of input transactions often contributes to efficiency of processing. However, while necessary to accomplish data processing, sorting itself does no data processing. Consequently, sorting should be kept to a minimum to maximize efficiency. One factor influencing the amount of sorting required is master file order. Master file order should be chosen to minimize the sorting required.

Master file order should not be subject to change. For example, keeping a payroll master file in order by badge number, the most significant digits of which are a departmental designation, necessitates stripping a man's master item from the file and reinserting it in its proper place each time the man makes an interdepartmental transfer. If possible, a master file order that necessitates such rearranging should be avoided. However, in the case given here, such rearranging is the lesser of two evils. The purpose of payroll data processing is to provide management with reports that reflect manpower utilization. Such reports are the basis for managerial decision. One thing that contributes to the usefulness of these reports is a breakdown by department. To get such a breakdown, either these reports must be produced by processing an employee master file that is in departmental order, or the output tapes from which the reports are to be printed must be sorted into departmental order before printing takes place. The computer time required to handle the occasional rearrangement of master file items necessitated by interdepartmental transfer is more than compensated for by the savings achieved in the sorting time this master file order avoids.

That master file order which minimizes sorting is to be preferred. If more than one order satisfies this criterion, choose that order which is least susceptible to change. The justification for both criteria is the consequent reduction of time required for running the system.

FILE MAINTENANCE

File maintenance consists of passing the master file through a file maintenance run, which applies transactions to the master file and produces an updated file. This system is shown in Figure 3-1. It is characteristic of file maintenance that the updated master file of one cycle become the input master file of the succeeding cycle.

There are two types of transactions. One type involves the alteration of some master item field; this alteration is taken to include the deletion of an item from the file. This type of transaction ranges from the simple substitution of information as is called for by a change of name, address, or pay rate, through the arithmetic operations called for by a clockcard transaction item, to the complicated analysis of the stock situation that may be touched off by an order for a particular stock commodity. All such transactions are referred to in this book as changes. The second type of transaction is the addition of new master items to the master file. Such transactions are referred to as additions.

Despite the distinction between change and addition items, there is no necessity to create two transaction files —a change file and an addition file— for a file maintenance run. Consolidation of the items into one file has advantages. The only possible problem created by a consolidation of transaction items into one file may be that optimizing the design of the transaction item will be more difficult than when a change file and an addition file are used.

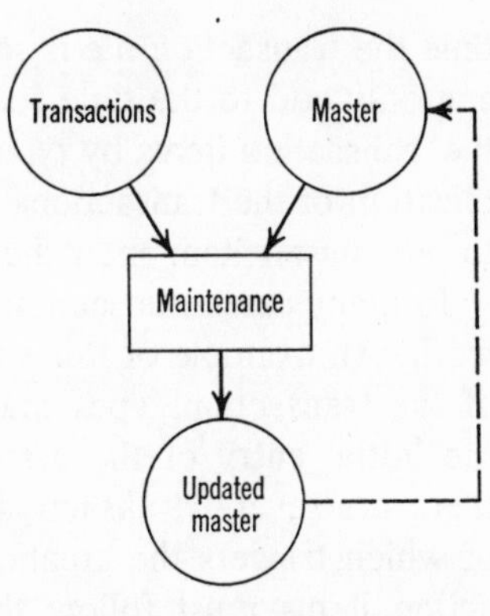

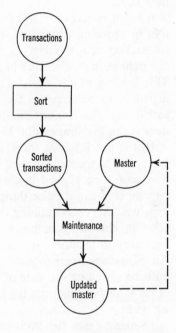

Fig. 3-1   File Maintenance

SORTING

Generally the transaction items to be applied to the master file are generated within the business in an order different from master file order. To apply efficiently the transactions to the master file, the transaction file must be in the same order as the master file. Consequently, a feature of file maintenance is a sort of the transaction file on the master item key before the transaction file becomes an input to the maintenance run. This addition to the file maintenance process is shown in Figure 3-2.

There is the possibility of several transaction items being present on the transaction file for the same master item. This situation may exist because there are different transaction types to be applied to the same master item during a cycle, or because there are several transactions of the same type to be applied to the same master item. In the former case, it may or may not be expedient to order these transactions by

Fig. 3-2   File Maintenance with Sorting

type. Against the ordering of the items by type is the fact that, although the operations to accomplish this ordering can be executed at the same time the transaction file is sorted by a master item key, these operations can only add to the time for execution of the sort. In favor of ordering the transaction items by type is the fact that it is easier to control the application of the transactions to the master file if all transactions referring to one master item enter the maintenance run by type in a known order.

In many cases transactions must be sorted by type to make the system work. An example of this situation is as follows. In many instances, one of the transaction types that can be applied to the master file triggers the initial entry of the associated master item into the master file. If there are several transaction items to be applied to a master item, one of which triggers the creation of the master item, then the other transaction items must follow the initiating transaction item on the transaction file. If such were not the case, the master item would be unavailable for other transactions to be applied. The remaining transaction items would have to be considered errors. In such a situation it pays to order by transaction type key all transaction items with the same master item key.

All that is necessary to order transactions as desired is to use discretion in choosing transaction type keys. For example, in the case of a transaction item to trigger a file item initiation, the transaction key for this item should be smaller in magnitude than any other transaction key. This loading of the transaction keys guarantees that, when all transaction items referring to the same master item are ordered by transaction key, the transaction item triggering the addition of the master item is the first transaction in the set.

If it is possible that there are many transactions of the same type to be applied to the same master item, it then becomes mandatory that these transactions be applied in chronological order. For example, if a man's payrate is changed twice during the same cycle, that employee's master item will end up containing the proper payrate only if changes are applied in chronological order. To achieve chronological ordering it is necessary to include a date of transaction field in the transaction item. All transaction items with the same master item and transaction type key must be sorted on this date of transaction field. This sorting can be done in the same run that sorts the transaction items by master item and transaction key.

In many cases the transaction file originates as a card deck. On a card computer, these transaction cards should generally be sorted externally on specialized card sorters. For other computers, the question arises of whether the transaction file should be fed to the computer and sorted there or sorted on tabulating equipment and then fed to the computer. One factor influencing this decision is the availability of idle time of card sorters. If this time is available, the question of which sorting technique is preferable may be real. If this time is not available, and idle computer time is available, it is likely that computer sorting will be preferable. In any event, the decision should be based on the incremental costs of the alternative procedures in the specific installation involved.

Some considerations involved in deciding how to sort are as follows.

1. The cost of sorting on tabulating equipment is more directly related to key size than is the case in computer sorting. On a card sorter each increase in key size results in a more than proportionate increase in cost. Cost of computer sorting is not independent of key size but increase in cost is in steps by word size of key, and is less than linear for fixed word-length computers. This same general characteristic is manifest even in character-addressable computers. The larger the size of the key, the less attractive card sorting becomes.

2. The sorting of keys containing alphabetics and special characters is cumbersome on card equipment. Such keys present no more problems to a computer sort than do numeric keys. When the key is alphanumeric, computer sorting gets the nod.

3. A further factor is item size. If card sorting implies handling headers and trailers because the item size exceeds the character capacity of the card, computer sorting is more economical.

4. The number of items is a consideration. Large volumes of cards are difficult to handle in a card sort. With computer sorting, large volumes of data present no particular problem.

5. It may be that the overall system calls for punched card processing of transaction data to precede the computer processing the data is scheduled to undergo. To do this card processing, it may also be necessary to sort the cards into the order required by the computer system. If such is the case, there is no reason why the computer system should not take advantage of the order of the card file. Some system designers maintain that requirement for some tabulating operation is the only justification for punched card sorting. In all other cases, sorting should be done on the computer.

6. It is faster to sort on tape computers than on card equipment. The former is measured in minutes and seconds, the latter in hours and minutes. If time is of the essence, transactions should be sorted on the computer. This statement may hold true even if the cards have to be sorted. Transaction cards can be converted to tape, the transaction items then being quickly computer sorted and fed into some computer process

where the time limit is tight; at the same time, the transaction cards can be more slowly sorted on tabulating equipment for some other purpose. This consideration may not apply in random access computers having no external tape handlers, since sorting is generally time consuming and costly in this case.

Even if transactions are sorted on card equipment, they do not completely escape computer preparation before they are fed into the maintenance run. Missorts in card sorting do occur. In a long deck, the probability that some lack of order exists is high. Experience indicates that a break in order occurs about once every 10,000 cards. A common technique for limiting the number of breaks is to subject the sorted card deck to a sequence check in a card collator. A few transaction items out of order on the transaction file can tie up the maintenance run. Consequently, transaction files that have been sorted on card equipment are put through a sequence check run before being matched against the master file. The sequence check ascertains that the items are ordered as expected. If missorts are detected, the misplaced items are stripped from the transaction file and reinserted in their proper places.

If an item is out of order when a sequence check on a file is made, it may take as long to complete the sequence check as it would have taken to sort the file in the first place. Since missorts on card equipment are not uncommon, the area for justifying a card sort of a file when that sort is not required for precomputer processing is small.

Sorting is subject to generalization and can be done by standardized routines generated in an automatic manner. Computer manufacturers develop such standardized sorts.

ERROR SITUATIONS

Another problem of file maintenance is brought about by the fact that transactions are prepared manually for introduction into the system. This manual preparation of transactions opens the door to the introduction of error into the system. Errors can creep in at two points. One is at the origination of the transaction, where the information concerning the transaction can be recorded incorrectly. The transpositions of digits in writing a man's new payrate is an example of this type of error. The other point at which error can be introduced into the system is the translation of the transaction into computer language. An example of this type of error is the striking of the S key on a keypunch when the intention was to strike the A key. The operations concerned with detecting the first type of error are known as validation. The operations concerned with detecting the second type of error constitute verification.

VERIFICATION

Verification characteristically involves a duplication of the translation process and is usually performed by some piece of equipment. If the transaction items are transcribed onto punched cards by means of a keypunch, verification consists of running the punched cards through a *verifier* which compares the holes in the cards with the key strokes made on the verifier by the verifier operator as he keys in the information from the source documents for the second time. Lack of agreement between a character punched in the card and the corresponding character struck on the verifier is automatically detected. The need for corrective action is indicated.

If it is a 90-column card in which the information is being punched, a different verification process is also available. After the card has been punched, the keypunch is set to the *verifier mode*. The card is punched again. The verifier mode of the keypunch causes the holes to be punched in the card to one side of where the holes are punched when the keypunch is in the *punch mode*. Consequently, every column of the card punched the same way during verification as it was punched during punching has only oval holes punched into it. Every column punched differently has at least one round hole. The cards are then run through a piece of equipment called a verifier, which checks for oval holes. Any card having round holes is rejected, indicating that a keypunching error has occurred.

Since the card transcription of data involves punching a hole in the card, the correction of any erroneous transcription usually necessitates the punching of a new card. To ease the burden of this repunching, card punches are equipped with a device that allows the correctly punched columns in the rejected card to control the repunching of the corresponding columns in the substitute card. Only the incorrect columns must be repunched manually.

Another medium of information transcription is punched paper tape. The punching of paper tape is verified in a variety of ways. One method involves the use of a paper tape verifier which operates in the same way as the previously described card verifier, that is, by comparing a punched tape with keystrokes on a keyboard. Another method requires the independent punching of the information into presumably duplicate tapes. The tapes are then matched by reading them simultaneously in a tape comparator. The comparator stops on the detection of a mismatch, and tape corrections then can be made.

Transcription of information on paper tape involves punching a hole in the tape. Correcting errors involves repunching the tape. Most keyboard devices used in the punching of paper tape have a paper-tape reader attached. The erroneous tape is inserted in the reader. The correct information is then read from the tape and automatically punched into a fresh tape. Finally, when the erroneous information is reached on the input tape, the automatic punching is halted, the erroneous information is skipped over on the reader, and the correct information is inserted on the fresh tape from the keyboard. Automatic reproduction of the rest of the tape is then made.

Paper tape often is used in communications systems. In some cases, information is keyed on a teletype board at one location, the information keyed is transmitted over a communications line, and the information is received at another point in the form of punched paper tape. In such communications systems, the cost of sending information over a line militates against dual transcription of the information for verification purposes.

Another approach to paper tape verification is to convert the tape to hard copy by means of a printing device and to proofread the hard copy. Since much paper tape is originated as a byproduct of the production of hard copy such as an invoice, this "conversion" and proofreading is an automatic part of the creation of the paper tape and can be accepted as an adequate verification procedure. In such cases, production of the paper tape and proofreading the hard copy go on concurrently. Similarly, a tabulator is often used to verify punched cards by proofreading against source documents.

In many instances the tape punch operator recognizes a key stroke error the instant it occurs. In such a situation the equipment allows the operator to punch a *delete code* over the erroneously punched frame on the paper tape. This delete code subsequently causes all paper tape equipment to use the tape to ignore the deleted code. After the delete code is punched, the operator can stroke the correct key and continue with the transcription.

In many instances in which paper tape is being produced as a byproduct of the creation of some document, portions of the document (and, consequently, portions of the paper tape) are automatically produced from another paper tape that is being read by a reader; the information which is read is being printed on the document and punched in the output paper tape. For example, in the case of an invoice, much of the header information, such as customer name and address, shipping address, and customer number, might be produced in this fashion. The input paper tapes that produce this information have been prefabricated, verified, stored, and are selected for use when appropriate. No verification of the portions of the output tape produced from these *prefabricated master tapes* should be necessary, since they are automatically reproduced from a tape known to be correct.

A third approach to paper tape verification is format control. Paper tape equipment allows *function controls* to be incorporated into its code. These function controls permit rigid format controls for printed output to be incorporated into the information being punched into the paper tape. The rigid format of the hard copy that results from printing a paper tape incorporating these format controls makes possible a relatively comprehensive verification of the punching of the paper tape by scanning the hard copy for deviations from this format. For example—if the format of paper tape is to print a field in a series of print positions; if the print positions surrounding those set aside for this field are to be left blank; if the field can consist of, at a maximum, four digits; and if the punch operator includes, in one item, five digits in this field—the operator's slip with respect to this item becomes obvious by scanning the column of figures which constitute the field.

The facility for format control also exists for punched cards. Tabulator listings of the cards are sometimes made to verify by visual inspection right and left justification of fields, segregation of alphabetics from numerics, and other common characteristics of the card.

One of the questions that arises with respect to verification is: How much of the information transcribed should be verified? Verification is a control procedure. Although important, and, in many cases, essential, it is of itself not productive. Consequently, there is pressure to reduce verification to a minimum.

There are instances in which verification is not necessary. For example, in a clockcard there are two types of data: data that contribute to the determination of a man's gross pay and data which are incorporated into labor distribution reports. There is an overlap between the two types of information. However, in many cases there are data which find their way into the labor distribution but which have no bearing on gross-pay determination. The clockcard data contributing to gross-pay determination must be verified. Correct pay is essential to good personnel relations. On the other hand, there is often a question as to whether the clockcard data which is material to the labor distribution alone needs verification. The labor distribution is statistical. If erroneous information is introduced into the compilation by keypunching error, the chances are that the difference in the distribution will not be managerially significant.

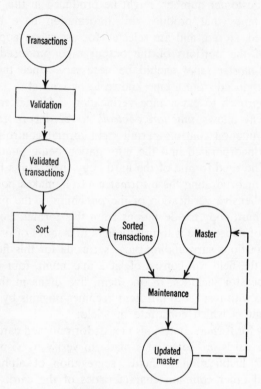

Fig. 3-3   File Maintenance with Validation

One fact bearing on the question of verification versus nonverification is that, when a field is not verified, the keypunching quality of that field drops. This situation is particularly the case when the verified and non-verified fields are segregated into two groups on the card. The knowledge that their work is going to be verified acts as an incentive to keypunch operators to keep the quality of their work high. One solution to the problem of keeping up the keypunching quality of those fields which would not otherwise have to be verified might be to verify these fields statistically; that is, to select small samples of the keypunching of these fields to be verified and to let the remaining keypunching of the fields go unverified. The Bureau of Census has developed statistical quality-control techniques for economical design of keypunching and key-verifying procedures.

The number of columns that are candidates for possible nonverification on a card is usually small. The size of the deck to be keypunched has to be large before savings due to nonverification of these fields can be realized. When the potential effect of nonverification on the accuracy of the keypunching of those fields is additionally considered, it becomes evident that the authenticity of promised savings should be seriously investigated before 100 percent verification of keypunching is abandoned.

VALIDATION

Validation of the transaction file is done by a run as shown in Figure 3-3. The purpose of the validation run is to check for the correctness and completeness of transaction data.

CONTROL TOTALS

One validation tool is the control total. A control total is a sum kept of some field or aspect of the data over a batch of data. For example, in the hourly payroll system each department may prepare, in addition to clock cards, a tabulator listing or adding machine tape showing a total of the number of hours worked in that department during the current pay period. Then, during the validity run of the clockcard items, the computer keeps a running total of the hours-worked field to compare against the department's total. This control total requires the clockcards from each department to be identifiable by department at the time they are introduced into the validation run, and segregatable upon the detection of error. Often, the clockcards are prepared and submitted to the data processing center by department and the controls necessary to maintain this departmental grouping throughout the data-preparation phase are not difficult to institute.

In the validation run for data batched by department, the hours-worked field of each clockcard is added to an hours-worked total, which the computer set to zero the last time the department designation changed, and which it has been accumulating ever since. When the department designation changes again, the computer takes the accumulated hours worked and checks it against the total supplied by the department submitting the involved clockcards.

This departmental total is made available to the computer by recording it on the clockcard tape as a bogus clockcard item either at the beginning or end of the set of items supplied by the department. This *control total item* may also be used by the validation routine to distinguish between the end of one batch and the beginning of the next.

The control total is a statistical method for determining that no data has been picked up or lost in the translation and communication of the data from its source to the computer. If an item has been dropped en route, or if an item gets duplicated, with the result that there are now two items where there should be one, the chances are remote that the control total created at the source of the data and the total accumulated by the computer are equal. Compensating errors are not that likely.

The reconciliation of a control total by the computer gives assurance that no data has been dropped or picked up within the batch to which the control total applies. However, it gives no assurance that a batch of data may not be mislaid. In those cases in which control totals are appropriate, it is generally the case that the number of batches of transaction data which should be received by the computer center from a data source for a data processing cycle is either fixed or is predictable from cycle to cycle. A checklist and count can validate that the computer center has received all batches of data from all sources for a cycle.

A problem intrinsic in checking control totals is that control totals refer to batches of data. A batch of data must be processed before the control totals associated with it can be checked. If the control totals do not check out, a good deal of data which has been proved to be invalid has already been written on the output tape of the validation run. One possible way this problem can be solved is to keep an item count on each batch of data. When the control totals for a batch do not check out, use this count to reposition the read-write head of the output tape to the beginning of the invalid batch of data. A more common practice is to create output which, upon use in a successor run, causes the bad batch to be discarded on an error file. The most common procedure calls for identifying all invalid batches to the computer operator and closing the validation run. These batches are later corrected and the run is attempted again.

Another consideration in the use of controls totals is the optimum size for the batch on which the control is kept. The batch size should not be too small, since each batch requires manual operations to create and maintain the control. It is undesirable from an economic point of view to require more operations in data origination than are necessary for provision of acceptable input data. On the other hand, the batch size should not be so large that it becomes difficult to locate an error, once it has been determined that one exists in a batch. For example, keypunching errors may occur at a level of about one half of one percent. Consequently, as far as detecting keypunching errors is concerned, batches of 100 cards are too small. There is too much investment in controls in terms of the errors that are expected to be caught. On the other hand, batches of 3000 cards are too large. When a control total does indicate an error, there are too many candidates for the card that does contain the error. Searching becomes difficult. A batch size of about 500 cards is probably optimum. A factor influencing the batch size is the type of keypunching to be done. If purely numeric or purely alphabetic keypunching is being done, the batch can be larger. If mixed numeric and alphabetic keypunching is being done, the probability of error is higher and smaller batches are called for.

Determination of batch size is not as academic as was implied in the last paragraph. Control breaks are set up in transaction data at points where there are natural breaks in the data. For example, in the clockcard illustration previously described, the control break was set up on a departmental basis, the points at which natural breaks in the data occurred. Other examples of natural breaks are stations and days.

While the basic purpose of a control total is to detect the inadvertent addition or deletion of items of data, the control total also provides a safeguard against the mutilation of individual items of data. For example, to return to the clockcard illustration described earlier, the reconciliation on the computer of the departmental total of hours worked does lend validity to the hours-worked field of the individual clockcard items in the batch. Because, if one of them had been perverted during transmission from the source to the computer, the control total would not check out. Because of this power of the control total to validate individual fields of data, the control total approach to the validation of a field is sometimes chosen in preference to performing some type of validation check on each field as it comes up. If a batch is in error with respect to control totals in some specific fields, then the batch will be subjected to other types of validity checks just for the defective fields in some successor run. In other instances, the erroneous batches and fields may be identified to the computer operator and the validation run closed out. This facilitates error identification.

One kind of control total is the item count. In this case the control total is the number of items in the batch. As the validation run processes the batch, it counts the items processed. When the end of the batch is reached, the computer's item count is checked against the previously prepared count for equality.

A validation procedure similar to the use of control totals is applicable when, because of some aspect of the application, a certain level of error in transaction data is acceptable. Then a sampling procedure can be carried out. Only those items of data selected need be verified. Moreover, no error items need be thrown out or flagged. All that is necessary is to monitor the validation of the sampled items and to make sure the error rate does not exceed the accepted level. Only when this level is exceeded need the batch be rejected. Only when the batch is rejected need every item be validated and erroneous items be marked for correction. This procedure is an application of standard, statistical quality-control techniques.

An alternative to control totals, which can be used to assure that no transaction items have been picked up or lost, is applicable when the computer system generates the items that are to be distributed to the field, acted on in some way, and then returned to the computer system. In such a case, the computer has a record of what transaction data to expect, since it generated the data. All that is necessary is that this record be preserved until the time at which the transaction items return to the computer system. Then the computer can check the returning items against this record to determine whether any items are missing or any extraneous items have been introduced.

An example of this technique is as follows. One company predicts, on a day-to-day basis, the work each of its hourly paid employees in a certain department will do. In this department, rate-of-pay is a function of the type of work done. An employee may switch from one type of work to another from day to day. The prediction of each employee's type of work for a particular day is based on a record of the employee's past work history maintained by the computer as part of the employee master item. Every day the computer punches out a card for each employee in this department. This card is the employee's clockcard. It has his employee number punched in it. It has printed on it the work description of the job the computer predicts the employee will work on that day. Each such card is a draft on the company for eight hours worth of pay at the rate indicated by the work description. It is imperative that none of these cards is mislaid. The control against such a loss of cards is the tape from which the cards were generated, which is used by the computer to determine that all clockcards issued are returned to the system, either to initiate payment for work done or to indicate to the system that the employee involved performed in some way other than is described on his preprinted clockcard.

Another method for insuring the completeness of the transaction file is to have all source documents numbered in sequence, either by prenumbering them when they are printed or by stamping them with a Bates stamp as they are completed. This identifying number is incorporated as part of the transaction item created on the basis of the source document. At the time the transaction file is fed into the computer system, the computer is given the range of numbers of the source documents used during this cycle. The computer checks to ascertain that all numbers in this range are present and that none is duplicated in a possible defalcation.

CORRECTNESS OF DATA

Correctness of data can be checked in many ways. Some validation checks used are as follows. Check digits can be used to make keys and other code fields self-checking numbers. The test on these numbers can then be carried out in the validation run. This is discussed extensively in a later section.

A check can be made to ascertain that the contents of a field are consistent with the rest of the data in the item. For example, if the work week field of a clockcard item indicates that the involved employee worked a normal work week, then those fields of the item which show hours overtime, days absent, and so forth, should all contain zeros.

A check can be made to assure that the data to be entered in a field does not extend over the limits of the field as set up in the item design. For example, in a fixed word-length computer, if a word in an adjustment item is set up in the following format:

$$OAAAAA$$

where A is the amount of the adjustment, a check can be made to verify that the first digit of the word is zero.

A refinement of the above type of check is possible when it is known that the value of a field can only vary between certain limits. For example, on one work day a man can work a maximum of 16 hours overtime. A validation run on a daily clockcard can check the overtime field of each item to make certain this limit is not exceeded.

In the case where a field is to contain nothing but numerics, the computer can be programmed to make certain the field contains no alphabetics or special symbols.

One of the sources for keypunching error is in the *right justification* of fields. A field that is right justified has all significant digits punched in the rightmost columns of the field. The *leading* columns of the field are blank. For example, if a field has been allocated six columns and a four-digit number is to be punched into the field, the card should end up with two blank columns followed by the four-digit number punched into the field. To punch a right justified number, a keypunch operator must tab to the beginning of the field and then space over as many columns as necessary to begin punching the number. It is in the spacing that the greatest possibility for error occurs. The operator may space over too many columns. He may not space over enough of them.

The way to detect this type of error is by blank-column detection. The card is designed so the column immediately following the right-justified field is blank. The computer then inspects the rightmost column in the field. This column should contain a number. If it is blank, the keypunch operator did not space over enough columns. The computer also inspects the column immediately following the field. This column should be blank. If it contains a number, the operator spaced over too many columns.

Another characteristic of transaction data that can be checked is header-trailer association and sequence. For example, suppose the addition items to a payroll file maintenance are to be punched on cards, converted to tape, and then fed into a validation run. Suppose also that, to keypunch one addition item, three punched cards are required. The addition item then consists of a header card and two trailer cards. These three cards should have a common field by which they can be associated. In the case at hand, the common field is the employee identification number. The cards should also be designed so they can be distinguished one from another. For example, one column can be set aside in all cards to identify the card by type, the header having a zero punched in this column, the first trailer a one, and the second trailer a two. The addition item should then be fed into the validation run in the order, header, trailer one, trailer two. The validation run can check for this order on the basis of the distinguishing column and can also ascertain, by means of an equality check on employee identification numbers, that the trailers following a header are associated with the header. If the number of trailers is variable, they can still be numbered in sequence in a type field, and the last trailer can have an entry in a *last-card field* to indicate that it is the last trailer. All other trailers must have a blank column in the last-card field.

A series of checks can be made against a code field to ascertain that it contains a legitimate code. For example, the transaction type-key field can be validated by such a procedure. There are only certain codes this field may legitimately contain. If the transaction key field of each transaction item is tested against an exhaustive list of the legitimate possibilities, those transaction items with illegitimate transaction keys will be detected.

This code validation breaks down into two types, depending on whether the code is used in a function-table lookup. If the code is used in function-table lookup, then its range is restricted. Moreover, it is well populated in that range. For example, the code might have a range of from 00 through 25. Most of the possibilities within these limits would be legitimate codes. Such a code setup can be validated by checking each case of the code against the limit of the possibilities. If it does not fall within the limits, it is not valid. If it does, it can be checked against the possibilities that lie within the limits, but which are not valid codes. If it proves unequal to all these possibilities, it can then be considered valid. It is important that such a validity test be performed, for if the code is used as the argument in a function table lookup, any invalid code will cause the run, of which the function-table lookup is a part, to go astray.

If the code is not used as the argument in a function-table lookup, there is a greater possibility that the range of the code is wide and that there are gaps between the occurrence of one legitimate code and the occurrence of the next. For example, arranged in ascending sequence, a partial list of legitimate codes might appear as follows.

14000—Sacks, Cotton
14025—25 pound sacks
14028—28 pound sacks
14035—35 pound sacks
14050—50 pound sacks
14056—56 pound sacks
14070—70 pound sacks
14100—100 pound sacks
14140—140 pound sacks

To test such a code for validity, a limit test is not adequate. It is necessary to resort to a sequence of equality comparisons that tests each code candidate against an exhaustive list of the legitimate possibilities. Although it is possible to perform this type of check during the validation run, the number of different legitimate codes is generally large enough to seriously add to the memory space and computer running-time requirements of a validation run incorporating such a check. These code fields are generally the subject of an exhaustive scrutiny during the file-maintenance run. For example, to return to the illustration of the transaction key field of the transaction item, the contents of this field for each transaction item are run against a complete list of the possible keys as a normal part of determining what the nature of the current key is. This type of validation check can be incorporated into the maintenance run as a byproduct of the normal maintenance operations with little additional demand on the space and time requirements of the run. It is customary to incorporate this type of validation check in the maintenance rather than in the validation run.

Codes such as the transaction key described here can be designed so the validation process of checking for legitimate codes is made as powerful as possible. This goal is achieved by choosing legitimate codes so the most likely types of errors, such as dropped, added, and transposed digits, lead to illegitimate codes. For example, if 24 is a legitimate code, then its transposition, 42, should not be.

One error type is the mismatch. A mismatch occurs when the master item key of a change item is incorrectly prepared and does not allow the change item to match up with any master item. Even self-checking keys will not catch all mismatches, since a key can be consistent with its check digit and still not match any key on the master file. It is not feasible to check for mismatches during the validation run. The list of legitimate possibilities is too large. However, the check for mismatches is a by-product of the maintenance operation of matching change items against the master file. Consequently, the validation check for mismatches is part of the maintenance run.

One way to validate that a change made to a field of a master item is being made to the right field of the right item is to have each change item incorporate not only a new information field, but also a field that contains what the master-item field currently contains. This *old-information field* can then be checked against the master-item field for equality before the change is made.

Another way of insuring that a change item is being applied to the proper master item is to carry in the change item, in addition to the master-item key, some other information identifying the master item to which the change applies. For example, in a payroll application in which the master-item key is the employee identification number, the change item can carry, in addition to the identification number, the first four digits of the employee's last name and his date of birth. When a match between employee identification numbers in the change and master files has been made, the name and date of birth data can also be matched to validate the correctness of the change item's employee identification number.

One area in which validity checking is important is where the possibility of negative quantities is involved. For example, consider a master-item field that cannot be negative, but which can receive negative adjustments. It is important to be sure that no negative adustment to this field can erroneously bring the value of this field below zero. This validation check is particularly important when the field to be adjusted occupies the least significant digit positions of a word, and an independent field occupies the most significant part of the same word. For example, consider the following word:

$$+120016$$

and suppose the 12 constitutes one field, and the 0016 another. Now suppose a negative adjustment of 18 is applied to the second field without field selection (masking). The resulting word would appear as follows.

$$+119998$$

Both fields have been perverted, the second particularly so.

Validation procedures are not confined to the validation run or to the operations associated with the application of transactions to the master file. They can encompass the whole system. Control totals, usually dollar controls, are kept on files. These controls are carried throughout the system. Periodically they are checked to protect against errors that may have crept into the system because of previously undetected illegitimate data or because of undetected bugs, a situation which is a possibility when a production routine has been patched to reflect some change in procedure.

Such a control total works as follows. At the beginning of a cycle, all inputs to the system may be known to represent a certain amount of dollars. At any point in the cycle, particularly at the end of the cycle, the dollars accounted for by the output of the system should equal the dollars entered into the system through the input files.

One problem associated with the use of such control totals is that, as a system progresses, the parts making up the total are allocated and reallocated, perhaps several times, among different files. During these allocations and reallocations rounding error creeps in. The control totals at the end of the cycle cannot be reconciled to the penny with the controls as they entered the cycle. One judgment that must be made in setting up such a control total is the determination of the limits within which the total may vary and still be considered correct.

One method for minimizing this variance is exemplified as follows. Imagine a run with one input and two outputs. Suppose for a particular input item the dollar field on which the control is kept is to be split between the two output files, 73 percent to one, 27 percent to the other. Instead of allocating 73 percent of the dollars to one control total and 27 percent to the other, allocate 73 percent to one control total and then allocate to the other the difference between the total amount of the field and the 73 percent already allocated.

Validation can also be performed after a data processing operation has been completed. For example, after an employee's gross pay has been computed, it can then be checked against some upper limit.

It is possible to sequence check a master file whenever it is passed. This may be particularly important in card deck files and others where unit records may be readily vulnerable. At first glance, it is hard to see how a master file can get out of sequence in a production system. Nevertheless, it occasionally happens. The possible causes are numerous— operator error, data error, tape error, machine malfunction, and so forth. Investment in such a sequence check is seldom warranted, because subsequent processing almost always contains inherent sequence checks.

Another type of validity check that concentrates solely on the accuracy of the master file is a special validation run that is executed periodically, say quarterly, to test the validity of the master file. The sole input to this run is the master file. The sole output is the validated master file. The sole purpose of the run is to check the validity of the master file. No validation procedure is exhaustive. As time passes, errors creep into master files. The advantage of a periodic validation run on the master file is that it avoids the bunching of the discovery of the master file errors at yearend, when summary reports revealing these errors are created. At yearend the pressure is on to get the work out. It is the least desirable time to be bothered with errors whose origin and consequent correction are difficult to determine.

Validation takes time. Judgment must be exercised as to the extent validation should be carried out. In some instances it may be less expensive from an overall viewpoint to allow certain errors to pass into the system undetected than it would be to incorporate validation procedures to detect those errors. However, this fact cannot be used as a justification for a haphazard approach to the integration of validation into a system. The philosophy with respect to validation must be that anything that can happen will happen, and that the computer, lacking in invention, must have incorporated in its program a course of action for every circumstance. Therefore, all possibilities for the occurrence of errors must be anticipated. If the integrity of the system requires that a particular error not be allowed to penetrate the system beyond a given point, some check designed to catch such errors must be incorporated into the system at some point prior to the time at which the error becomes critical.

For example, it is imperative that the first data card from a deck which has been placed in the card reader be validated in as much detail as possible, not so much to validate the fields on the card, but to guarantee that the card belongs to the file constituting the input to the run at hand. The presumption is that, if the first data card belongs to the proper file, then the other cards in the deck also belong to the file.

When a deck is placed in the input hopper of the reader, it is preceded by an identification card identifying the file being entered. The program can check this card to ascertain the identity of the file. But this check alone should not be relied on, since it is possible for an operator to place the right identification card in front of the wrong card deck.

One way to minimize the erroneous association of label cards and data decks is to have the label card keypunched at the same time and place as the data deck, and in every way to treat the label card the same as the data cards. Another protective device for correct label card and data deck association is to punch in the label card a hash total of some number of columns in the card deck. When the hash total checks out, assurance is given that the correct data deck has been read in.

Given that a validation check is incorporated into a system, the question then arises: What action should be taken when an error is detected? The most desirable course of action is to have the computer system automatically correct the error and then continue normal operation. In many cases this approach is feasible. For example, the case of addition items to a payroll file was described previously as requiring three cards each to be represented and as being required to be fed into the validation run in the order: header, trailer one, trailer two. If the validation run ascertains that an addition item is being entered out of order, say, header, trailer two, and then trailer one, the validation run can rearrange the information into proper order before recording the information on an output tape.

The choice between an automatic and a manual correction procedure is economic. Which procedure is least expensive? If the difference between the costs of the two procedures is close, the nod should be given to the automatic procedure. Automatic correction makes for a system less susceptible to breakdown and crisis. Also, automatic correction will enable a system to be run in less calendar time, since it will not be interrupted by intermittent manual operation. Such manual operations present additional data integrity control problems to the system. If automatic correction is possible, it is usually time that determines the amount of automatic correction. As much is done as the system schedule and computer room schedule allow.

If it is not possible for the computer system to automatically correct an error, then some indication that an error exists must be sent by the computer outside the computer system. This indication must contain sufficient information to specify the nature of the error and the steps required to realize its correction. In tape computers, such indications are produced on error tapes which are used to prepare hard copy to form the basis for the instigation of the manual error-correction procedure. In other computers, error tallies may be made on console typewriters, in tabulator listings, in punched decks, and so forth. Since validation goes on in both the validation and maintenance runs, both may produce error tapes. A process chart incorporating these error tapes is shown in Figure 3-4.

It is not necessary for both the validation and maintenance runs to produce error tapes. An alternative is as follows. During the validation run error items are flagged but are written on the validated transaction file. During the maintenance run these flagged items, as well as the error

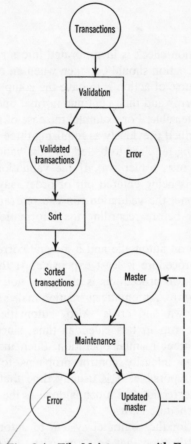

Fig. 3-4   File Maintenance with Errors

items detected during the maintenance run, are written on an error tape produced by the maintenance run.

Despite the fact that provision has been made for ejecting errors, as little use should be made of this mechanism as is feasible. When an item is placed on an error tape, a complicated procedure that should be avoided when possible is initiated. The item must be edited into a format such that, when it is printed, it is legible to the clerk to whom it is given for investigation and correction. The clerk must go through a seldom used and unfamiliar procedure to correct the item. On the basis of this correction, information must be prepared and reinserted into the system. Controls must be maintained to insure that all items going out on the error tape are handled and that appropriate corrections do return to the computer system.

Even though it may not be possible to devise any automatic correction procedure for a certain class of errors, it may be possible to come to an agreement with the line organization on some arbitrary method of handling the error. As long as no out-of-pocket losses or gross distortions of information are involved, the arbitrary handling of errors is a possibility. For example, if in a labor distribution, an illegitimate account number is encountered, there is no gross distortion of information if the amounts associated with the illegitimate account are absorbed by one of the large volume accounts or are spread proportionately into all accounts in accordance with their totals for nonerror items.

Even if the system does handle errors either by automatically correcting them or by arbitrarily altering them, a record should be kept by the program of which errors occur. Such a record may be of particular importance in the case of arbitrarily handled errors, where no harm is done if a few errors are handled in a summary fashion, but where trouble could occur if many error items were to get this arbitrary treatment. Monitoring an error record would allow a program to take extraordinary action when the incidence of a certain type of arbitrarily handled error exceeds a safety limit. In addition, such a record can be used as a basis for the analysis of the system error experience with an eye toward additional clerical training and revising input procedure to reduce the occurrence of error.

If it is impossible to either correct an error automatically or to handle it arbitrarily, the offending item is committed to an error tape. After the error item has been deposited on the error tape, the question arises: What should the system do now that an error has been detected? Should it stop and wait while the erroneous information is corrected? Or should the system continue processing regardless of the fact that some erroneous information has been found? If possible, the system should continue. Two considerations underlie this decision. For one thing, systems operate under tight schedules. The paychecks must be out by such and such a date. If the production schedule does not meet its deadline, the efficiency of the plant is impaired. It is not reasonable to jeopardize the system as far as meeting its deadline is concerned because a small amount of data deviates. This deviating data can be handled to the side on an exception basis. The first consideration is that the system continue on to process the large bulk of data which is normal.

The second reason for maintaining system operation regardless of the occasional failure of data to become validated is an economic one. Tearing down a computer equipment setup at the termination of one run and setting up the equipment for the next run are not simple. Perhaps tapes must be dismounted from tape handlers and labeled appropriately. Other tapes must be mounted. Certain tape files must be returned to the tape library and correctly filed away. Other files must be withdrawn for use. Forms must be changed in the printer. Plugboards may have to be changed in some units of the machine system. In some computers, even cabling interconnections may have to be altered. If a run is discontinued when an error is found, the computer cannot remain idle while the error is corrected. The current run must be torn down and another instituted. Later on, the run that has replaced the run with the error may have to be interrupted to allow the previous run to get back on. A significant amount of setup and takedown time is created, time that is unproductive. To eliminate this unproductive time, keep the system running regardless of error occurrence.

Despite the aptness of the prejudice toward keeping the system running even though there are errors, there are situations in which the system must be brought to a halt. For example, in a payroll system, if the total of the hours worked for the employee roster fails a reasonableness check against some predetermined total by a wide margin, there is no question about whether the system should be stopped. There is something radically wrong. The system must be halted until the cause of the error is detected and corrected.

Given that an error has been detected by the validation process, that it is not within the ability of the computer system to either automatically correct or arbitarily handle the error discovered, that an indication of the occurrence has been recorded on the error tape, and that the nature of the error is such that the system can continue to operate, the question then arises: What should be done with the error item? Should the system digest it even though it is in error? Or should it be eliminated from the system and allow processing to continue without it? The answer to this question is a function of the operation at hand.

For example, suppose the purpose of the application is to produce some type of statistical report or gross distribution, such as labor distribution. The fact that a few items of information which should have been applied to the master file were tossed out of the system has little impact on the validity of the output. These invalid items can be corrected, fed back into the system at a later cycle to correct the records on the master tape, and still not significantly influence the results in the reports this system turns out. Thus, in a weekly payroll system, erroneous clockcard items can be tossed out of the system. They can be inspected manually. If the amounts involved are significant, payment can be made manually. If the amount involved is small, the transaction can be held over until the next week. However, in either case, special input must be prepared for the succeeding week's run. In the case where payment was not made, the corrected clockcards must be reentered. If payment was made, an adjustment item must be fed in to bring the totals kept in the employee's master item up-to-date. During the labor distribution that follows the payroll run, time and money are considered in a particular week which belong to the previous week's distribution. Money that does belong to the current week's distribution is not considered until the following week. However, for the purposes of the labor distribution, these facts are hardly significant.

In the preceding example the integrity of the individual items—the paychecks—was the important thing. A slight error in the summary information, exemplified by the labor distribution, was not considered important. Errors were eliminated from the system as they were identified. In other instances the integrity of the summary information may take precedence over the integrity of the individual items, in which case the error items may continue through the system regardless of the fact that they have been identified. Although this approach may appear hard to achieve, with a little ingenuity it is almost always possible to devise some method for handling most errors capable of being identified. For example, if a mismatch occurs, the system can set up a bogus master item with the missing master key and apply the offending change to the bogus item. Such a procedure requires that, at some later date, the change item with the erroneous master item key not only must be corrected and reentered into the system, but a transaction item to delete the bogus master item also must be introduced. However, despite the creation of a bogus master item and the necessity for later steps to delete the item, the procedure does allow the change item to contribute to whatever summaries may be being made on its fields regardless of the fact that it has an erroneous master item key.

Unfortunately, it is impossible to have the computer process every error that can be detected even if that is desirable. It is impossible to anticipate every possible error situation. For those that can be anticipated, there is no problem in building into the program an ability to recognize these error situations and to process the errors which fall into a particular category in any way desired. However, if a class of error is not anticipated, then the system cannot incorporate the ability to recognize that class of error and handle it in some particular way. The best that can be done (and not so incidentally, the least that should be done) is to build the system so that when some unanticipated error does occur, the program has the ability to say, "My gosh, I've never seen anything like that before," commit the offending item to the error tape, and go on to the next item.

RUN CONSOLIDATION

The process chart in Figure 3-4 indicates that validation and sorting take place in separate runs. Such is not necessarily the case. It is possible to perform the validation required during the first and last passes of the sort. Last passes are included in this assertion because some types of validation are better effected when transaction items are in sequence. The combination of the two runs is a distinct possibility when the sort is a sequence check. A sequence check requires very little central computer time. Adding a sequence check to the validation already planned will add relatively little or nothing to the total run time. Since such a run generally is limited by the rate of delivery of transaction items to the central processor by input devices, there will be no penalty in run time paid for sequence check. In those instances where the validation is so extensive that the run is limited by the rate of validating items within the central processor, the addition of sequence check to the run computation will add at most a very small percentage to the total run time. The decision of whether validation and sorting should be one run or two is dependent on which approach is least expensive in terms of computer time, including setup and takedown.

Figure 3-4 indicates that the transaction file originates as a tape file. Generally, such is not the case. More often, the transaction file originates as punched cards, documents for machine sensing, or paper tape. When transaction files in such media are to be delivered to the computer processor via on-line reading mechanisms, a conversion run may precede all other computer operations on the transaction file to convert the file to magnetic tape form. Validation procedures can be incorporated in the conversion run. Control totals, particularly, are most appropriately checked during file conversion. In other cases of on-line conversion, the validation and conversion may very well be combined with the first pass of a sort run.

It should be borne in mind that, in organizing file maintenance on a random-access processor, sorting of the transaction items might not exist at all as a run or portion of a run. Then one needs to investigate the possibility of combining validation with file maintenance in a single run. For example, each transaction item would be validated, and for all valid transaction items the corresponding master-file location would be computed from the validated key within a single run. The nonvalidated items would be placed in a special output for further investigation and recycling.

ERROR HANDLING

When an error item is recorded on an error tape, then regardless of whether the error item is subsequently processed or is eliminated from the system, a discrepancy remains in the system. Some correction procedure is necessary. Some control must be set up to insure that the correction is made. For example, suppose some operating unit originates a source document in error and the validation system snares the error and records it on the error tape. The item is converted to hard copy and returned to the clerical unit, where it is established that the transaction was erroneously initiated. The unit cannot drop the matter there. Some indication that the item should be cancelled must be returned to the computer system. Otherwise, the computer system has no way of knowing whether the whole transaction is in error or whether the transaction is valid but has been so mangled that it is unrecognizable to the computer system.

To insure the return of corrected information for every error item issued, a journal should be set up in the computer center. This journal is an accounts receivable ledger. When an error item is issued by the computer center it should be debited to the office to which it is sent. When a correction is received by the center it should be credited to the office to which the associated error was delivered. It may also be used to wash out the debit of the error. Generally, this error journal is a manual system although, if voluminous enough, it could be kept on the computer.

In connection with this journal and its maintenance, it is well to provide each error item with some serializing or other identifying key on the error list. This key will be used in a field of the correction item to identify the error journal item which needs to be washed out. This same key may be used as a low-cost reference within the correction item to all the nonerroneous fields within the error items. Thereby, the amount of information required to be re-entered into the computer as part of the correction item can be reduced. For example, the correction item may be a punched card with only the identifying error item key field and the corrected fields punched in prescribed columns of the card. Field identification is on a column number basis. The use of prepunching and preprinting for reducing cost of correction reinsertion is discussed subsequently.

The journal kept to control the correction of errors can also be used as a historical document for purposes of analyzing errors according to type and frequency. The results of such an analysis can be used to improve input organization techniques and may suggest some automatic error-handling technique that can be incorporated into the validation procedures of the system. Some deficiencies that such an analysis may point up are poor manual procedures, poor documentation of procedures, low-quality printing or poor formating of coding directories, and poor clerical supervision and training.

It is possible that, if an error item is ejected from a computer system, the procedures that the item would have otherwise caused the computer system to carry out may have to be performed manually. Example has been made of the payroll system that rejects erroneous clockcard items. Generally, it is not possible to ascertain what is wrong with these items, correct them, and reintroduce them into the computer system in time to have them contribute to the automatic production of paychecks by the computer. The payroll system schedule is too tight to allow a wait for this correction procedure. By the time the corrected clockcards are ready to be reintroduced into the computer system, the system has completed the computation of gross and net pay and is printing the checks to meet the deadline at which the checks are required. Even though the pay based on the corrected clockcards cannot be generated by the computer system, the employees involved must be paid. Paychecks that arrive on time are essential to good employee morale. The only alternative is to resort to a manual procedure to compute the pay and prepare the paychecks for rejected erroneous clockcard items.

All checks prepared by the computer system have contributed to certain totals such as year-to-date gross, year-to-date withholding tax, and quarter-to-date FICA tax being kept in the employee items on the payroll master file. The checks prepared by the manual system should contribute to these totals. As far as the totals kept by the computer on magnetic tape are concerned, the manually prepared paychecks do not contribute.

It is possible to keep two sets of records, one on tape for the computer system and one in a ledger for the manual system. One can combine the information from these two sets when it becomes necessary to use this information to prepare some report to which they contribute, such as W2 forms (the annual reports to the U.S. Treasury Department and to the employee on his gross pay and withholding taxes). Such a procedure is complicated, as in the case of the W2 form. At the end of the year the tape file would have to be used to prepare a W2 form for each employee earning wages during the past year. Then for every employee to whom a manual payment had been made during the last year, and consequently, for whom there is an entry in the manual ledger, the W2 form produced on the computer would have to be used as a source document, together with information from the ledger, to produce a second, final W2 form for the employee.

The procedure is more straightforward if, after a manual paycheck is produced for an employee, adjustment items designed to be introduced into the computer system during the next payroll cycle are created to modify all accumulations in the employee's master file item by whatever amounts were involved in his manual payment. In this way the record of these accumulations are consolidated in one place—the tape file. When the time comes to prepare a report based on these accumulations, it can be produced by printing from the tape file. Consolidation of such accumulations is of particular importance when the company requires a reconciliation of these totals with an independently derived control. The purpose of the consolidation is to simplify the process of reconciliation.

Where accounting transactions are involved, and especially where defalcation is a possibility, the error journal is a necessity. Without it, audit trail to the clerical organization and return to the computer is lost and normal precautionary controls on computer operations are vitiated. The error list accounts for some dollars in the transactions subjected to validation. The other dollars are in the validated items. The correction procedure must ensure that error items do not grow stale in the error *accounts receivable file.* Over-age items must be the subject of special investigation to determine why corrections were not received.

The manual operations involved in investigating and correcting computer detected errors constitute an exception procedure. The process of investigating and correcting such errors may not occupy a man full time. Consequently, to some extent, the procedure remains unfamiliar to him. Therefore, in setting up this procedure, every means should be used to make the process simple, straightforward, and easy.

Errors can be detected at many points in a system. They should, however, not be tossed out of the system as they are detected but should be collected at one point. They should there be edited for easy discernment and integrated into as many reports as there are correction points to which the errors are routed. On these reports the errors should be classified according to type so all errors requiring a particular error correction procedure are grouped together on the report. The error report should give a clear indication of what each error is, what probably caused it, and the steps necessary to correct it.

One problem involved in error correction is that to effect a correction a new document must be fed into the system. In many cases an item is put out for correction, but only one field of the item is in error. The rest of the information in the item is good. In several instances, not only does the corrected field have to be fed back into the computer system, but all the other already correct information also has to be reintroduced. The job connected with this reintroduction of information can be minimized by prefabricating on the computer the document used to reintroduce the data. If the corrected information is to be reintroduced to the computer system via a punched card, the computer system can prepunch the already correct information in a card leaving blank only that field which requires correction and printing the information relating to the nature of the error and what is to be done about it on the card. A deck of such cards then constitutes the error report to be sent to a correction point. At this correction point the error can be investigated and corrected, the correct data can be punched into the blank portion of the otherwise prepared card, and the card can be returned to the computer center for reinsertion into the system.

As already mentioned, another procedure is to identify each error on the error list by a serializing key and to require only this key and the corrected fields to be reinserted into the computer. The nature of the corrected fields can be identified by a change-type key or by coordinate position on the input document for the correction item. Where error lists are in perforated tape form, the error tape may be used to reperforate the corrected tape with the operator stopping the tape at the point of error for keyboarding the corrected field.

As an aid to easy error correction, every person involved in such procedures should have access to an error correction-procedure manual that describes in detail how the computer presents each error on the error report, lists in detail the probable causes of each error type, and explains in detail how to go about correcting each error.

For easy error correction, a filing procedure for source documents that must be referenced as part of the error correction procedure should be set up to make this reference as convenient as possible. The filing procedure should be set up on the basis of ease and economy in filing the source documents. Then the computer system should be designed to prepare the error report so that ease of matching against the source document file is optimized.

Another consideration in the area of error handling is: At what point should an error be corrected? The closer to the computer center it is possible to get an error corrected, the sooner the correction returns to the computer center. On the other hand, a policy of sending errors back to the point at which the information originated has a felicitous effect on error rate. The correction of errors has an educational effect which enables people to avoid making the same errors in the future. Perhaps the conclusion to be drawn is that errors should be corrected as near the computer center as possible, but in those cases where the errors result from a misunderstanding of procedure, adequate information concerning the errors should be funneled back to the information source points for educational purposes.

For example, consider a set of source documents on which control totals have been created on a desk calculator. These documents are keypunched. Then, because the cards are to be sent over a considerable distance to the computer center, they are tabulated and the proper fields are accumulated to check the control totals. This operation provides assurance that the card deck to be sent to the computer center reflects the source documents from which they were punched and that no documents were dropped or duplicated during the keypunching operation. The tabulation produces the summary cards for the batches of data cards on a summary punch. The tabulation output constitutes a transmittal list that accompanies the cards when they are sent to the computer center.

If in converting and validating the cards it is discovered that a control total does not check, the first step in the error correction procedure is to print the information on the cards belonging to the batch whose control did not check and compare the resulting listing with the transmittal list. This check often shows why the control total did not check, the discrepancy is remedied, and the batch is reintroduced into the system.

It may be that the error discovered can be attributed to some procedural failure in the preparation of the cards. For example, suppose the cards reveal that a calculator-prepared control total does not check. The tab shop corrects the error in the batch of cards failing the check but neglects to alter the summary card prepared during the tabulating. The computer center receives a correct deck of cards and an incorrect batch summary card whose control totals will not check. This error could result from a temporary lapse of attention on the part of some tab room operator. If the error persists, there is an indication that someone misunderstands this aspect of the data preparation procedure. Some information of an educational nature should be passed back to the tab room.

APPLYING THE TRANSACTIONS

The application of the transactions to the master file takes place during the maintenance run. In some instances, the number of transaction types applied may be large—large enough to cramp the memory as far as space to code all the transaction application procedures is concerned. Some of the transaction types occur infrequently. The pressure on memory space can be lessened if, during the validation run, the coding to effect the less frequently occurring transactions is recorded on the transaction file following each transaction to which the coding applies.

Then, when such a transaction is read into the maintenance run, the coding associated with the transaction is read in with it.

Another way to effect this insertion of coding into the transaction file is to have this coding prepunched on cards and to insert these *coding* cards immediately behind the transaction cards to which the coding refers. This approach is not a good idea. It would place more of a burden on the validation run than the insertion of the coding by the validation run does, since the validation run would not only have to validate the transaction items, but would also have to validate any coding inserted in card form.

These remarks are heavily imbued with programming considerations. However, these have so great an impact on the run organization of the process chart that they merit attention. If the file maintenance computation planned within the run is overly complex, it may not be feasible to accomplish it in one run. The process chart may have to designate two runs in tandem, each sharing part of the file maintenance burden. Although each will require a pass of the file, the total computer time of both runs will not necessarily exceed the time of one awkwardly complicated single run. Considerations for dividing processing between runs to achieve minimum overall computer time are discussed in a subsequent chapter.

THE CHANGE JOURNAL

When the application of a transaction item to the master file causes a field to be altered on that file, the old information in the field disappears as far as the master file is concerned. The master file is not a historical record. Each cycle, the old master file is read into the maintenance run and a new master file is produced. This new master file contains only up-to-date data. The old master files are not kept any longer than are necessary for regeneration purposes unless there is some legal requirement involved. Magnetic tape is too expensive a recording medium to be used in this way. Unless there is some normal printed output from the system that reflects the changes made to the master file during maintenance, there is no record of these alterations unless one is deliberately provided. Since it is advantageous, particularly from an auditor's point of view, to be able to retrace the changes in the life of a master item, a change journal is incorporated as one output to a file maintenance system to hold all necessary information concerning changes to the master file not documented in some other report. A process chart incorporating a change journal is shown in Figure 3-5.

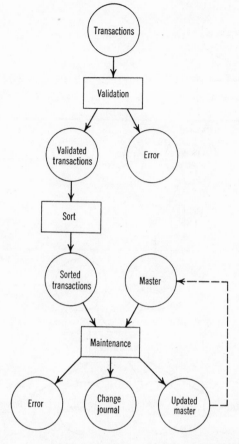

Fig. 3-5   File Maintenance with Change Journal

HANDLING TRANSFERS

The possibility of sequencing the master file on a key subject to change has been mentioned. While such file changes may not be troublesome in random access processing, they can be in tape computer or punched card system batch processing. The volume of such changes varies. The change can involve less than six master items to hundreds or thousands of items. What is the most efficient method of effecting the change and restoring file sequence? Some approaches are as follows.

1. Introduce two transaction items: one a change item to delete the master item with the old key, the other an addition item with the new key to be merged into the master file.

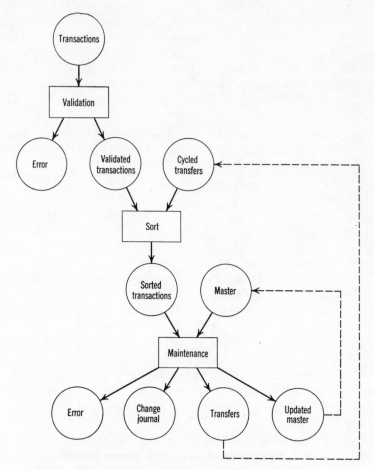

Fig. 3-6 File Maintenance with Transfers

2. Introduce a change item to substitute the new key for the old. To maintain master file order under this system, the file must be sorted after the maintenance run.

3. Introduce a change item to substitute the new key for the old, write the altered item on a transfers file, and delete the item from the master file. The transfers file is then sorted and merged into the master file during the next cycle. Figure 3-6 depicts the system just described.

The first approach is applicable when the number of changes and the size of the master item are small. Under other conditions the approach is not feasible, since each change involves introducing an additional item to the system. The number of changes does not have to become numerous, nor the master item size large, before the information origination required becomes unbearable. If the master file incorporates accumulation fields, such as the on-hand amount or year-to-date taxes normally kept in the computer system, there may not be sufficient information available outside the computer to allow the creation of the bogus *addition item* which is required by this method of handling transfers.

The second solution is feasible when the change to keys is wholesale. Under other circumstances the cost to sort the master file each time a transfer occurs becomes unreasonable.

The third approach is the most general and is the one seized on in most systems in which transfers occur. One drawback to this method is that, at the end of the maintenance run, there is no single file containing all the master items. The first approach avoids this drawback.

It is possible to build the system with options to handle the transfers in a variety of ways, depending on their volume. A combination of the second and third approaches is particularly feasible, since both require the same transaction item type. The number of transfers can be determined during the sort or validation run. The computer can decide which option is more appropriate. The choice is an economic one.

Combination with the first approach is less feasible, since different transaction item types are needed in this approach than are needed in the others. Hence, the decision as to which alternative is to be elected during a given cycle must devolve to the clerical group preparing the transactions. Such a situation may be tenable but should probably be avoided.

One problem is the possibility of a change item coming in under the old master item key after the item has been reinserted in the master file under a new key. If such a situation is possible and it is desired to have the computer handle the problem automatically, then an item consisting of the old key, new key, and date of change can be inserted in the master file at each point where a master item is deleted because of a transfer. These *shadow items* are used to update the keys of all change items referencing old keys. These updated change items then are written on an output tape and are reintroduced into the system during the next cycle with the transactions normal to this cycle. At some later date, when the possibility of a change being introduced under the old key is nonexistent, the corresponding shadow item can be stripped off the master file on the basis of its date-of-change field. The costs of such a system are twofold: procedures must be built into the maintenance run to monitor the shadow items, and the master file length is increased.

BASIC OPERATIONS

A flowchart incorporating the basic operations in a maintenance run is shown in Figure 3-7. This flow chart presumes that all transactions are on one file. There are $n + 1$ different transaction keys identified as $0, 1, 2, 3, \ldots, n$. If the transaction key is zero, the transaction item is an addition. Otherwise, it is a change. Transaction key $n - 1$ indicates a transfer, which is handled as indicated in Figure 3-6. Transaction key n indicates a deletion. Every other transaction key indicates some type of alteration to the associated master item. The major key on which the transaction items are ordered is the master item key. This file is also in order on a minor key constituted by the transaction key. The consequence of this order by minor key is that, if more than one transaction item has the same master item key, and if one of these transaction items:

1. Is an addition item, then the addition item precedes all the other such transaction items.
2. Initiates the deletion or transfer of the associated master item, then that transaction item follows all the other transaction items with the same master item key.

The flow chart presumes that all error items are recorded on an error tape and that after this error-handling procedure normal processing continues without interruption. The errors could be prepared as printed listings, punched cards, and so forth. Notice how the normal procedures of the maintenance run automatically siphon off three error types characteristic of file maintenance operations.

1. Addition items with a key identical to an item already on the master file.
2. Mismatching change items.
3. Change items with illegitimate transaction keys.

FREQUENCY OF UPDATING

One problem in setting up a file maintenance system is the determination of how frequently the master file is to be cycled. To a considerable extent this decision is forced by the timing considerations inherent in the system. How often is output required from the system? In random access computers and real-time on-line processors, file maintenance is on demand and is essentially instantaneous. The more dynamic the operation, the more frequent the cycle. If both weekly and monthly out-

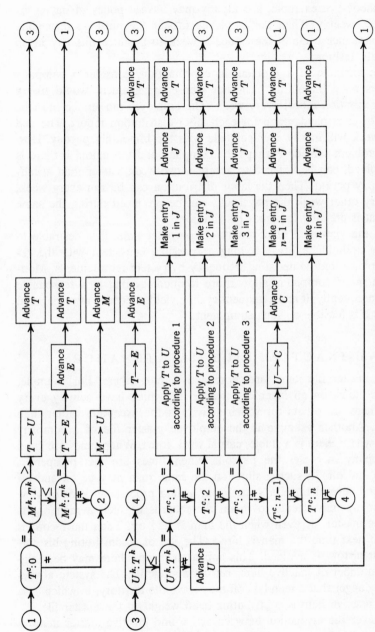

Fig. 3-7 Basic Operations of a Maintenance Run. ($M =$ the current master item; $M^k =$ the key of M; $U =$ the current updated master item; $U^k =$ the key of U; $T =$ the current transaction item; $T^k =$ the master item key of T; $T^c =$ the transaction key of T; $C =$ the current transfers item; $J =$ the current change journal item; $E =$ the current error item.)

put is required from the system, how is the production of each to be coordinated? For example, a company may have a policy of paying its employees weekly. Then the employee master file must go through a file maintenance cycle at least once a week to produce this pay in an up-to-date fashion.

As an example of a problem in coordination, consider a company that pays on a bimonthly basis but whose management would like a labor-distribution report every week. The employee master file must be cycled for each payday and for each labor-distribution report. The end of the week will hardly ever coincide with the bimonthly payday. How is this problem solved? Perhaps the company and the union, if there is one involved, can be induced to accept a two-week, rather than a half-month, pay period. Then the labor distribution can be run every week, and every other week the paychecks can be produced during the same cycle that is creating the labor distribution.

From the viewpoint of economy of computer time, it is desirable to keep the updating interval as long as possible consistent with the re-straints placed on the updating frequency by system requirements. Modern high-speed computers allow more frequent cycling at a reasonable cost. Consequently, if more frequent cycling yields evidence of managerial benefits, it is feasible on such equipment.

ACTIVE-INACTIVE FILE MAINTENANCE

Some master file items are more active than others. For example, there are items on an inventory master file which have activity every cycle. There are others for which activity is the exception rather than the rule. Another example is the employee master file of a company situated where there is a stable, casual work force. When times are good the company increases the payroll. When times are less prosperous men are laid off. In such a situation the same man may be on and off the payroll several times a year. From a data processing point of view the company may decide to retain the records of such a man on its employee master file even when the man is laid off. Then the record is there the next time the man is hired. The job of reconstituting his em-ployment history is avoided. This approach means there may be a sig-nificant number of inactive items on the master file. The system always runs the danger that a man laid off may leave the territory, in which case a really inactive item is contributing dead weight to the master file.

Whenever the distinction between active and inactive master items is significant, it may be more economical to have two master files—one consisting of active items and the other of inactive items—rather than have one master file on which active and inactive items are mixed.

There are no distinct classes of items, active and inactive. There is only a gradation. There are items that were active during the last cycle, items which have been inactive for one cycle, items inactive for two cycles, for three cycles, and so on. Without asking what basis is used to distinguish an active item from an inactive item, let us agree that an active item can become an inactive one, and vice versa. A system that handles an active and an inactive file and allows transfers between the two is shown in Figure 3-8.

Procedures operate in this system in the following way. Mismatches must be distinguished from all other error types during the maintenance run, since a mismatch can now represent one of two things: a true error, or a change item for a master item on the inactive rather than the active file. Also, during the maintenance run, whatever criteria have been decided on for distinguishing active from inactive items are applied to all items on the master file that are not active this cycle. All items satisfying these criteria are culled from the file. The mismatch and cull items are written on a file that constitutes the transaction file for the inactive maintenance run. In this run the culled items are merged into the inactive master file. At the same time each mismatch item is run against this inactive master file. If a match between the mismatch item and the inactive master file does not occur at this point, the mismatch item is a true error and is handled appropriately. If a match does occur, the change item is applied to the matching inactive master item. The master item is written on a reinstatement file. This reinstatement file is merged into the active master file during the maintenance run of the next cycle.

The inactive master file can be culled in a way similar to the way the active master file is culled. In this way dead master items are eliminated from the system.

This discussion embodies the assumption that the inactive master file is maintained on tape. Such need not be the case. An active-inactive file maintenance system may utilize a card inactive master file.*

To institute an active-inactive file maintenance system two requirements must be met. For one thing, each master item must contain usage data. For example, on the simplest level, there might be a field in each master item containing the count of the number of cycles since the master item at hand has been active. This usage data is necessary to determine whether an item is to be considered active or inactive. The determination is made on the basis of criteria set up for evaluating the usage data.

The second requirement for an active-inactive maintenance system

* Sherman Blumenthal, "A Dual Master File System for a Tape Processing Computer," *Journal of the Association for Computing Machinery* (October 1958).

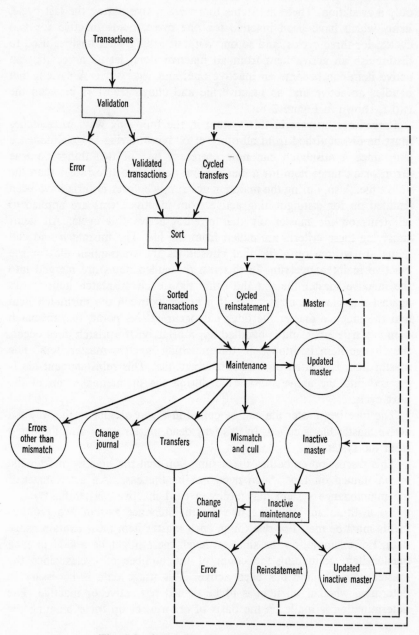

Fig. 3-8 Active-Inactive File Maintenance

is the existence of these criteria. They must be of such a nature that the maintenance system is optimum from an economic point of view.

There are three costs in an active-inactive file maintenance system: file cost, updating cost, and reinstatement cost. File cost is the cost to handle the active master file internally and to read and write the file. Updating cost results from the performance of those operations required when a match between a transaction item and a master item is found. Reinstatement cost is the cost to analyze mismatches when they occur, select items off the inactive master file, and reinstate them in the active master file. The criteria for culling inactive items from the master file must be such that when an item is culled, it is more probable that the reinstatement cost of reinstating the item on the master file when it becomes active is less than the sum of the file and updating costs of maintaining the item on the master file until this activity occurs. These criteria can be gross and still do a satisfactory job. Consequently, the method by which they are determined can be gross. One method is as follows.

The longer the master file, the larger the file cost of the file. However, the incremental file cost to add another item to the file decreases as the file grows. Graphically speaking, the file-cost curve looks like curve F on the chart in Figure 3-9.

A truer picture of the file-cost curve appears in Figure 3-10, in which the steps in the curve indicate the expansion of the file size to the point where another tape is required. Curve F in Figure 3-9 is a close enough approximation of the curve in Figure 3-10 for the purpose at hand.

The longer the active master file, the fewer are the mismatches that occur because the associated master item is on the inactive rather than the active master file. Consequently, the reinstatement cost for the file involved is lower. When the active master file is short, any increase in length results in a sharp reduction in reinstatement cost. The longer the file becomes, the less significant this incremental savings becomes. Thus, the reinstatement cost curve looks like curve R in Figure 3-9.

The longer the master file, the greater the updating cost—but decreasingly so, since the possibility of a match grows with the file size at a diminishing rate. The updating cost curve looks similar to curve U in Figure 3-9.

There should be no difficulty in constructing a file cost curve for a file. If statistics on the activity on the file are available, it should be possible to construct reinstatement and updating cost curves. There is then available all the information necessary to arrive at a determination of what the optimum active master file size is.

If there are not sufficient statistics to allow the creation of reinstate-

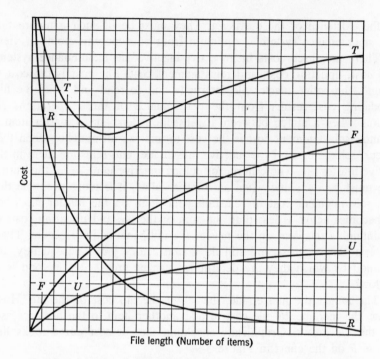

Fig. 3-9   Active-Inactive File Maintenance Costs vs. File Length

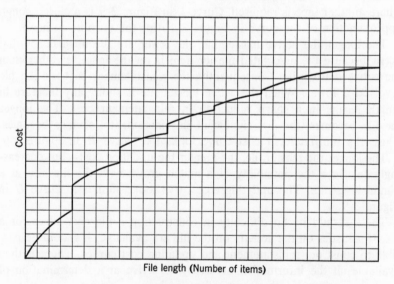

Fig. 3-10   File Cost vs. File Length

ment and updating cost curves, these statistics can be developed in the following way. The system can be designed as shown in Figure 3-8 replete with mechanisms for developing usage data. The only thing left out of the system is the operation of the decision as to whether to cull an item. Consequently, all master items are on the active master file, no culls are made, and the inactive maintenance run is unused. However, cycle after cycle the system is developing usage data, which can be used to develop reinstatement and updating cost curves. Then, when culling criteria have been established, they can be incorporated into an active–inactive file system that is otherwise ready to go.

When file-, reinstatement-, and updating-cost curves have been developed, they can be added together graphically to produce curve T. Curve T is the total-cost curve for the system. The total-cost curve has a low point which represents the optimum active master-file length for the system. Notice the long, low belly of the total-cost curve, which is characteristic of this situation. The implication of this belly is that there is a large number of different file lengths all along it at which the cost is so close to minimum that in practice it makes little difference which of those lengths is chosen. This is the reason why the criteria for culling can be gross and still be satisfactory. Once the limits of optimum file size have been determined in this manner, the only remaining job is to determine the culling criteria that will maintain the file at a size stabilized between these limits. These criteria can be simple or complex as the case requires. For example, it might be necessary for the criteria to take seasonality into consideration. A period of inactivity that would justify the removal of an item from the active file during one season might not constitute sufficient justification during another.

This discussion is concerned with static situations. It has been assumed that reasonable culling criteria remain static, and that once they have been identified, they can be incorporated into the active-inactive file maintenance system in the form discovered where they will, forever after, perform as well as they do on the day in which they are installed. In many situations such an assumption is valid. However, if the situation is dynamic, then a different approach is called for. Not only must the designer determine what the criteria are at a particular moment in time, but he also must determine the laws by which the criteria change in the dynamic situation. Once these laws are discovered, the criteria and the necessary mechanisms for adjusting the criteria according to their laws of change can be incorported and used in the active-inactive file maintenance system.

If a system incorporates a long master file on which there is a low level of activity, one approach is to pass the master file once, copy those master items active this cycle onto a separate file, and use this active file for all subsequent processing in the cycle. This approach embodies the problem of how to merge the master items processed back into the master file at the end of the processing cycle. Yet, this is a very common practice for punched card processing systems.

In random access processors, master files frequently occupy very substantial portions of an expensive memory facility limited in capacity. Hence, there is a premium on purging a master file of its relatively inactive items and setting them into a subsidiary punched card file for manual or machine matching. Other lower-cost, more capacious, slower-access memories are also used—even printed lists are used. While the capability of the system to respond to random inquiries or to make on-line postings into the file is compromised to the extent of culled items, it is usually admissible to subject low-activity items to reasonable delays in updating or inquiry response. Thus, the principle we have described here applies to random access and other computers as well as to batch-processing tape computers.

4

OTHER GENERAL RUN TYPES

The run complex constituting the file-maintenance operation is the most general feature of computer systems. However, there are other common run types. These types are discussed in this chapter.

CONVERSION RUNS

In a computer equipment array in which the peripheral equipment, such as the card reader and paper printer are on line to the computer, one run type is the conversion run. Examples of conversion runs are the card-to-magnetic tape conversion run shown in Figure 4-1; the magnetic tape-to-printed paper conversion run, Figure 4-2; magnetic tape-to-card conversion, Figure 4-3; paper tape-to-magnetic tape conversion; mag-

Fig. 4-1   Card-to-Tape Conversion

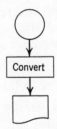

Fig.   4-2   Tape-to-Printed   Paper
Conversion

netic tape-to-paper tape; and document reader-to-magnetic tape conversion.

Especially where conversion is consolidated with other processing within a single run, as in random access processing, or where conversion is accomplished on a satellite computer, the conversion may be from one nonmagnetic medium (cards, paper tape, documents) to another. Special purpose converters may be used for this latter purpose also; for example, paper tape-to-punched card converters.

Some magnetic tape computers do not permit on-line peripheral equipment. In such a case, special purpose converters transform data from one medium to magnetic tape, others from magnetic tape to various media—for example, off-line card-to-magnetic tape conversion, line printers driven from magnetic tape, and so forth. In these instances, medium conversion can be combined with editing and other processing capabilities generally built into these special purpose devices.

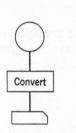

Fig. 4-3. Tape-to-Card Conversion

Another method of dealing with the conversion problems presented by the tape computer with no on-line peripheral equipment is to support it with a satellite computer. The satellite computer is generally a slower speed, less capacious, lower cost, computer system permitting on-line peripheral operations as well as magnetic tape input and output. It is used as an omnibus converter, enabling transforming from any one of a number of media to any other, including to and from magnetic tape. Since it has quite complete computer capability, it permits the consolidation of conversion with a modest amount of other processing. The satellite computer may be looked upon as not essentially different from the numerous special purpose converter devices mentioned previously. In fact, it may function largely as a multi-programmed array of such converters time sharing a common central computer processor.

SORTING RUNS

Sort runs, already discussed as part of the file maintenance operation, appear in other parts of systems. Although sorting may be accomplished by card equipment or by special purpose, off-line tape sorters, the attention here is to the use of general purpose tape computers and to sorting runs which are an integral part of a large process chart.

The function of a sort is to arrange the items on a tape in sequence by a given key. Most sorts are probability sorts, which take advantage of sequence bias in the input data to shorten the length of the sort.

A tape sort consists of several phases. The first assembles strings of items in sequence and disperses the individual strings onto two or more collation tapes. The second phase consists of repeated merges of strings

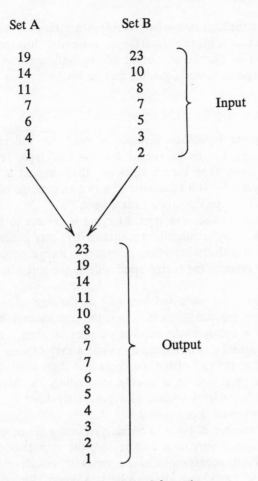

Set A   Set B

19	23
14	10
11	8
7	7
6	5
4	3
1	2

Input

23
19
14
11
10
8
7
7
6
5
4
3
2
1

Output

Fig. 4-4   Merge Schematic

into ever-lengthening strings. The last phase of the sort is the final collation which produces a single string of items in sequence.

The multiphase structure of the sort is such that processing can be
profitably incorporated into phases other than that required by the sort
itself. For example, during the initial phase, conversion, validation, input
editing, and other such functions can be accomplished before items are
delivered to the sort process. During the second phase, which may consist of several intermediate passes of the data through the central processor, merging may be supplemented by collapsing items of like key into
one item. During the last phase, a wide variety of run consolidation possibilities are open to the system designer. For example, as the items are

delivered from the final merge before outputting, they can be immediately applied to the master file in normal file maintenance. Other possibilities are summarization of like items, output editing and conversion, validation procedures dependent on sequence, and so forth.

MERGE RUNS

Most computer tape sorts produce at most one full tape of sorted items. When the file to be sorted exceeds one tape, tapes must be sorted individually. The sorted tapes are then merged to form an ordered file. Figure 4-4 is a schematic of a two-way merge of two ordered sets of numbers to produce one ordered set.

The merge is another run type. Merging is subject to generalization and can be done by standardized routines. The sort generators created by computer manufacturers often incorporate merge generators. These automatically produce the merge applicable to the sort whose generation is requested.

Merges have been discussed formerly as the final phases of a sort. However, there are situations in which the merges may appear in the process chart a considerable number of runs or even cycles after the sort which supports it. For example, a system may process a transaction file daily, and at the end of the week, the five daily transaction files are merged to be processed as a weekly transaction file. Merging implies that the data in each of several files previously have been put into a common sequence on a prescribed key.

Where the number of tapes to be merged into a file or the number of files to be merged is very large and exceeds the number of tape handlers available, it will be necessary to have a series of runs all effecting merges of some of the tapes and files involved. Methods for construction of optimal run patterns of multilevel merging are described in a later chapter.

As in sorts, other processing may be incorporated into the pass of data which takes place in a merge. In multilevel merges, the same supplementary processing can be effected in the intermediate levels as described for the intermediate phases of a sort. In the final merging pass of a multilevel merge or in a single-level merge, the same processing as described for the last pass of a sort can be introduced.

SEQUENCE-CHECK RUN

The sequence-check run is a run type that may be part of a file maintenance function or may appear in other parts of systems. The function of a sequence check is to determine that a file presumably in a desired order is actually in that order. Normally a sequence-check run incorporates automatic error-correction procedures. These take the form of sorting the out-of-sequence items detected and their subsequent merging with that portion of the file which was found to be in the prescribed sequence. Hence, a more complete and accurate name for such a run would be *sequence check-sort-merge run.*

Where the break in sequence is from reel to reel in a multireel file rather than within a reel, the system designer provides for the correction of this by computer center instructions calling for a merge of the tapes at fault.

ITEM EXPANSION RUNS

Some files are passed frequently in a system. Their length is often minimized by storing the information in these files in a compact, encoded form. For example, the files in a railroad freight accounting system might carry commodity identification in a three-digit decimal, ICC commodity code form rather than incorporate the more lengthy alphabetic commodity descriptions. At some point in such a system it may be necessary to produce a report about the encoded information stored in some file. It may be desirable to print the information in a clear (decoded) rather than, or in addition to, an encoded form. If such is the case, the report printing run must be preceded by a collation run. This latter matches the file forming the basis of the report (the detail file) against a file that constitutes the transaction dictionary (the reference file). This reference file provides the information to be printed in both a coded and a clear form. This run expands the items in the detail file by adding to each item the translation information found in the reference file. This may consist of substituting the clear information for, or appending the clear information to, the encoded information. The output of this expansion run is an expanded detail file ready to be printed.

For example, one file in a freight accounting system might contain all waybill information for a given period of time summarized according to commodity. The key identifying each of the items on the file might be a three-digit decimal commodity code. Suppose it is desired to print the information summarized on this detail file in commodity code order. Suppose that, in addition to printing commodity codes, it is desired to include the commodity descriptions in the report. It may not be feasible to carry these descriptions on the detail file. In such a case, before printing can occur, the detail file must be matched against a reference file, each item of which consists of a commodity code and the associated commodity description. The output of this expansion run is an expanded detail file; each item in the output file contains all the information making up the corresponding item on the input detail file supplemented by the appropriate commodity description.

The run that expands detail items on the basis of a reference file is another general run type. A more familiar instance of this type of run is in the payroll system in which daily pay items are keyed by employee number. Only once a pay period is the net pay file passed against a master file of employee names and addresses to recover these in preparation for check printing.

EDITING RUNS

Information in a computer data processing system is handled by a variety of equipment. The code structure and format in which one piece of equipment handles the information may not be the same as that required by another piece of equipment. For example, a computer may read information from a card in six-bit character code and require that the information be in four-bit numeric code before it is processed arithmetically. The information may then have to be returned to six-bit character code to actuate a printer. The editing run may provide a check on the validity of the initial character and the accuracy of the character translation. Or the sequence of characters in which the information is most readily keypunched on a card and the character sequence in which it is desired to print this information may be different. In such a case, at some time between the point at which the information is read from the cards and the point at which it is printed, the information must be rearranged from one character sequence to the other. If the editing is done on information just read into the computer system, it is called *input editing;* on information about to be put out of the computer system, it is called *output editing.*

Input editing may consist of a variety of processing operations at the character, field, item, batch (reel, deck) or file level. The operations may consist of translation, deletions, additions, replications, rearrangements, and so forth. Character code conversion has been mentioned already.

The characters within a field of an item as delivered in the input record may not correspond exactly to the structure desired in further processing of that field. It is common to delete from the field in the input edit run those characters that had control or other purposes in prior processing on other equipment or in other runs but are not required any further. For example, control signals on perforated tape may be used to establish item beginning, field marks, choice of alphabet, and so forth, and then are dropped from the item produced by the input edit. An input item may carry a check digit for validating a particular field and this redundant digit may no longer be necessary after validation. It is common in character-addressable computers and in records where the right or left justification of the field is known from order or field within the record to suppress unnecessary zeros or spaces from the input record. In other instances, characters may be inserted into a field during input editing. As an example, one often inserts zero- and space-fills into fields of items to be processed in computers preferring items with fixed field sizes. Characters in a field may be aligned for ease of subsequent processing. For example, an input field may be converted from one fixed decimal form to a rounded, truncated, or filled version in another fixed-decimal or floating-decimal form. The radix of a numerical field may be altered.

In addition to character and field modifications, entire fields may be dropped or added from an item. For example, an input card deck may bear a transaction type code in each card, which is no longer necessary after validation. Another example is the deletion of serial numbers, after sequence checking and validation establish than no items are missing or repeated. In general, one would drop any field not required by subsequent processing.

In other cases, fields may be inserted in the input edit. A common one is the insertion of item count or serial number into each item. Another is the plugging of a transaction type key into each item so that subsequent processing may batch different types. In some cases, this transaction type information or the date of the input may be delivered in the form of a header item to the input file for insertion into each item of the file in the input edit. This is similar to gang punching, just as dropping fields is equivalent to selective reproduction in card processing.

Rearrangement of field sequence within an item is a very common function of an input edit. The sequence in which fields appear in an input document may be determined by the requirements for economy in preparation of the document and in subsequent encoding and conversion to machine legible form. This field sequence may not necessarily be the most effective arrangement for exploiting the special characteristics of the system used in computer processing. For example, fields may be re-arranged within an item to contribute to sorting efficiency. Fields may be shifted so as to provide common alignment of decimal point for arithmetic operations. They may be grouped to exploit opportunities for multifield transfer and other operations. Many other instances could be cited.

The input edit may operate on items as well as on characters and fields. For example, items may be tested in some respect, and certain items dropped on the basis of the results of the test. In other cases, several items may be collated and possibly summarized into one. This can be desirable within the items of a single file, as in header-trailer sets, which will be discussed further, or among the corresponding items of two or more simultaneous input files to the edit run. The summary item may replace the detail items from which it is derived or may supplement them. In the latter case, it may be interfiled with copies of the detail items or dispersed independently into a special file of summary items. An example is the instance of summary items developed for each of several transaction types present in the input file, or for each one of several input files. Another example is the construction within the input edit of special items carrying control, identifying, and other "housekeeping" information for batches of items or an entire file.

It is not uncommon to have header-trailer combinations to represent a single input item. This arises where the data required in the input is so extensive as to exceed the carrying capacity of the unit record medium. Hollerith punched cards have only 80 columns and it is rarely convenient to use all 960 bit-positions possible on the card. More commonly, header-trailer sets are used for lengthy items as described in the earlier discussion of file maintenance. One function of an input edit is to assemble such header-trailer sets into a single item, stripping out fields whose sole purpose is to establish linkage and sequence between header and trailers. In other instances, a header-trailer set may be used to convey information from a batch of input items bearing much common data. In such a case, the header item may carry the common fields and the trailer items the detail differing from item to item. The input edit must replicate the information from the header item into each input item to complete its unit record. It is likely that the header input item will thereupon be disestablished as an independent item for further processing.

It has been remarked that several input files may be present in an input edit run. Since files come from different processing subsystems, each input file may present an individual editing problem. In addition, there may be an interfiling of items prescribed by the edit, dropping of like items, combining of corresponding items from two or more input files into one or more output items with expansion of the fields present in any one of the items or dropping of duplicated fields, and so forth.

Analogous to this on the output side of the input edit run is the accomplishment of a dispersion or even a replication and dispersion of items on to two or more output files. These items may have been arranged in one or more inputs to the input edit run. For example, the input edit may provide for the test of transaction type of each input item and for the dispersion into independent output files of each transaction type, especially where each type is to be subjected later to quite unique processing.

One use of the input edit has such important system design implications that it is worth special mention. If the input items are ultimately to be required in two or more sequences on different occasions in the process chart, the input edit may replicate each input item, plug a type key into each copy, and place it in the output in as many copies as required sequences. Each copy will have its own field arrangement within the item so that a single sort with common coordinate definition for the sequencing key will produce several copies of the file, each batched by transaction type and further sequenced within transaction type as required by the various subsequent processes for each type.

Output editing also provides many possibilities comparable to those discussed with respect to input editing. In principle, the problem of character code conversion is identical to that in input editing. A new code structure must be formed that will actuate devices used further in the processing. Characters may be dropped, added, or rearranged within a field. Function control signals may be inserted for punched paper tape output. Characters may be right- or left-justified within a field. Zeros and spaces may be inserted to complete appropriate fields. Decimal points, commas, and other punctuation may be inserted into a field. Dollar signs may be provided either left-justified or floated to the next left position of the most significant digit of a dollar amount field. Zeros in the input item to the output edit may be suppressed for preparation for printing or punching. Numerous other special symbols may be inserted for subsequent printing. Overpunches and various other control punches may be edited into the output of the output editing run for subsequent card punching.

An output of the output editing run may contain only those fields and items from the various inputs to the run which are required for subsequent processing, other data being dropped within the run. Fields and items may be added or rearranged as in input editing. For example, in the use of exception reports as a management control device, the output edit may test each item against prescribed control limits perhaps delivered from a standards file. Only those items outside control limits would be selected for output of the output editing run. An example of field selection occurs in the creation of output from a payroll master file for subsequent printing of paychecks. Only the employee name and identification number, date, gross pay, net pay, and deduction detail would be delivered for printing actuation. Other fields in the master file, such as year-to-date accumulations, would be ignored in the current output.

An item which appears as a single entity in the input to the output edit may require formatting so as to appear as several items in the output of the output edit run. This is particularly the case where printers and card punches are subsequently to be actuated. The input item may be formatted into a header and several trailer subitems for punching into a header-trailer set or for printing as a multiline entry on hard copy with each subitem providing the detail for each line of printing.

In the course of forming the output detail, various heading items or summary items may be formed for significant batches of output and even for the entire file. For example, in preparation for printing, a report heading the summary item may be prepared for the entire file; each page may have its own heading and summarizing items; each control break within a page may have its own identification and subtotals. Preliminary to this, another function of the output edit run will be to batch the output items in accordance with the pages on which they will be printed and to provide the necessary controls for vertical formatting. If items are to be printed side by side but in columns in sequence (two-up, three-up, etc., printing) on a line printer, the output edit must effect substantial item rearrangement within the input file sequence and proper interlacing of the corresponding line subitems from the side by side items.

As in input editing, there may be one or more inputs to an output edit. Similarly, there may be one or more outputs from the output edit. Hence, one function may be the dispersion from one or more streams of some or all of the fields present in the various inputs, each output stream being provided concurrently with the editing required to adapt it to the subsequent processing peculiar to it. Editing is a very general process. In fact, every run can be considered to have an input edit and an output edit phase. Editing is so common a requirement of computer processing that all computers have some special provision for easing the editing burden. For example, basic machine instructions may be provided for simplifying editing—shift, character extraction, field selection, word masking, zero suppression, special symbol insertion, automatic character conversion, and so forth. The computer and its supporting peripherals often are provided with hardware features incorporating edit capabilities—coding and decoding matrices, multilevel and format control plugboards, symbol-fill and column-split, zero suppression, error detection, and vertical format controls. Perhaps the most extensive instance of omnibus editing capabilities is the satellite computer.

Computer software (programming systems) may be provided with editing capabilities. These may include data conversion-edit routines, input/output subroutines, and extensive report generators and editing compilers. The more flexible of these provide for the incorporation of other operations within the run beyond editing.

In fact, editing is very frequently combined with other functions within a single run. This is particularly true of conversion and validation procedures for input and conversion procedures for output, where the item processing contains many features in common with editing. In the description of sorting and other general runs, it was mentioned that editing could be accomplished in first and last phases.

Editing is very important in random access processors. It cannot be delayed but must be combined with conversion and validation so that an input item can be processed against the master file upon receipt. In particular, random inquiries from on-line input devices designed to match capabilities of human beings will probably require conversion and substantial editing to a form economical to computer processing. Similarly, responses from the computer system will have to be converted and edited for the particular output display device used in the man-machine system.

COMPUTATIONS RUNS

Most computation in business data processing is incorporated within other general run types, and particularly file maintenance. However, there are occasions when the detailed computation pertaining to each item of a file is so extensive that memory or other limitations prevent the consolidation of computation with other significant processing. A computation is one run which, except for modest input/output subroutines, is devoted to computation. For example, in some pay systems, the rules of development of gross pay from clockcards are so complex that little else can be accomplished in the gross pay computation run other than the application of these rules. Computation runs are more likely to occur in small-scale, mathematical programs. Large-scale mathematical programs usually involve as much data shuffling as is normally present in mundane business data processing.

5

ITEM DESIGN

PERSPECTIVE

The computer application determines the information content of a computer system. However, it determines generally, but not specifically, the variety and sequence of items to be processed, the field complement of each item, the sequence of fields within an item, and the choice and arrangement of characters to encode the information content of each field. The specific limitations are imposed by two factors. The first is the need to accommodate the computer system design to the requirements of the input preparation group and the clerical, managerial, or scientific organization consuming the results produced by the computer. The second is the need to design for characteristics of a scientific computer and of its supporting peripheral equipment.

Every computer system begins with the solution of problems of the initial recording of events and transactions—the encoding and transmission of this information to the computer and its support equipment. The techniques for dealing with this *source data problem* effectively tend to condition the medium, format, and other characteristics of the information as it appears at the threshold of the computer. Even the code structure for a particular datum may be made easy for application by manual means, or easy for conversion from the physical output of a device used to sense some event. Similarly, the medium, format, code structure, and other evident aspects of the data considered efficient for use by those who are being served by the computer system must be considered in the design of data for internal computer processing. A physical device may have to be actuated by the computer output, and this will influence the form in which information is processed and delivered. In later sections of this book, forms design and other input and output problems are discussed at length. The emphasis here is on the form of information for efficiency within the narrower confines of the computer process.

Computer characteristics are all important to the present considerations. One must know the media—punched card, perforated tape, document for character recognition, magnetic tape, printed copy—in which the information will be delivered to the computer threshold and in which intermediate and final output will be recorded. Conversion runs as well as peripheral hardware and satellite computers have been discussed in this connection. Furthermore, editing runs have been discussed as a means of obtaining structural designs of information efficient for internal processing. The fundamental computer characteristic influencing data design is the character mode of the computer. Is the system binary, octal, hexadecimal, decimal, alphanumeric, or multimodal? Other characteristics affecting data design are:

1. The nature of memory addressing—character or field addressing, word addressing
2. Run-to-run communications (basic input/output)—card, magnetic tape, perforated tape—and the efficient use of these recording and reading media
3. The capacity and cost of file storage—drums and disks in random access processors, tapes and cards in batch processors
4. Operand size permitted in instruction repertoire for data movement, logical and arithmetic operations

These are mere insinuations of the complex elements of machine design influencing information design.

It is indeed impossible to discuss data design without specific computer characteristics in mind. Since the computer system which probably presents most of the problems in item design, is a tape-oriented, batch processor with fixed word length and word addressed memory, prime attention is focused on such a computer system. However, there are frequent references to the applicability of the item design principles to other types of computers, or to the corresponding principles for other systems.

Subsequent chapters deal with the design of a file on tape, in card decks, or other media. The current discussion is limited to the design of items within the file.

OBJECTIVES AND SCOPE OF ITEM DESIGN

Information is dealt with in the computer in the form of reports on events, transactions, and other unit records gathered to form files of individual items. The information in each item is determined by the demands of the application and usually is in two categories. The first is a body of data identifying the item from others. This is called *indicative data*. It is generally moved or operated upon logically but seldom is manipulated arithmetically in the processing. Another body of data within the item gives specific values of certain observations assigned to the item. These values are not necessarily unique to the item—many items may have identical sets of values. These data are often operated upon arithmetically and otherwise. Each of these bodies of data is subdivided into fields. Each field represents a particular datum of interest—the recorded characteristic, such as marital status; assigned parameters, such as hourly rate of pay; measurement, such as number of dependents; and so on—in short, what the mathematician calls a variable and the physicist a dimension. Each field consists of a collection of one or more symbols from the computer's symbol complement, which will be called the computer's alphabet. Each symbol in turn is represented by a configuration of one or more bits.

Although the nature of the fields in an item is strongly constrained by the application requirements, the choice of fields within an item is an important aspect of item design. Because not every field of interest need be represented in every item and, for other reasons cited subsequently, this selection of fields may present a significant design problem.

Item structure requires the designation of the sequence of the fields within the item, including the indication of blank fields and variations in use of field space for different types of transaction items in a file. Finally, the manner of encoding the information content of the field is within the scope of item design.

Virtually all of these considerations can be related to two basic aspects of the item: the way information is arranged in the item and the item size. Item design reflects the application system. In item design the system designer neglects any aspect of the application at his peril. However, in theory, item design is simple. There is but one principle— economy of computer running time.

There are two kinds of time: input/output (I/O)—the time to move an item past the input sensing or output recording mechanism; and processing time—the time to process that item inside the computer. The time to move an item past the read-write head of a tape is an example of I/O time, as is also the time to read a punched card or to punch one. The I/O time is in magnitude dependent, of course, on the I/O device used and its speed characteristics. When concern is with data arrangement in an item, attention is directed to the conservation of processing time. Given an item size, the way data are arranged in an item has little to do with how long it takes to read, write or punch the item. However, it has a great deal to do with the length of time necessary to process that item. When interest is in item size, concern is with the conservation of tape length, number of card trailers, lines of print, and, hence, with I/O time. The longer the item, the longer it takes to pass the item over the read-write head. The more tape time is increased. Similarly, the more trailer cards per item, the more card cycles required per item; and the more card reader time is increased for input, card punch time for output. As for processing time limitations, the reader with punched card experience will recall that a nominal 150-card per minute tabulator can be found to be slowed to a substantially lower throughput if extensive arithmetic is required for each card. Item length has no necessary connection with processing time.

There are indeed other objectives to be served in item design beyond direct computer running time. Economy in the use of bits in the design of a file may serve to solve problems of limitations of the size of file storage in a random access processor. Here, the only possible alternative might involve enlargement of the computer hardware complement as well as adding to computer running time.

In a card-handling system, the number of trailers per item will influence card consumption and the cost of card stock. In a paper tape-handling system, costs for tape rolls can be reduced by effective item design. In magnetic tape-handling systems, tape inventory for master files and transaction files in transit may occasionally be reduced. Conceivably, forms design and paper costs for printing may be affected.

For on-line and off-line data conversion equipment, including satellite computers, the equipment demand and operating costs are conditioned by file sizes and this, in turn, by item design. Generally, medium more remote from the computer determine the rate of item handling.

GROSS CONSIDERATIONS IN I/O AND PROCESSOR TIME

The issue of I/O-computer balance is not as simple as has been intimated. The more "loosely" information is arranged in an item (the more space there is between fields), the more quickly it can be processed. Arranging information loosely in an item increases item size. That increase may mean an increase in I/O time. Packing information tightly into an item reduces item size and possibly I/O time, but the item may have to be unpacked to be processed. The time to do this unpacking must be added to the processing time. Information arrangement and item size are not unrelated. In item design the most satisfactory compromise between the conflicting goals of minimization of I/O time and processing time must be made.

Computer limited runs should have item design oriented toward information arrangement; and I/O limited runs, toward item size reduction. Arrangement of data for easy processing may increase I/O time, but this is of no consequence in a computer limited operation. Compressing item size may increase processing time, but in a I/O limited operation it will not increase running time.

Speaking of a run as being computer or I/O limited is a simplification. Some runs may be computer limited at one point in a file and I/O limited at another, depending on how much processing is required by the activity of the particular items at any given point in the file. Taking his knowledge of this activity into consideration, the system designer must come up with the item size and information arrangement that minimizes total running time.

The notion that all runs are either computer limited or I/O limited is not entirely applicable for all types of computers. Some computers are not provided with facilities for buffering between I/O devices and the computer memory. In such a computer, total control of the computer and its memory access is seized during a continuous portion of the document cycle of the I/O device. This portion is a significant percentage of the cycle of the I/O device and no computing can proceed concurrent with it. The computer running time in such a system is the sum of the I/O data transfer time and the internal processing time. The object of item design for such a system will still be to minimize computer running time; however, now both elements, I/O time and processing time, will have to be considered rather than just their maximum.

This situation is complicated by the fact that not all items contain information in all fields. This situation extends from the simple case, in which an employee may or may not have dependents, to an insurance application, in which a policy holder may or may not elect a variety of options. There are two ways this information variability can be handled. One is to design the item so there is space for every field possibility. Those spaces allocated to fields not pertinent to a particular item are filled with blanks. The other approach is to have each item contain only those fields with significant information and allow item length to vary from item to item. The first approach is referred to as *fixed item size;* the second, as *variable item size.* Of course, the variable sized item must contain a special fixed field (transaction type) identifying the fields present in the item, be so organized that the conditional fields are in trailer subitems, or use some similar technique for orderly collapse of the item.

For a file, it must be decided whether the item size will be fixed or variable. This decision is one aspect of the primary item design problem. Should information in the item be arranged to minimize processing time or item size?

A fixed item size contributes to minimizing processing time, since the location of each field is fixed and can be addressed simply. In variable sized items the location of fields is variable. When it is desired to operate on a field, it must be located, and this location takes time. I/O time is minimized with variable item size, since nothing is recorded or read that is not pertinent. With fixed item size, every time a field does not apply to an item, an equivalent number of fill characters is carried in I/O devices.

This is the problem. Should the item be designed to make for easy processing or minimum I/O time? A major aspect of this question is, "Should item size be fixed or variable?"

ARRANGEMENT OF INFORMATION

The reason for directing attention toward the information arrangement is to reduce processing time. The processing to be done in a run is fixed. It cannot be reduced or increased unless an unwary programmer introduces redundant operations. Item design cannot increase or decrease the amount of processing a run requires. The area in which item design has an effect on processing time is not in the area of processing to be done. It is in the arranging of information preparatory to and subsequent to processing—in other words, in editing. If interest is in reducing processing time, concentrate on designing the item so editing is minimized.

Editing is minimized by arranging fields in items so a field to be operated on can be accessed and results of processing can be stored with no editing. In a word-addressable computer, the computer operates on a word or series of words; one way this goal can be approached is to restrict the contents of a word to a field or part of a field. This device is particularly helpful if the field is operated on arithmetically. The field, isolated in a word or series of words, can be operated on without the need to separate it from other fields. A result can be stored without fear that the process will destroy other needed information. This approach minimizes the use of field selection, masking, or character extraction, which cost processing time. Similarly, in a character-addressable computer, the characters constituting an operand should be contiguous within the item to minimize assembly before operation.

It should not be assumed that an uncritical segregation of fields among words in a word-addressable computer necessarily results in a processing time reduction. For example, if there are two key fields, each of which must be tested for equality with some constant at the same point in a program, it is to the system's advantage not to have these fields in distinct, separated words, but to have them in the same word or series of adjacent words. In this way, the fields can be tested with one set of comparison and jump operations rather than two.

To pursue this example further, suppose the two key fields are to be tested simultaneously for equality against a constant at some point in the system, but that at another point it is necessary to operate on the fields individually. Assume that each field is less than a word in size. To minimize processing time, the fields should be stored in separate words to allow immediate access to them for individual processing. If the computer is equipped with multiple precision instructions in its repertoire they should be stored in adjacent words so they can be accessed as a two-word operand when it is necessary to compare them against the constant. Correspondingly, in character-addressable systems with flexible operand size, placing the fields in adjacent character positions would enable simultaneous operating on both fields with one order.

A more general statement of a principle embodied in the preceding example is as follows. If a series of fields is to be operated on in the same way, and if it is possible to perform the operation on all the fields at the same time, then the fields should be arranged in a contiguous sequence so the fields can be treated as a multiple operand and be operated on with one instruction. For example, if several fields of an item are to be transferred to another location, these fields should be stored sequentially so they can be transferred as a multiple operand.

In a fixed word-length computer, a field should not be split across more words than is necessary. The purpose of this rule is to minimize the number of words to be accessed to access the field, since the more words there are in a multiword operand, the longer it takes to operate on that operand. There are great costs in processing time for extracting, shifting, and rearranging the characters required to form the desired operand.

If it becomes advantageous to have the least significant portion of a sorting key field and some other field share a word in a word-organized computer, place the key to the left of the other field.. Then the sort can proceed without the necessity of extracting the key. The other field can enter the sequencing comparisons without effect, since it enters as the least significant digits. Of course, this problem does not exist in character-addressable computers.

Sort and merge routines are made available by computer manufacturers. These sorts and merges have conventions with respect to how to find the keys of the items to be sorted and merged. It is advantageous to incorporate these runs into a system, since each incorporation means one more run in the system that is programmed and debugged. To gain this advantage, the keys of items shoud be laid out to conform with the requirements of the standard routines.

Program decimal and binary points should be taken into consideration in laying out fields that are to be operated on arithmetically. For fields that are involved in addition or subtraction, processing time is minimized if the program points of the operand fields and the result field are lined up. Such an approach eliminates shifting. For fields that enter or contain the result of multiplication or division operations, the same rule applies. Arrange the points so shifting is minimized.

Another technique is also applicable to fixed-word computers. A total may be accumulated in a field. It may be possible for the length of this field to extend beyond one word in size. Suppose all fields to be added to this accumulation field are one word or less in length: In such a situation arrange the accumulation field so that as many of the least significant digits as possible are in one word. For example, if the computer word is six digits long and the accumulation field is seven digits long, the six least significant digits should be stored in one word and the most significant digit in another. By designing the accumulation field in this manner, it is possible to program the addition or subtraction of the increment fields to the accumulation field with one word operands, the six least significant digits of the accumulation field constituting one of the operands. Such an approach requires that, when overflow occurs, a special subroutine be coded to increase (or reduce) the most significant digit of the accumulation field by one. This approach is less expensive than providing two-word operands for the increment fields and performing a two-word operand addition every time an incrementation of the accumulation field is necessary. There are some instances where a corresponding device can be used in character-addressable computers.

If a field can be positive or negative, a sign bit or character must be assigned to it. The field must be laid out so this sign bit or character is associated with it during arithmetic operations. Suppose it is a characteristic of the computer that a field which is field selected or extracted cannot have any sign bit selected. To avoid editing for sign handling, fields which can carry either a plus or minus sign should be arranged so that field selection is never necessary.

For those fields not requiring a sign, the sign bits or characters of the fields or words in which they are stored can be used for additional information. For example, a sign is sufficient to indicate whether a person is male or female. If the sign is used this way, be sure the operand does not enter any arithmetic operations.

CHARACTER MODE AND FIELD DESIGN

There is a considerable connection between the mode in which fields are encoded and the information arrangements possible in an item. Hence, the influence of mode on item design will be considered further in preparation for the completion of the discussion of field arrangement. The use of a sign bit or character for indicative data has been discussed already. Of course, the modes available reflect details of the computer characteristics. Although the computer is binary on the simplest engineering levels, it may or may not be organized to recognize one-bit characters or to perform binary operations on binary operands. In fact, most older and many current computers use a single mode with a fixed number of bits required to represent each character in the computer's alphabet. In such a computer, there is no choice of mode in field design. However, some of these computers use a single bit for algebraic sign of operand; this may be available for use as a simple two-valued field. Other computers permit the use of an additional compact mode for a restricted portion of the alphabet. The most common instance is the use of a four- or five-bit code for decimals in computers requiring six or seven bits for the general alphanumeric symbol complement including the decimals. Some early computers were limited to decimal operands, others were indeed binary, octal, or hexadecimal. Recent trends have been toward multimodal computers. In the design of fields for such a computer, the bit structure of characters in each mode is of consequence. Also, the instruction repertoire must contain direct functions on operands in the various modes or the computer cannot be said to function in these modes. There may or may not be special characters or fields used to designate the mode of an operand and this must be provided in the item design where required. Some computers require prescribed modes in conversion from and to external devices. This may require editing of fields into and out of other modes for efficiency of other internal processing.

Where the mode is inflexible, there is no problem of choice of mode for field design as a contribution to optimizing item design. Where there is latitude, as is more commonly the case in modern computers, the interest in exploitation of binary representation is high.

Information representation in pure binary form is not restricted to use of a sign bit. Most computers have the ability to handle information in binary regardless of where it is in a field or word. Since binary is the most efficient method of representing information in the computer, it becomes ideal for use with respect to indicative fields and even numerical fields when the system never requires the fields to be converted to another mode. This is the situation if the field is never used outside the computer.

In the case of numeric fields that must be handled in decimal form (for computation or output, for example), the information is not necessarily carried in the computer in the form required for handling. The cost of converting from binary to the desired mode, or vice versa, must be compared against the space savings afforded by carrying the information in binary. If the field is used infrequently enough, the nod may go to binary representation.

Whether a field can be stored in less space in binary than in another form is determined by the following rules. Let us suppose the field is numeric and a decimal number is represented in d bits within the computer. Further, let m be the number of bits required to represent the field in binary, and n the number of digits required to represent the field in decimal. Then when dn is greater than m, space is saved by storing the field in binary. Similarly, let the field be alphanumeric and an alphanumeric character be represented in the computer by α bits. Further, let x be the number of bits required to represent the field in binary, and y the number of characters required to represent the field alphanumerically. Then when αy is greater than x, space is saved by storing the field in binary. When space is not saved there is no point in going to binary mode. If space is saved, binary still may not be the most efficient storage form, if it entails more processing time than another mode, but an investigation into the possibility is indicated. In some computers, binary operations are executed faster than decimal ones; this should favor the choice of binary mode.

Comparable space savings can be obtained by use of a decimal mode for numerics rather than an alphanumeric mode in computers permitting it. One popular computer permits packing three decimal characters in the same bit space as two alphabetic versions of the same decimals. This capability has to be exploited in item design.

As an example of steps to facilitate this exploitation, let us imagine a word-addressable computer in which alphanumeric characters are represented by six bits, but decimal digits can additionally be represented by four bits for operations in the decimal mode. The word organization of the memory, as contrasted with character addressability, may make it difficult to extract the advantages of the efficient four-bit decimal representation, unless the fields are suitably arranged within the item. In general, space savings can be realized if all alphanumeric fields are grouped in one part of the item, front or back, and all decimal data are grouped in the remaining part. The alphanumeric fields can then be packed into contiguous characters in an unbroken string of alphanumeric words. Similarly, the decimal fields can be packed into a sequence of decimal words. This generally will save bit space and also facilitate the use of multiword operations in each mode in the handling of adjacent words in order to effect internal processing savings. A concrete illustration may clarify the issue. Suppose that a computer word contains 24 bits plus sign bit, and that there are four fields in the item—a two-digit decimal, four-digit decimal, five-character alphanumeric and three-character alphanumeric. Since the five-character alphanumeric already consumes one word and six bits of a second word, one might be tempted to place the 16 bits of the four-digit decimal in the second word, leaving two bits to spare. Now, these two bits are inadequate for even decimal representation; hence, the three-character alphanumeric must go into 18 bits of a third word, laving six bits to spare in it. This is inadequate for the remaining two-digit decimal which must go into a fourth word. Contrast this with the result obtained by putting both alphanumeric fields into two adjacent words and both decimal fields into a single word. Here, three words are adequate where four were required by the previous item design. Of course, in those computers using a fixed number of bits for every character, there would be no opportunity for and no problem of a more effective use of bits in field and item design of the kind described.

As remarked earlier, data conversion from and to input and output devices may influence choice of mode. An alphanumeric code read into a computer from a transaction card may be read in six-bit alphanumeric character mode even though the numerics in the code need only four bits for representation. Here is an instance where six-bit characters and four-bit numerics can possibly be combined in one word. The comparison instructions that investigate the code must be able to make a binary comparison. If by packing the characters and numerics of an alphanumeric code in as few bits as possible enough space can be saved in a master item, it may pay to take the time to effect this packing as the codes come in from the transaction cards. On the other hand, if the time to do the packing is significant, it may be better to avoid the packing and settle for a larger master item size. Number of items in the master file is a factor in this determination. The greater the number, the less desirable the increase in item size.

Of course, the design of each field is largely determined by the computer application. One needs to ask what the range of variation of the field is, what precision of measurement (number of significant digits) is required, what the number of possible values to be found in a field is, and so on. All these questions are usually resolved in the design of the input system and will be discussed later in this text.

MORE ON ARRANGEMENT

In computers in which field selection, masking, or extraction are controlled by specifying the beginning and ending bits of a field it is important to keep the characters in a field contiguous. In computers in which field selection is controlled by masks or extract patterns this requirement is not as important.

An example illustrates an important technique: Let us suppose the information in, perhaps, the name field of an employee master item must be arranged first name, middle name, and last name. Let us suppose further that it is necessary to sort the employee master file alphabetically by last name. Then, a special symbol, such as an ampersand can be placed in the character position immediately preceding the first character of the last name. This special symbol can be searched for by the sort to locate the last name. This approach is more economical than providing three fields: a first-name field, a second-name field, and a last-name field.

If most of the entries for a field consist of, for example, six digits or less, but a very few entries require many more digits, one may try the following: Allocate six digits to the field, assign special six-digit codes to the nonconforming entries, and on the basis of these codes, look up these entries in an internal table of program constants.

Much information is read into the computer from master and transaction files, moved through the computer in conjunction with associated processing, and put out on some output unit, such as the printer, with no change in the nature of the information. Badge numbers, names, addresses, and other indicative information are subject to such handling. The way information is printed on a line is a function of the way the information is arranged in the memory at the time the print instruction is executed. The way information is punched in a card is also a function of the way it is arranged in the memory. Similar remarks can be made for all output equipment. The more this output format of indicative information is retained in the item design of the file in which it is introduced into the computer, the fewer instructions it takes to move this information through the data flow in the computer until it is recorded on the output unit.

The rules just stated are not all compatible. When it comes to information arrangement, every instance a field is used in a system must be conceived of. That field must be fitted into the item so that overall efficient manipulation of this field is optimized. It may pay to reduce the efficiency of a run to increase the efficiency of the system of which it is a part. To concentrate on system efficiency as affected by item arrangement, identify the family of runs in the system which a particular item design pervades and optimize the efficiency with which the fields in the item are handled using the following considerations:

1. Try to improve those items used in a run or a family of runs involving the greatest computer running time with due consideration for length of run and frequency of running. Presumably, this defines the area of greatest potential for gain.

2. Improve those items in a run or family of runs where the internal processing is most extensive, that is, most likely to be heavily computer limited.

3. In the course of this item rearrangement, investigate those fields most frequently used.

Such an approach requires that the system designer be familiar with programming so he can make this analysis competently. The approach also implies that, short of programming the system, there is no way of telling whether efficiency of field manipulation has been optimized. As programming of the system advances, changes in item design may manifest themselves as desirable. The system designer must make himself available for suggestions on modification of item design and evaluate these suggestions for adoption or rejection.

ITEM SIZE

There are two purposes for reducing item size. To reduce the number of tapes or cards in a file or, generally, to fit a file into a random access storage system and to reduce tape, card, or other I/O time. A reduction in the number of tapes or cards in a file results in a reduction in tape inventory and consumption of card stock. If the number of tapes in a file is reduced to one, tape swap is eliminated, tape handler allocation and computer center controls are simplified and runs may be eliminated. An example of such run elimination occurs with respect to a file that must be sorted at some point in the system. If the item size is initially such that it makes this file a two-tape file, and if by packing the item the file can be reduced to a one-tape file, a merge following the sort can be eliminated. If a card file contains no trailers, there is still the prospect of reducing item size and using a single card for two or more items. If trailers exist, there is the prospect of eliminating them through improvement in item design.

When a tape file consists of one tape an item size reduction is aimed at reducing tape time. There has been too much emphasis on minimizing item size for this purpose. Not enough consideration is given to the relatively high proportion of the tape time devoted to setting up and taking down the tape reel. For example, if tape passing time is 12 seconds and setup and takedown are 30 seconds each, a 100 percent reduction in file length only reduces the sum of tape passing, mounting and dismounting time from 72 seconds to 66. Also, if a run is computer-limited, reducing item size does not reduce running time. It may increase running time. In a computer-limited operation, running time is determined by processing time. Squeezing item size means more instruction per field processed. Hence, instances in which significant benefit can be derived from item size reduction in smaller files are few.

The importance of minimizing item size is a function of data volume. The smaller the volume, the less important the minimization. Making it easy to handle an item results in lengthening it. If a file is short, why make it a difficult programming job to handle the items in that file for the sake of a microscopic reduction in the file size?

To underline the relationship between file size and I/O time saved by item size reduction, consider the following: Suppose an effective (overall, not instantaneous) I/O data transfer rate is s seconds per character. If this is multipled by c, the number of characters in an item, the result is effective transfer rate (R) in terms of seconds per item.

$$R = sc$$

Multiplying R by n, the number of items in a file, yields tape time T, for the file.

$$T = snc$$

The quantity s is a constant. T varies directly with n and c. The smaller n is, the less a change in c affects the value of T. In other words, item size for a short file is not as crucial as for a long file.

This relationship is shown graphically in Figure 5-1. The lines on this chart represent I/O time as a function of item size for various numbers of items. The larger the number of items, the steeper the slope of the line. The steeper the slope of the line, the more drastic the change in I/O time as a result of a change in item size. Packing master items may be more sensible than packing transaction items. Master data volume is usually greater than transaction data volume. When this is the case, master item size reduction has a more significant effect on I/O time than transaction item size reduction.

Another consideration that may argue for larger item size even at the cost of some increase in running time is the existence of already coded routines. Generally, computer manufacturers will deliver with the equip-

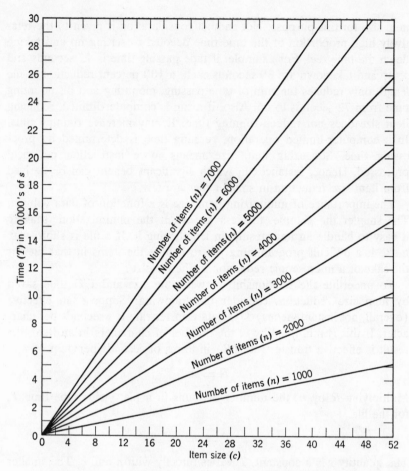

Fig. 5-1   I/O Time as a Function of Item Size and Number

ment software packages providing a large number of general runs of the kind discussed earlier. Among these are sort runs, merge runs, sequence check-sort-merge runs, edit runs, report generating or editing runs, file maintenance runs, and data conversion runs. The software may include significant subroutines encompassing important functions within a run such as input/output functions, item advance, mathematical processing, and so forth. Although many of these software elements are of a general nature, there will usually be some restrictions on the family of items to which they can be applied or on the structure and location of certain critical fields within items. In such cases, the system designer will have to adapt his item design to restrictions imposed by those portions of the software he intends to utilize. The interest will be on saving programming time and placing an application into production on the computer at an earlier date, rather than on attaining minimum computer running time through optimal item design.

The more the output format of indicative information is retained in the item design of the file in which it is introduced, the fewer instructions it takes to handle this information. Because of output editing considerations, such a format may result in a larger item size than is otherwise required. Reducing the item size does not necessarily result in gain. With the larger item size, operation may be I/O limited. With the smaller item size, operation may be computer-limited. Running time may be longer than with the larger size. The complexity of the programmer's job is increased with the packing of the item. This latter also should be of direct concern to the system designer, who is interested in the cost of the programming effort and the time delay in installing a computer application.

Certain hardware characteristics discourage an overconcentration on reduction of item size. For those computers dealing basically with punched card input/output, once an item design corresponds to a single card or less, there is seldom any value in further reduction of item size unless it is possible to compress two or more items into one card. In some tape computers, the magnetic tape is blocked in a fixed number of characters per block and a limited variety of multicharacter or multiword transfer operations is provided. The number of characters or words transferred by such operations is generally a submultiple of the block size. It will be found to be convenient, less likely to produce a computer-limited runs, less likely to engender memory limitation, and less likely to waste tape space, if the item size for such a computer is a submultiple of block size. Reduction of item size in this case would be undesirable unless it could be made in an acceptable quantum to the next lower submultiple of the block size.

One of the most compelling reasons for increasing item size beyond the bounds set up by any concern for processing ease is the possibility of combining low-volume files onto one tape in a tape computer. For example, suppose there are three transaction files feeding into a run. Suppose the item size on each of these files is fixed, and each file must be sorted before it can be introduced into the main run. The standardization of item size on these three files by increasing both other item sizes to the size of the largest allows all three files to be handled on a single tape. This consolidation of files has the following advantages.

1. All three files can be sorted with one sort run. Such an approach results in less running time than would three sort runs, one for each file.
2. Use of one combined tape rather than three individual tapes re-

duces the setup and takedown time required in the main and sort runs.

3. One transaction file rather than three feeding into the main run has many effects on the programming of that run.

a. Only one input area rather than three is required. This reduction in input area requirements frees locations for other use.

b. Housekeeping subroutine requirements for transaction files are cut by two thirds. This means more computer time available for other operations and less locations required to store the subroutines.

c. The number of tape handlers used is reduced.

The effect of these programming ramifications is that enough time and space may be freed to allow more work to be packed into the main run by the system designer and fewer runs required in the process chart.

Another consideration in item size is expansion space. If an item has been designed to be tight, later addition of fields is going to increase item size. Such an increase results in system redesign and reprogramming. Some investment in system flexibility can be made on the basis of intelligent anticipation. However, leaving space for the insertion of more fields in an item should be done with caution. Field addition usually occurs as a concomitant of such significant system changes that system redesign is required independent of change in item size. In the meantime, the blank space allocated for expansion has been "pulled through" the system every time the associated file is used.

FIXED VERSUS VARIABLE ITEM SIZE

Fixed item size contributes to computer time minimization; variable item size to tape time reduction. On the basis of this principle several rules of thumb can be developed.

1. If those fields for which variability exists within an item constitute a small portion of the item size, relatively little benefit can be derived from use of variable item size. Hence, it will be less likely that the benefit will be adequate compensation for the processing complexity introduced by variable item size.

2. If the number of items in a file for which reduction of item size through use of variability is relatively small, the penalty in I/O time for carrying these few items in the larger item size of the remainder of the file will be relatively small. It may be compensated for by the savings in internal processing time arising from uniform item design.

3. There is no point in going to variable item size for a one-shot job. The running time of such a job is usually not a matter of great concern. The objective here is to expedite the coding and running. In such cases

it is adequate to adopt some fixed item size and not worry about the running time that might be saved by going to a variable item size.

4. Variable item size should be restricted to files of large volume. If the information in a file is of small volume, adoption of a fixed item size is not going to significantly increase running time.

5. Variable item size is of use only if activity on a file is low. If activity is high, there is a good possibility that the run is computer limited, in which case variable item size buys nothing and may cost in increased computer time.

In summary, the following are indicators that fixed item size should handle the job.

1. Little variability of data
2. One-shot job
3. Small volume file
4. High activity

The opposite of these indicators points to the use of variable item size. These opposites are

1. Large amount of variability of data
2. Repetitive operation
3. Large volume file
4. Low activity

The chief use of variable item size is to cut down on tape when there is a low frequency of long items and a high frequency of short items in a tape limited operation.

It is more reasonable to use variable item size on a master file than on a transaction file. Master data volume is greater than transaction data volume. Activity on a master file may be low. Activity on a transaction file is 100 percent.

There are all sorts of compromises between fixed and variable item size. The more fixed the item size, the easier it is to process the items, easier in the sense that:

1. Fewer instructions are needed to do the operation.
2. Less computer time is required to execute the operation.
3. The programmer's job is more straightforward.

Choose enough variability to give good computer to I/O balance. Go no further, and the optimum in item size variability is achieved.

The remainder of this section is devoted to a description of the possibilities existing between the extremes of fixed and variable item size.

In fixed item size each item in a file is of a fixed length. The item layout contains space for the storing of all necessary data. For any item where not all information for which space in the item layout has been allocated is applicable, those locations set aside for the inapplicable data are filled with a filler code: spaces if the field is alphanumeric, zeros if numeric.

There is room for variability of information in fixed item size. For example, consider a file containing two item types, renewal and cancellation items. If each renewal item carries a renewal date, and each cancellation item a cancellation date, then it is not necessary to have a renewal date field and a cancellation date field in the item layout. There can be one date field. In renewal items this field is filled with the renewal date, in cancellation items with the cancellation date. The extreme logical extension of this idea is a file containing two or more item types, each type containing information totally different from the information contained in all other types, but all types being of the same item size.

This principle may apply equally well to punched card input/output. For example, suppose the file consists of items having fixed fields well within card capacity and a complement of variable fields which, in total, exceed the remaining card capacity. Suppose further that no item need contain more variable fields than the residual card capacity. Then, one could assign an item type key representative of the particular combination of variable fields in the item. Each card would be punched with this key, the fixed field structure, and the variable fields represented by the key. This puts every item in a single card as an alternative to using a larger uniform item size encompassing all possible fields and requiring header-trailer card sets for each item.

With variable item size the idea of a fixed length for every item in the file is abandoned. Every variable sized item consists of two parts: a header and one or more trailers. No trailers is also a possibility. Header and trailer here mean logical subitems, rather than physically distinct documents.

The header of a variable sized item is a fixed size for the file to which it belongs and contains the fields appearing in 100 percent of the items. However, a field does not have to meet this criterion to be considered for inclusion in the header. The same considerations as were involved in whether item size should be fixed or variable are involved in whether a field should be included in the header, as a fixed part of a variable sized item, or in the trailers, or variable part. If the field appears in a large proportion of the items; or if it is active, whether it is present or not (that is, its presence must be tested for): then the field should be included in the header. Those items for which the field is not applicable can carry fill characters in the space allocated for the field. If the field appears infrequently, then it should be carried as a trailer or part of a trailer when it does occur. The touchstone for the decision is, "Will putting this field in the trailer part of the item contribute to shortening running time?"

Trailer fields occur in groups. For example, in an insurance policyholder master file, a policyholder may elect to have his dividends paid to him or he may elect to let them accumulate. If he elects to let them accumulate, then several fields are necessary. These include current dividend accumulation balance, total dividend accumulations, total dividend accumulation interest, tax credit balance, and current interest. If the policyholder does not elect to let his dividends accumulate, then none of these fields are necessary. It is on the basis of these groupings that the trailers for a variable sized item are determined. In certain instances it may be advantageous from an ease of processing point of view to repeat crucial fields in more than one trailer.

Every item consists of a header and as many trailers as are required. Nonapplicable trailers containing only fill are not carried in the file.

The simplest type of variable sized item occurs where the number of trailers is restricted. For example, suppose there are two mutually exclusive trailers possible for a file, and that one of the two must be present. In such a situation there are two item types possible. The easiest approach is to have a field in the header of each item that identifies the item as to type. All the program has to do is interrogate this field to find out which of the two types the current item is. When the item type is determined, the program knows the item with which it is dealing and the operations called for.

If the number of item types is too large to be handled on a type basis, then some other technique must be adopted. Such a technique must allow each item to communicate to the program what its nature is. There must be some indication to the program of the length of the item in order that it tell where the next item begins. The nature and location of the trailers that make up this item must also be communicated to the routine. These indicators should be designed and located in the item so they can be used by the program with minimum difficulty.

If trailers are arranged in some order by type following the header, the trailer processing is more straightforward than if the trailers were aranged in random order. In many cases it is required that trailers be processed in a prescribed order; in which case it is advantageous to have the trailers so arranged.

Try to make all trailers the same size as the header. This approach makes the item-advance or record-move routine easier. In practice, using headers and trailers of the same size is as far as variable item size has been pushed. Many more sophisticated variable item size techniques have been proposed, but none is in general use.

INFLUENCE OF HARDWARE AND SOFTWARE ON ITEM DESIGN

In computer data processing, items are read into the computer through a variety of input equipment, moved about in the computer's memory, and recorded on a number of different output devices. Reading and recording may be possible in a number of modes. Items may be read and recorded as unit documents or handled in groups. If in groups, the items may be stored contiguously or they may be scattered in memory. Internally the items may be moved with multiword transfer instructions or located by instruction modification or by indexing. Software to handle the operation of the input-output equipment and to deliver items to and receive items from the worker program may embody a variety of techniques. Each possible item-handling operation in the computer has certain advantages and disadvantages, as may the software techniques. One may conserve space at the expense of time. The opposite may be true of another.

A technique that is advantageous to one run may be disadvantageous to another. The system designer must consider these factors in fixing on a technique for a particular run. In many cases, once this choice is made, it has implications as far as item design is concerned. Any restrictions thus imposed on item design must be taken into consideration by the system designer.

EXAMPLE

Consider a maintenance run in which changes and additions are applied to a master file. A variation in the size of change items can be expected. For example, take the most simple type of change, substitution of information. At a minimum such a change item consists of a master item key, a change key, and a new information field. The new information field size has a range of variability, since it can contain information for any of the master item fields subject to change. In this particular master file, most item fields are one word in length. There are, however, few fields that extend over several words. For example, in a payroll master item the name and address fields are longer than the other fields. If the new information field is made large enough to accommodate the largest possible amount of new information, the majority of the time the new information requires less space, and a part of the new information field will be dead space.

Since it is a transaction file on which this variability in information is occurring, variable item size is not the answer. A more feasible solution is to consider the larger new information fields to consist of a number of subfields and have a change item for each subfield. For example, if a new information field of six digits handles most possibilities, but some need 24 digits, the latter can be considered to consist of four six-digit subfields, each subfield containing one-fourth of the new information. When the rare change requiring 24 digits occurs, it requires four change items to accomplish the change. The net result of such an approach is profitable, however, since the size of all change item types is kept to a minimum.

Addition items are longer than change items. The subfield approach may allow addition items to be incorporated on the same file with change items. If the addition item size is too large and the volume of additions is considerable, it may be necessary to split the transactions into two files —a change file and an addition file.

6

BLOCKING

TAPES AND TAPE RECORDING

In the previous chapter, the discussion of optimal item design was obliged to include concern for the time to handle items into and out of the computer as well as within the computer central processing unit. For tape-computers in particular, one must consider how data are recorded on and read from magnetic tape in order to determine what I/O time will result from a proposed item design. In addition, the alignment of data on tape will determine the length of the tape and possibly affect material and operating costs. Thus, a discussion of item design is hardly complete without consideration of data layout on tape as well as in computer memory.

The basic recording and reading mode for magnetic tape systems in digital computers is binary. Other modes are represented in binary codes for uniform or various levels. The tapes of a pure binary computer are likely to be recorded in pure binary. If a decimal mode is permissible, decimals may be represented by a 4-, 5-, 6- or higher level binary code. If an alphanumeric mode is available, it may use a 6-, 7-, 8- or higher level binary code. If multiple modes are possible, the decimal mode may be at a reduced code level from the alphanumeric mode. In addition, there may be redundant bits for each character for error-detecting and possibly for error-correcting purposes. There may be clock-synchronizer bits also, but these are of hardware interest only and do not enter into the item design. There may be special characters or bits to indicate character mode, to start or stop of various integral units of data, and so forth.

In character-addressable computers, the tape record is also character organized. It may be completely unbuffered from the main memory of the computer or there may be character buffers, since memory read-write rate is always much greater than tape read-write rate. In addition, tape data in character-addressable computers are record organized, usually with *record mark* characters to set off a record. The record may be an item or sequence of items extended to be read from or recorded on tape by a single tape instruction. Similarly, word-addressable computers will be buffered from internal memory by buffers with the capacity of one or more words. The data will be record- or block-organized, with a record or block consisting of an integral number of words, except possibly for the special characters or bits to be mentioned subsequently. In some systems, block size is fixed in bit, frame (bits simultaneously read or written by multiple heads of the tape mechanism), character, or word count. In others, the block size may be variable but restricted to an integral number of words or characters. Blocks or tape records may contain not only characters inherent to the information of the computer application, but also special recording patterns for error detection and error correction on a block basis, and for regulating hardware functions and other such purposes outside the control of the application system designer or the programmer.

Between blocks or records, there are areas of gap which may or may not contain signals. If the gap does contain signals they will be for control of hardware and of no item design interest. However, length of gap and time consumed by gaps will be of interest. This time is of special significance because tapes are generally read or written discontinuously in blocks even if buffered from internal memory by large buffer storage units. Some computers permit continuous reading and writing, that is, nonstop between blocks, as well as the usual discontinuous read/write; however, this does not eliminate the need for a tape length devoted to gap.

In addition to the variety of characteristics mentioned, the tape-handling system may permit recording at only one bit density (number of bits per lineal inch in each tape recording channel); be switchable to one of several densities, at only one tape speed (lineal inches per second); be switchable to one of several tape speeds, on only one size of tape reel (length in feet); or accept alternative lengths. Some computers may even be harnessed simultaneously or alternatively to a variety of tape handlers with different characteristics.

In some computer systems, there may be a choice of the number of channels of communication between tape handlers and the central processor which can be procured. Also, each channel may be seleted as buffered or unbuffered, as bidirectional (read/write) or unidirectional (read only, write only), and so on. In connection with tape channels, it will be found that buffering and supplementary control units permit the tight interlacing of memory cycles for the word transfers involved in reading, writing, and computing. Hence, computers will be said to permit "simultaneous" read-compute, read-compute-write, read-read-compute. It is assumed that choice of the equipment configuration is not within the scope

of the individual application system designer but has been previously made in terms of the needs of the complex of applications arrayed by the entire using organization. This is explicitly stated here because the preceding hardware aspects will have a distinct bearing on the balance point between a run being tape limited or computer limited and, hence, on block design. This will be seen in later sections of this chapter.

In the discussion to follow it is assumed that the type of tape handler has been selected if an option exists. However, length of tape reel need not be considered prescribed unless the tape handler chosen permits no option. The interrelationship between item design, block design, and tape length will be discussed.

PRELIMINARY CONSIDERATIONS IN CHOICE OF BLOCK SIZE

Obviously, for those machine systems in which block size is fixed, the application system designer must accept the restrictions imposed on him. His latitude is in the design of item for best utilization of dictated block size in accordance with the principles cited in the previous chapter. The ensuing discussion is restricted to tape handlers that permit a choice of block size.

There are other general considerations which bear on the selection of block size, and it may simplify matters to dismiss these quickly. In the first place, where off-line conversion equipment supports a main computer, these peripheral units usually produce or demand magnetic tape blocked in a predetermined manner. Since no block design decision is required, this fact alone is germane to the present discussion. Where the off-line converters permit choice of block size and where on-line conversion equipment is used, the usual considerations of tape time and processor time are overshadowed by the fact that the conversion is I/O limited, not by tape but by relatively slow-speed electromechanical devices. As a result, item layout on tape and block size will tend to be dictated by the requirements of the rest of the tape-to-tape runs in the process chart supported by the conversion equipment. Thus, tape associated with conversion runs is given little consideration below, although some of the remarks concerning saving of tape length well may apply.

Finally, the system designer should seek to exploit the availability of the software packages provided by the computer manufacturer and user information exchange or developed previously within the user's own organization. In these, there may be prefabricated read-write and item advance routines calling for prescribed tape blocking characteristics or permitting only a limited number of alternatives. To the extent that there is a choice, the selection can be guided by the issues subsequently discussed.

Still other hardware considerations in choice of block size are the method of error detection and correction and the reliability of the tape quality and tape-handling subsystem of the computer. Some computers have error detection and correction procedures pertaining to block rather than to frame, character, or word. In such a case, excessive block length may vitiate the effectiveness of the error procedures. On the other hand, if blocks are made short for such a tape system, the fixed investment per block in error-control recording will constitute a substantial percentage of the total block, perhaps an undue sacrifice of tape time and length. It is assumed that standards for the range of block sizes have been established for a computer installation using such tapes. These standards will reflect the reliability statistics of the entire tape-handling system and the power and cost of the particular error detection and correction procedures provided. The system designer will be obliged to live within these standards and apply accordingly the principles developed here.

In fact, the investment in recording patterns for error procedures is only one of a set of special patterns which may appear on tape and not be directly related to the data of the computer application. Record marks, mode marks, block start and stop marks, control signals, and so forth, have been mentioned. There are numerous others used in various type systems. In general, there is a distinction drawn between data words or data characters, information peculiar to the application system, and nondata words or characters. The latter are characteristic of the hardware and software systems used independent of application information. They have special purposes related to the control of hardware and operations.

VARIABLE BLOCK SIZE

This section is devoted to the system design problem of block size for those computers in which variable block sizes are permitted. Where hardware and software characteristics permit variation of block size on a tape, the system designer still has a choice of fixing the block size for each file or allowing the block size to vary over the file. When file block size is fixed, the input or output area in which the block is stored in memory will be completely used by each block. When file block size is variable, the memory area set aside for blocks on the file must be equal in size to the largest possible block. In this case, many blocks on the file will have a size smaller than maximum. When these blocks are in memory, the difference between the file block size and the area set aside for maximum block size is not used. Fixed block size on a file contributes to memory utilization and, where possible, should be adopted.

With fixed item size, fixed block size is always possible and should be adopted for programming simplicity and memory space saving. Here, to minimize housekeeping further, it is advantageous to fix block size at some multiple of item size to avoid splitting an item across blocks.

If fixed file block size is used with variable item size, splitting items across blocks and possibly even across successive reels of the file becomes unavoidable. The system designer then has a choice of living with this situation, or of letting block size vary to avoid it. This consideration is one more factor encouraging caution in the use of variable item size. By all odds, the use of fixed item sizes and fixed block sizes is preferable.

MINIMIZING FILE TAPE CONSUMPTION

Tape reels are of a fixed length. The longer the block size, the fewer the blocks recorded on one tape. The fewer the blocks, the fewer the interblock gaps. Interblock gap length is fixed and independent of block length. Consequently, the fewer the interblock gaps, the greater the percentage of tape on which information is recorded.

If block size is increased to the point where the number of tapes in a file is decreased, a savings in the investment in and control and handling of tapes is realized. The size of the tape library is reduced, particularly when the retention of past generations of files is involved. The cost of controlling the library is reduced. There are fewer setups and takedowns of tapes.

Tape savings is one of the possible advantages of increasing block size. However, if increasing block size does not decrease the number of tapes in the file, no tape savings can be realized by any increase in block size.

The number of items that can be recorded on one tape reel is determined as follows. The block size for the file to be recorded on the reel is fixed at some number of data characters or data words, depending on whether tape recording is character or word organized. In the following discussion it is assumed that the recording is word organized, although the discussion can readily be altered to reflect character organization by substituting the term *character* for the term *word* wherever it appears in the discussion. Let the number of data words in the block be w.

If the item size is fixed, it is advantageous to fix block size at some multiple of item size. Let the number of items in a block be n. If the item size is variable, it is necessary to break the item size down into some number of common sized subitems. The number of words in each subitem must be a divisor of the number of words in each variable item. The term *subitem* should then be substituted for the term *item,* and n would represent the number of subitems in a block.

An item consists of a number of data words, x. The length of tape required to record one word is some constant, t. Therefore, the length of tape required to record one item is tx. The length of tape required to record one block of items is tnx.

In many computers the recording of a block of data words requires the recording of some number of nondata words, such as segment separators, sentinel words, mode definitions, or other control words. Let c be the number of nondata words recorded per block. In some cases c may be a function of n, x, or both. For purposes of this discussion c will be assumed to be fixed for the block. The length of tape required to record the nondata words for a block is tc.

Between blocks on tape there is an interblock gap. Thus, for every block on tape but the last, there is an associated interblock gap. It is realistic to assume one such gap per block. In some computers interblock gap length is fixed (except for statistical fluctuation in hardware performance not relevant to application system design). In others, it is variable. When variable, gap length is not usually predictable per block, and for use in the technique developed here, an average figure must be chosen. Let fixed or average interblock gap length be g. Then, the length, b, of tape required to record one block is as follows:

(1) $$b = t(nx + c) + g$$

Prorating b over the items recorded in the block gives h, the *fully distributed cost* in inches for each item, that is, the effective item length.

(2) $$h = [t(nx + c) + g]/n$$

The number of items in a block equals the number of data words in a block divided by the number of data words in an item. That is

(3) $$n = w/x$$

Substituting from (3) into (2) gives

(4) $$h = [t(w + c) + g]x/w$$

The number, Q, of items recorded on a tape reel is the effective length, L, of the tape divided by h; the effective length of the reel is the physical length minus provision for control blocks containing no data words.

(5) $$Q = wL/[t(w + c) + g]x$$

Solving (5) for the number of data words in a block gives

$$(6) \qquad w = \frac{(ct + g)xQ}{L - xtQ}$$

Expression (6) can be used as a tool for choosing block size to minimize the number of tapes in a file. For example, assume the following values:

$t = 0.003$ inch $\qquad\qquad L = 42,000$ inches
$g = 0.73$ inch $\qquad\qquad c = 23$

Substituting these values into (6) gives

$$w = \frac{0.799xQ}{42,000 - 0.003xQ}$$

If a file has 300,000 25-word items, this formula specifies that, to record all these items on one tape reel, block size should be at least as large as follows:

$$w = \frac{0.799(25)\,(300,000)}{42,000 - 0.003(25)\,(300,000)} = 267$$

Presuming that block size is to be a multiple of item size, block size in this case should be at least 275 data words.

OPTIMIZING BALANCE

Another advantage of increasing block size is that tape time is reduced. The larger the block, the greater the effective (not instantaneous maximum) tape transfer rate. This is true because the larger the block, the less interblock gap there is per unit of data. This fact is demonstrated as follows. If one word is passed on tape in 0.00003 seconds and 0.0073 seconds are required to pass over the interblock gap, the time to read a block w words long is $0.00003w + 0.0073$. Dividing this time into the words in a block yields the effective tape transfer rate, E, in words per second.

$$E = \frac{w}{0.00003w + 0.0073} = \frac{1}{0.00003 + 0.0073/w}$$

As w increases, the denominator decreases. Therefore, E increases. That is, effective tape transfer rate increases with block size. There are two limitations to savings in this area:

1. The larger the block, the larger the memory I/O area. It should be borne in mind that other input and output files for the run will also require memory I/O area. At some point any further space demands by an I/O area will strangle the run.

2. In a buffered computer, savings stemming from use of a larger block size are real only in a tape-limited run. At some point, further increase in block size will make the run computer limited.

The optimum block size for computer to tape balance on a buffered computer is determined as follows. Instructions in a program break down into two groups: those whose execution actually processes items by computing gross pay, determining reorder quantity, and so on; and those concerned with housekeeping, reading and writing blocks, handling interrupt, advancing items, and so on. Call the first type processing instructions and the second, housekeeping instructions. For a given run, it takes a certain number, N, of processing instructions to process a given item. The execution of these instructions takes a certain amount of time, P. For any given instance this information is adequate to determine the block size that optimizes computer-to-tape balance. To make the discussion general, the concept of average instruction execution time is introduced.

Different instructions take varying amounts of time to execute. Multiplication characteristically takes longer than addition. The longer the operand, the longer the instruction execution time, and so on. For a given family of runs, the instruction mix may be such that an average instruction execution time can be fixed. This is the time it takes to execute the average instruction. That is, the number, N, of processing instructions to process an item; the time, P, to process the item; and average instruction execution time, a, have the following relation:

(7) $$N = P/a$$

To have computer-to-tape balance, the time to process an item must equal the time, B, available to process a block of items in tape time divided by the number, n, of items in the block. That is, the following must hold

(8) $$P = B/n$$

Substituting from (8) into (7) gives

(9) $$N = B/an$$

The time available to process a block of items in tape time equals block read time, R, less the time, A, to transfer the block between the tape handler and memory and the time to execute the housekeeping instructions for the block. The nature of the housekeeping instructions depends on the computer being used. For purposes of this discussion assume that housekeeping time per block consists of the time, I, to handle the interrupt for the read or write; the time, H, to execute the block handling routine; and the product of the time, D, to execute the item advance routine by the number of items in the block. That is

(10) $$B = R - A - I - H - nD$$

Block read time equals the sum of the time, T, to pass over the block on tape plus interblock gap time, G. That is

(11) $$R = T + G$$

In the case of a tape handler with the facility to read or write in a continuous mode, tape time becomes two-valued. When operating in continuous mode, interblock gap time is the time to pass over the interblock gap. When operating in discontinuous mode, interblock gap time is the time required to stop and start tape motion as well as to pass over the interblock gap. Discontinuous interblock gap time is usually significantly longer than in continuous read/write. This fact has the following ramifications. If it takes less time in a given run to process a block than to read or write the block in a continuous mode, the run is definitely tape limited. If it takes just slightly more time to process a block than to pass a block in a continuous mode, the run may still be tape limited, but at a higher tape time, since blocks must now be handled in a discontinuous mode. Under the latter circumstances, it pays the system designer to pack more processing into the run to achieve balance at the higher tape time.

The time to pass over the block on tape equals the time, W, to pass a word on tape multiplied by the number, $w + c$, of words in the block. That is

(12) $$T = W(w + c)$$

Substituting from (12) into (11) gives

(13) $$R = W(w + c) + G$$

Tape time involves both the time to read and to write tape. On computers that allow only reading or writing to occur concurrently with processing, tape time is the sum of read and write time. On computers that allow simultaneous processing, reading, and writing: tape time is the greater of read time and write time. On this latter type of computer, the amount of internal processing that can be done in tape time is at a minimum when for every block read one and only one must be written. For purposes of this discussion, assume such a computer and consider the "worst possible case" just described. Then the time to transfer the block between the tape handler and memory equals twice the memory word-access time, M, this product multiplied by the number of words in the block. That is

$$(14) \qquad A = 2M(w + c)$$

Substituting from (13) and (14) into (10) gives

$$(15) \qquad \begin{aligned} B &= W(w + c) + G - 2M(w + c) - I - H - nD \\ &= (W - 2M)(w + c) + G - I - H - nD \end{aligned}$$

Substituting from (15) into (9) gives

$$(16) \qquad N = \frac{(W - 2M)(w + c) + G - I - H - nD}{an}$$

An alternative expression for the number of items in a block is given in (3). Substituting from (3) into (16) gives

$$(17) \qquad \begin{aligned} N &= \frac{(W - 2M)(w + c) + G - I - H - wD/x}{aw/x} \\ &= \frac{[(W - 2M)x - D]w + [G - I - H + c(W - 2M)]x}{aw} \end{aligned}$$

Solving (17) for w gives

$$(18) \qquad w = \frac{(G - I - H + c[W - 2M])x}{aN + D + (2M - W)x}$$

Given a number of instructions to be executed per item of a given size, (18) can be used as an aid in choosing a block size optimizing tape-to-computer balance. For example, assume the following values:

$c = 23$ words/block $\qquad$ $H = 1$ millisecond/block
$G = 7.3$ milliseconds/block $\qquad$ $a = 0.014$ millisecond/instruction
$W = 0.03$ millisecond/word $\qquad$ $D = 0.35$ millisecond/item
$M = 0.004$ millisecond/word $\qquad$ $I = 4$ milliseconds/block

Substituting these values in (20) gives

$$\begin{aligned} w &= \frac{(7.3 - 4 - 1 + 23[0.03 - 2(0.004)]x}{0.014N + 0.35 + (2[0.004] - 0.03)x} \\ &= \frac{2.806x}{0.014N - 0.022x + 0.35} \end{aligned}$$

If a file has an item size of 100 words and it is estimated that 200 instructions will be executed to process an item in a given run, this formula specifies that, for a balanced run, block size should be as follows:

$$w = \frac{2.806(100)}{0.014(200) - 0.022(100) + 0.35}$$

$$= 296$$

Presuming that block size is a multiple of item size, block size in this case should be 200 words to produce a computer-limited run, 300 to produce a slightly tape-limited run.

This formula yields optimum block size for a given run. Block size should never be determined on the basis of one run. All runs the file enters must be considered. For example, 250-word blocks may be fine for a transaction file in a maintenance run, but it may place a liability on the sort of the transaction file. Choose the block size that is best for the whole system.

Activity on a transaction file is 100 percent. If activity on a master file is low, it may be advantageous to block the master file in large blocks and the transaction file in small ones.

OTHER CONSIDERATIONS

The preceding discussion of optimizing balance is simplified in the sense that it does not take into consideration numerous other factors, such as number of I/O channels available for communication with memory, the bidirectionality of these channels, and input-output technique utilized with special reference to the number of backup storages (internal buffering) allocated to each file. For example, the smaller the block size, the more buffer block storages that can be supplied internally in the same amount of memory. As discussed in a later chapter, multiplicity of such storages tends to reduce interlock, the time during which the computer is waiting for information to be transferred to memory for processing or from memory for recording. However, this is not usually of as much importance as minimizing the number of interblock gaps required to be passed, since any interlock time avoided by a smaller block size is usually small compared to the time required by the extra interblock gaps. Also, availability of extra I/O channels reduces the possibility of interlock and increases the prospect of a run being computer limited for a given block size.

With a concurrent processing computer, a further consideration in choosing block size is the necessity to conform to installation conventions concerning memory allocation. These conventions are generally set up to minimize the possibility of conflict in memory requirements between runs which may be scheduled concurrently on the computer.

7
USE OF A CONCURRENT
PROCESSING COMPUTER

The purpose here is to outline how commercial computer application systems should be set up to efficiently use various hardware configurations. As the chapter title indicates, special emphasis will be given to the utilization of a concurrent processing computer.

To develop the principles to be stated in this chapter, a simple, abstract computer application will be assumed. This application has the following characteristics. A transaction file is brought up to the computer threshold in the form of a card deck. The transaction file is applied to a master file for updating purposes. The master file is stored on magnetic tape, and the updated master file is produced on the same medium. As a by-product of the updating process, a printed report is prepared.

MAGNETIC TAPE COMPUTERS WITH OFF-LINE PERIPHERAL OPERATIONS

One common computer hardware configuration is a central processor, the only mass input and output of which is magnetic tape. Typically, such a central processor is serviced by a collection of peripheral devices, each of which has the capability to perform one conversion function between magnetic tape and some other medium. Thus there is a card-to-magnetic tape converter, a printer driven by magnetic tape, a paper tape-to-magnetic tape converter, a magnetic tape-to-card converter, and so on. The central processor can be serviced also by a satellite computer, which combines the ability to do the required conversions, card-to-magnetic tape, magnetic tape-to-printed copy, paper tape-to-magnetic tape, magnetic tape-to-card, and so on.

On such a computer configuration, the example application described at the beginning of this chapter is implemented in the following way. The transaction card deck is converted to tape, either on the special card to tape converter, or on the satellite computer. The resulting transaction tape is applied to the master file by the central processor. The output of this processing is an updated master file and another magnetic tape with the information to be printed in the report recorded on it. This report tape is then used to produce the printed report, either on the special magnetic tape-driven printer or on the satellite computer. A process chart of this procedure is shown in Figure 7-1.

NONCONCURRENT COMPUTERS WITH ON-LINE PERIPHERALS

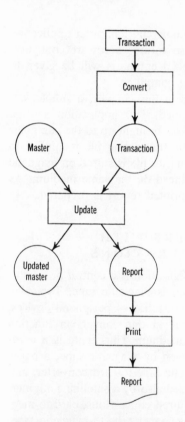

Fig. 7-1 Process Chart for a Magnetic Tape Computer Serviced by Off-Line Peripherals or Satellite Computer

Another common computer configuration type is one in which, in addition to having magnetic tape input and output, all the peripherals units, the card reader, the printer, the paper tape reader, the card punch, and so on, are online to the computer. In such a configuration the central processor can read information from magnetic tape and directly from cards, paper tape, documents, and so on. It can write information on magnetic tape, print reports, punch cards and paper tape, and so on, directly. The utilization of such a computer depends on whether the computer has concurrent processing capability. First, consider a computer that does not have this facility. In this instance, the computer is continuously under the control of a single program.

It is possible to use such a computer to perform the simple file maintenance used as an example here in the same way the computer with off-line peripheral equipment is used. In such a case, the process would be as shown in Figure 7-1. In this case, the computer would first be used as a card to tape converter to convert the transaction deck to magnetic tape. The computer would then be used as a magnetic tape computer to update the master file and produce the magnetic tape report file. Finally, the computer would be used as a magnetic tape-driven printer to produce the printed report. The procedure results in a three-run system. This approach, however, is not the best utilization of the equipment.

Another approach to the utilization of a computer with online peripherals is shown in Figure 7-2. Here the transaction file is read into the updating process in card form. The report is produced directly on the printer. Introduction of timing figures will demonstrate the superiority of the second approach over the first. Suppose the speed of the card reader and the volume of the transaction file set the time for reading the card deck at 15 minutes. Suppose the speed of the central processor, the speed of the magnetic tape units, and the volume of the master file set the time for updating this file at 5 minutes. Finally, suppose the printer speed together with the volume of the report file set printing time at 20 minutes. Running time for the process shown in Figure 7-1 is the sum of these times—40 minutes. If the

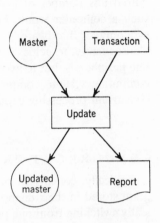

Fig. 7-2 Process Chart for a Nonconcurrent Computer with On-Line Peripherals

computer is buffered so that card reading, printing, magnetic tape reading and writing, and internal computer processing can occur simultaneously, running time for the second approach shown in Figure 7-2 is the largest of these times—20 minutes. If the computer is partially or totally unbuffered, running time for the second approach is greater than 20 minutes but is always smaller than 40. Clearly, the technique exemplified in Figure 7-2 is the appropriate one for a nonconcurrent computer with online peripherals.

Such computers are characteristically medium scale with an average instruction execution time in the range of 200 microseconds. If the card reader of such a computer can read one card in 400 milliseconds, 2000 instructions can be executed in card read time. This is not an unreasonable number of instructions to perform the housekeeping operations associated with the control of the tape handlers, card reader, and printer; to do the processing associated with applying the transaction to the appropriate master item; and to edit the card image for this application and the one or more line images required to produce the prescribed information on a printed report. Hence, such a computer configuration functions as a well-balanced system.

However, there are computers with on-line peripherals whose average instruction execution time is about 14 microseconds or less. With a 400 millisecond per card reader, upwards of 28,000 instructions can be executed in card read time. It would be an unusual application that required this number of instructions to be executed per card. Generally, such a computer would be hopelessly peripheral limited. Nevertheless, economy of hardware construction legislates for on-line peripherals. Consequently, to achieve the construction economies associated with on-line peripherals, but to avoid the disutility of a seriously peripheral-bound computing system, computers with high internal speeds generally have concurrent processing capability.

CONCURRENT PROCESSING COMPUTERS

Typically, concurrent processing computers have more than one program stored in their memories, with the control of the computer periodically switching from one program to another. To achieve this concurrent processing capability, the computer requires the following features.

1. Some type of executive system is required. It may be hardware, software, or more typically, some combination of the two. This executive system performs several functions.

A. The executive system determines which of the several programs in memory is to have computer control. There are two aspects to this control.

a. The executive system periodically must be able to snatch control from the program currently executed and pass this control on to another program. This feature prevents one program from dominating control to the detriment of the other parts of the hardware system. For example, this feature prevents a heavily computer-bound program from retaining control, to the point where the operation of input-output equipment is slowed. This aspect of executive system control may be connected with the interrupt system, another necessity for concurrent processing, which will be noted subsequently in further detail.

b. The executive system must be able to accept control from some program and pass it on to another. This allows a program that is input or output limited to relinquish control when it has completed processing on the items currently in memory and is waiting for more items to be delivered or for the items in the output area to be recorded.

B. The executive system generally determines where programs are to be loaded in memory and loads them there. This feature implies that programs are written in such a form that they are relocatable. This ability is generally required on a concurrent processing computer because, at the time of loading a program, P, into memory, there are usually other programs already loaded in memory. These previously loaded programs are typically not the same from one running of program P to another. Consequently, different portions of memory are occupied from one running of program P to another. Program P must have the ability to be loaded in that part of memory which is available at the time of its loading. One technique for avoiding the necessity for relocatability will be pointed out later.

C. Similarly, the executive system generally determines what logical peripheral and magnetic tape units are to be assigned to program P for each running. This, in turn, implies that program P must have the ability to address input-output units symbolically. The reason for this necessity is similar to that for relocatability. Program P knows the complement of input-output equipment required for its running, but it generally cannot predict which logical units will be available for assignment at running time. As will be pointed out later, this is not necessarily true. Arrangements can be worked out for fixed input-output assignment to programs.

2. A concurrent processing computer requires an interrupt system. An interrupt is a hardware feature that, as the result of the occurrence of some event, causes control to go to some fixed memory location. At the very least, there must be one interrupt that periodically returns control to the executive system so it can cycle control among concurrent programs. More typically, interrupt is supplied whenever an input-output unit completes a cycle.

USE OF A CONCURRENT PROCESSING COMPUTER

One reason for not using a concurrent processing computer in the way shown in Figure 7-2 already has been stated. Such a processing scheme generally results in seriously peripheral-bound programs. On the off-chance that a program calling for peripheral as well as tape input-output consumes more computer time than peripheral time, it is still not a good idea to mix tape units with the peripheral units in this program, since the peripheral units are then not operated at top effective speed.

The other reason for not mixing tape units with peripherals in one run has to do with scheduling. If any program can require any array of input-output equipment, it will be difficult to achieve a constant program mix on the computer that makes full utilization of the peripheral units. Also, there will probably be many instances when a particular program cannot be loaded because one or more of the peripheral units it requires are already in use.

The alternative is to design systems in the manner exemplified in Figure 7-1. That is, application systems for a concurrent processing computer consist of tape-to-tape runs—programs utilizing only magnetic tape input and output—and of peripherals runs—programs with one magnetic tape input or output and one peripheral unit. Thus, peripheral runs are divided into two types, input peripheral runs and output peripheral runs. In an input peripheral run, information is read from some peripheral unit such as a card reader or paper tape reader and is written on magnetic tape. In an output peripheral run, information is read from a magnetic tape and is put out on some peripheral unit such as a printer or card punch.

The program mix on a concurrent processing computer then may consist of one tape-to-tape run and one or more peripheral runs. For example, the program mix at one point in time might consist of a tape-to-tape run from the payroll system, a card-to-tape run to convert transactions for the inventory system, and a tape-to-printer run to produce a report for the billing system. When the tape-to-tape program reaches completion, it calls in another tape-to-tape run as its successor. When the card-to-tape conversion winds up, its successor is another tape-to-card conversion. Another printer program succeeds the current one. And so on. In this manner, all peripherals are kept busy; and, with the possible exceptions of adequate memory space or adequate numbers of tape handlers, no program about to be loaded need be delayed because of unavailable facilities. Also, all peripherals are kept running at maximum speed. A schematic of such concurrent processing is shown in Figure 7-3.

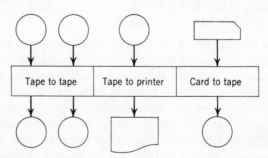

Fig. 7-3 Schematic of Concurrent Processing

TAPE UNIT ASSIGNMENT ON A CONCURRENT PROCESSING COMPUTER

It can be guaranteed by installation convention that each program will find an adequate number of tape handlers available when it becomes time to be loaded. For example, suppose a configuration of input-output equipment consists of 14 tape handlers, a printer, a card reader, and a card punch. The installation is on single shift; application demands require that the printer be run a full eight hours, the card reader four hours, and the card punch for two hours. An instruction tape is required. Then one tape handler can be set aside for the instruction tape, one for driving the printer, and one used for four hours by the card reader and two hours by the card punch. The installation can then set up as a system design requirement that no tape-to-tape run be designed to use more than 11 tape handlers. In this fashion, each program will, on loading, always find adequate tape handlers available for it.

Some installations may wish to go further and assign a particular logical tape unit to the instruction tape, to all printer runs, and to all card-to-tape and tape-to-card runs. This leaves a specific 11 logical tape handlers available for tape-to-tape runs. Programs can then address tape handlers directly, and the executive system function of allocating input-output equipment to programs as they are loaded becomes unnecessary.

MEMORY ASSIGNMENT ON A CONCURRENT PROCESSING COMPUTER

Adequate memory space for each program can also be assured by installation convention. In this case, each run type is assigned a maximum amount of memory within which it must be designed. For example, if the computer's memory consists of 32,000 locations, 5000 of which are required by the executive system, 2000 memory locations might be assigned to each peripheral run that must run concurrently. This would be 2000 for the printer run and 2000 for the card-to-tape or tape-to-card run. Twenty-three thousand locations then remain as the upper limit within which all tape-to-tape runs must be designed.

To make the most effective use of memory, a minimum amount of memory is usually assigned to each peripheral program. This leaves a maximum amount available for tape-to-tape runs. Such an approach dictates that peripheral runs be limited to little more than straight conversion, all editing being handled by the tape-to-tape runs. This also provides further assurance that all peripherals will operate at maximum speed.

A characteristic of peripheral runs is that they frequently require restarting. Paper in the printer tears, or a card jam occurs on the card reader. In such instances, the process must be backed up for a number of items and restarted. Restarting procedures are simplified if peripheral runs are limited to conversion. This simplification leads to smoother and more standard computer-center operating procedures—a desirable system-design goal.

Memory limitations by run type need not be made binding in all cases. For example, suppose that once a year it is required to prepare an omnibus report made up of year-to-date summaries maintained on the master file. It is not necessary to design a tape-to-tape run to produce an edited version of the master file for subsequent printing. Once a year, all tape-to-tape processing can cease and the master tape be fed into a large-scale printer run that both edits and prints the required information.

Once the memory has been partitioned by convention, it becomes possible, if the installation so desires, to assign fixed memory locations to each run type. For example, presuming that the executive system pre-empts memory locations 00000–04999, locations 05000–27999 can be assigned to tape-to-tape runs; 28000–29999 to printer runs; and 30000–31999 to card-to-tape and tape-to-card runs. Programs can then be written with fixed memory locations and the program relocatability function of the executive system can be dropped.

INSTRUCTION TAPE HANDLING ON A CONCURRENT PROCESSING COMPUTER

Because it usually cannot be predicted which program currently in the computer will wind up first, some rocking of the instruction tape to locate successor runs seems inevitable. One way to minimize this rocking is to use *wired in* peripheral programs. For example, an installation may have a sole printer program that requires input in a specified format. All tape-to-tape runs producing tapes for this printer program must produce these tapes in the specified format. The same can be true of the card-to-tape program and the tape-to-card program. Then, at the beginning of the shift, the printer and card-to-tape programs can be read into memory from the front of the instruction tape. These remain in memory and service all printer and card-to-tape operations. The tape-to-tape programs can be arranged on the instruction tape in the order in which they are to be run. As a consequence, if the schedule is adhered to, no instruction tape rocking is necessary until the card-to-tape program is replaced by the tape-to-card program. After this has been done, the only other event which can cause instruction tape rocking is a change in schedule.

MULTIPLE USE OF PERIPHERALS ON A CONCURRENT PROCESSING COMPUTER

On a concurrent processing computer, there is a temptation to hang more than one peripheral on a peripheral program. For example, if a computer has two printers, there is the possibility of using both simultaneously to print different reports from information on a single input tape. This temptation should be avoided. Peripheral equipment is electromechanical and subject to more frequent breakdown than electronic equipment. The more units of peripheral equipment that must be up concurrently before a run can be executed, the greater the possibility that the run will be delayed because of equipment failure.

Moreover, such a run design requires that all peripheral gear involved be free before the run can begin to operate. In the preceding example, both printers must be free and set up before the run can begin. Both printers will not generally become free at the same time. One printer will have to remain idle until the other becomes free and set-up before the run can begin. A third reason for avoiding such run design is pertinent when the volumes that the peripheral gear are to handle are disparate. For example, in the two-printer run described, if one printer is to produce a detail report of the input tape while the other is to produce a summary report, the speed of the run is limited by the printer producing the detail report, and the utilization of the other printer during the run is low.

MIXING OF TAPE-LIMITED AND COMPUTER-LIMITED RUNS ON A CONCURRENT PROCESSING COMPUTER

It is sometimes proposed that computer-to-tape balance can be achieved on a concurrent processing computer by running a tape-limited, tape-to-tape program concurrently with a computer-limited program. Although this is theoretically possible, there are several considerations that militate against the approach.

The proposed approach presumes that two or more tape-to-tape programs of different characteristics are to be run concurrently. This generally requires an increase in the number of tape handlers and in the memory size of the computer required. To justify such an acquisition, the installation must have sufficient computer load to keep several tape-to-tape runs in the computer concurrently for the greater part of a shift. Even in such cases it may be less expensive to settle for a more modest configuration, only run one tape-to-tape program at a time, and run into overtime. The proposed approach also presumes that, whenever a computer-limited run is scheduled, there is a tape-limited run which can be scheduled concurrently, and vice versa. Such a program mix is exceptional rather than common. Moreover, even if such programs existed, the approach presumes a timing fineness, predictability, and static content in scheduling that is not generally realizable.

RANDOM ACCESS ON CONCURRENT PROCESSING COMPUTERS

Random access devices such as drums or disks generally have an access time significantly larger than that of central processor memory. Consequently, random access memory falls into the same category as peripheral units. Thus, if information in a random access memory is to be used in a tape-to-tape run, rather than put this memory on-line to the tape-to-tape run, it is preferable to record the information from it on magnetic tape in a *peripheral* run. The resulting tape can be used as input to the tape-to-tape run.

A common use of random access memory in a concurrent processing computer is exemplified as follows. The random access memory may hold a master file such as an airlines reservations file. Inquiry and display units are on-line to the computer. When an agent wishes information concerning a specific flight, he can key in his request on an inquiry unit. This may cause an interrupt, which allows the executive system to transfer control to the program doing the lookup in the random access memory. When the lookup is complete and the information requested has been routed to the agent via the display unit, this program returns control to the executive system. Thus, when this program does not require control to service inquiries, control is given to other programs concurrently stored in memory and designed to perform tape-to-tape and peripheral operations for batch processing as already described.

USE OF CONCURRENT PROCESSING COMPUTERS AS CONVERSION EQUIPMENT

Suppose an installation with a concurrent processing computer, a number of tape handlers, a printer, a card reader, and some other peripheral equipment. Suppose the installation is on a one-shift basis, but that the application demand on the printer and card reader is four hours a day from each. During the other four hours of the 8-hour shift, the printer and card reader can be used in a peripheral run to read cards and print the information read. Such utilization lowers the installation's need for punched card tabulators. Other combinations of peripheral gear are possible: paper tape reading to paper tape or card punching, paper tape to printing, and so on. It should be emphasized that such use of a concurrent processing computer is economical only when there is idle time on the peripherals involved. The use of the computer as a card reader to printer device is usually particularly well balanced, since the document speeds of card readers and printers tend to be similar. Such planned use of the computer still suffers from design deficiencies mentioned earlier and should be approached cautiously. Simultaneity of availability of the peripherals involved is required. This is not only a scheduling problem, but is also one of peripheral equipment reliability.

8
COMPUTER SYSTEM DESIGN CONSIDERATIONS

THE GENERAL APPROACH TO COMPUTER SYSTEM DESIGN

The system designer's goal is to design a system to "produce the required output from the given input [while] minimizing the sum of computer time cost, related manual effort cost, [and] related machine costs, yet allowing flexibility and practicality, and ensuring accuracy commensurable with [the] job to be done." This statement is a glowing enunciation of the system designer's goal and can hardly be argued with. The system designer must keep these desirable system characteristics in mind as he builds his system. But how these characteristics are optimized and what determines when the optimum system has been arrived at is not yet clear.

One of the first steps is to investigate the system presently in operation. A result of this investigation is a complete definition of the system output requirements. The next step is to review this output. How much duplication of information is there between output documents? From where does each field of output derive? Source documents? Unchanging records? Accumulations? Computation? What factors enter into these computations? From where do these factors derive?

One way to carry on this investigation is by means of an output analysis chart. An example of such a chart is shown in Figure 8-1. All the output types are listed down the left-hand side of the output analysis chart. All the information fields that appear in the output documents are listed across the top of the form. The purpose of the analysis chart is to describe the reports in terms of the fields that make them up by marking the intersections of the row on which each report is listed with the columns in which the fields making up this report are entered.

The chart accomplishes more than this description. The intersections are marked with symbols. If the field is picked off of a transaction source document, the intersection is marked with a T. If the field is derived from an unchanging record or an accumulation, it is marked with

120

DATA FIELDS

		KEY FIELDS	CLOCK NUMBER	BADGE NUMBER	NAME	ADDRESS	UNION DUES KEY	BLUE CROSS KEY	WEEKLY BD. DED. AMOUNT	HOURS WORKED	ADJUSTMENT KEY	ADJUSTMENT AMOUNT	GROSS WAGES	NET PAY	INCOME TAX	BOND ACCOUNT NUMBER	SIZE OF BOND KEY	SOCIAL SECURITY NUMBER	QUARTER TO DATE FICA EARNINGS	QUARTER TO DATE FICA TAX	NO. DAYS ABS. (CLASSIFIED)	NO. DAYS ABS. (PERSONAL)	NO. DAYS ABS. (MEDICAL)	NO. HRS. LAID OFF-13 WKS.-2 DIG.	TOT. HRS. WORKED-13 WKS.: 3 DIGITS	YEAR-TO-DATE GROSS EARNINGS	NO. INCOME TAX EXEMPTIONS	YEAR-TO-DATE INCOME TAX WITHHELD	YEAR-TO-DATE FICA EARNINGS	CUMULATIVE TOTAL BOND DEDUCTION
Number of Digits per Field		3	5	26	28	1	1	4	3	3	12	5	6	6	6	1	9	6	4	26	26	26	39	52	78	8	2	8	6	4	5
	HARD COPY OUTPUT																														
DAILY	Employee Termination	2	M1	M2	M	M	M	M	M						M	M	M	M	M	M	M	M	M	M	M	M	M	M	M	M	M
WEEKLY	Pay Check	2	M1	M2	M	M	M	M	M	T	T	T	C	C	C																
WEEKLY	Bond Listing	2	M1	M2	M	M										M	M														
WEEKLY	Payroll Register	2	M1	M2	M	M	M	M	M	T	T	T	C	C	C																
WEEKLY	Check Register	2	M1	M2	M	M							C																		
QUARTERLY	FICA	1	M	M	M													M1	M	M											
QUARTERLY	Attendance Report	2	M1	M2	M																M	M	M	M							
QUARTERLY	Earnings Report	2	M1	M2	M																				M	M					
ANN.	W–2	2	M1	M2	M	M												M								M	M	M	M	M	

Fig. 8-1   Output Analysis Chart

SOURCE:

Master Record	M
Transaction	T
Computed	C

an *M* for master information. If the field is computed, it is marked with a *C*. The fields have been segregated as to source. A step has been taken toward the definition of the master item and the characteristics of the source documents that will be necessary. The fields marked *M* must be provided for in a master item. The information for the fields marked *T* must be solicited by means of a source document.

The fields marked *C* present a different problem. In these cases it is necessary to determine the factors involved in their computation and decide if the factors can be taken from master or transaction documents or are computed. This process continues until a complete list of input fields is created and dichotomized into master and transaction fields.

Another piece of information included on the output analysis chart concerns the sequence in which each output document is turned out. This information is imparted by showing the number of fields on which the report is sequenced in a column. The major field on which the field is sequenced is marked not only with an *M, T,* or *C,* but also with a *1.* The second field in the sequencing from major to minor is marked with a *2,* and so on. In this way it can be determined whether two reports have the same sequence. In Figure 8-1 all reports, with the exception of the quarterly FICA report, are sequenced on the same two keys; the clock number is the major key field, and the badge number is the minor one. The quarterly FICA report is sequenced on social security numbers.

Reports are listed according to frequency. Because of this arrangement and the inclusion of the sequencing information, the columns and rows on the chart can be rearranged to emphasized similarities or reports on three characteristics: frequency of appearance, sequence, and field complement. The columns of the chart in Figure 8-1 are arranged to maximize this emphasis.

An output analysis chart arranged in this way provides a tool for analyzing the present system's output array. The resequencing of reports or change of frequency required to combine reports is indicated. Even if consolidation is not possible, the chart identifies reports similar enough in frequency of appearance, sequence, and field complement to make producing the reports side by side on the printer a possibility. The output chart indicates output fields bearing useful information but which are not included in any current report by implication of the fact that the fields are absent from the chart.

On the basis of a review of the output requirements of the present system, and an understanding of company objectives in the data processing area, a definition of what output the computer system should turn out can be arrived at. Because of the use of the given method of output analysis, a listing of the input fields required to generate this output and a breakdown of this input into master and transaction data is available. The next step is to identify the processing required to produce this output from the input and arrange these operations in a sequence to implement this production.

The identification of the operations to be performed and the arrangement of the sequence in which the operations are to take place go on concurrently. In any data processing area there are operations that must be performed regardless of the sequence of operations finally chosen. However, the complement of operations which must be performed is also a function of the sequence in which the operations are arranged. One sequence requires operations, another does not. For example, suppose it is necessary to look up entries for a number of arguments (the problem arguments) in a table in which the arguments (the table arguments) are arranged in some order. If the problem arguments are made available in random order, there are two solutions to the problem. One is to sort the problem arguments into the same order as that in which the table arguments are arranged and to select the proper entries by a match merge on the two lists of arguments. Another is to select the problem arguments one at a time in their random order and select the entry associated with it by searching the list of table arguments for the corresponding argument. In this example, both the operations in the two solutions and the sequence in which they are performed are different, yet they are both solutions to the same problem. Moreover, it is impossible to detail the complement of necessary operations without specifying the sequence in which they are to be performed. One solution involves the repetition of a searching operation, the other a sort followed by a match merge.

The tool used to identify these operations and their sequence is a block diagram. An example of a block diagram is shown in Figure 8-2.

There are no standard symbols used in making block diagrams; in Figure 8-2, circles are used to symbolize master information on the input side and information feeding into other data processing systems on the output side. Cards are used to symbolize transaction information; rectangles for operations; and ovals for decisions. The process chart symbol for printed output is used as the symbol for final reports, and the flow chart symbol for connectors is used in the same way it is used in flow charts.

Several block diagrams are produced in the course of determining what the sequence of operations should be. The first of these is gross. The detail of the chart is refined with each succeeding version. As this amount of detail increases, operations that should be done on the computer can be identified. However, no operation should be dropped from the block diagram because it has been decided that the operation will not be performed on the computer. The block diagram is a description of the com-

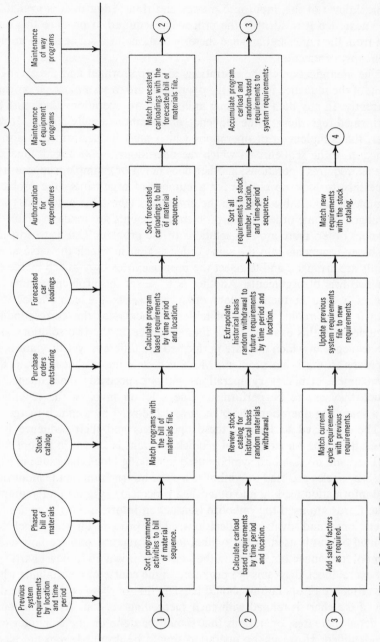

Fig. 8-2 Example of a Block Diagram; Railroad Requirements Planning and Inventory Control Procedure

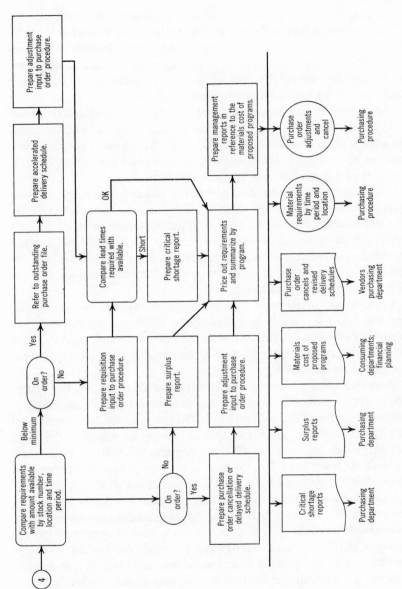

Fig. 8-2 Example of a Block Diagram

plete data processing procedure. It is not like a process chart, which shows only those operations in a data processing procedure performed on the computer.

The determination of what operations are going to take place and the sequence in which they will occur sets the mold for the system. It is at this point that the decision concerning the fundamental approach to the system is made. This determination is not an easy job and a significant amount of time should be devoted to it. The sequence of operations should be set up to minimize the amount of sorting.

Once a final block diagram has been produced, a final determination as to which operations are to be done on the computer can be made. Then the process chart to show the division of computer operations into runs can be developed. The completed process chart is a symbolic representation of a computer data processing system.

In evaluating a computer data processing system by itself, the measure of its merit is the extent to which it minimizes both computer running time and *handling* time for the system. Handling time consists of the time required in the computer center to get ready to run a system and to clean up after a system has been run. It includes mount and dismount time for tape handlers, time to tear down the printer from the previous run and set it up for the next, and so on.

A rough way to estimate how successfully a system minimizes running and handling time is by counting the number of runs. Given two proposed computer systems for accomplishing the same objective, the one with the lesser number of runs is the one that more likely does the best job of minimization.

However, when evaluating the effectiveness of a system, the system should not be looked at in a vacuum, a tendency that is evidenced in statements such as "the best system is the one with the least number of runs." It is true that, given two systems which are aimed at the same goal and which are equal in all other respects, the better system is the one with the fewer runs. But this fact is no basis for the contention that the number of runs in a system should be minimized at all costs.

A system does not exist in a vacuum and cannot be evaluated in one. The system designer may be working on an accounts receivable system, a stockholder records system, or some other kind of system to the exclusion of all other systems, but when he is finished his product is just one more system in his company's data processing spectrum. It is in relation to these other systems that the system designer's current system is viewed for evaluation purposes. These systems are vying with each other for running time on a limited equipment facility. For example, a company may have one computer. In such an instance all systems must have their runs executed on this computer. One characteristic that should be incorporated in a system is flexibility as far as scheduling computer time for it is concerned. This flexibility makes less possible the situation in which a company has a fully loaded computer with idle time. For example, if the systems presently designed for a computer use all the computer time available during the last week of each month, then no other system also requiring some time during this last week can be put on the computer even though there may be large amounts of free computer time during the other weeks of the month. If the systems designed for a computer are flexible from a scheduling point of view, periods of peak demand such as the one illustrated can be avoided.

Flexibility of computer scheduling is a function of how much the work load of the system can be spread over its cycle of operation. For example, if the transactions for a system enter in batches over a period of time, one batch a day, for example, the system should be designed so each batch is processed as far into the system as possible as soon as it is received. The alternative to this design approach is to collect the transactions and process them all at once at the end of the week or whenever the cycle point occurs. The latter approach makes for a system consisting of fewer runs and also reduces system running time, but it also peaks computer utilization at the end of accounting periods.

It only takes a few systems that incorporate the same scheduling inflexibility and conform to the same accounting period to aggravate this peaking to a point where the computer becomes fully scheduled for lengthy periods of time even though the schedule is light at other stretches of time. The former approach to system design gives the computer center a choice, in the case of many runs in the system, as to when the run can be put on the computer, with the result that scheduling can be smoothed out and the presence of peaks and valleys in the demand for the computer can be reduced. In addition, the validation of the batches on a daily basis allows some of the transactions to become validated, and if in error, corrected, before the production runs at the end of the week are entered.

The system should be constructed so the operations showing whether the system is in accounting and statistical balance and producing those reports most important as far as action is concerned are executed first.

Also influencing run sequence is the desire to use up most fields early and strip down input as soon as possible. That is, get rid of the heavy traffic first with a minimum of runs. There are then fewer fields to drag through the rest of the system. In the same vein, specialized input should not be introduced into a system until the system is ready to use it. Otherwise it constitutes dead weight carried through the system until it does become of use. Finally, using a sample of transaction data in a system rather than the universe of this data may be considered. This approach is used to cut the volume of operations in the quality control procedures connected with production processes. There may be instances where the technique is applicable to data processing operations, particularly in those cases where interest is centered around performance with respect to some criteria.

THE DIVISION OF THE PROCESSING INTO RUNS

Previous to the advent of concurrent processing computers there was little question concerning the validity of the maxim that operations should be divided between runs so that I/O time versus computer time balance could be optimized. There was acceptance of this proposition, because if the time required to process information exceeded the time required to handle this information on the input or output devices, then the input-output equipment was required to stand idle for undesirable periods of time. Conversely, if the time to read information exceeded the time to process the information, the central computer had to mark time while awaiting new information to process. Consequently, to avoid making portions of the computer system idle for significant periods of time, a balance between processing and I/O time was required.

With the introduction of concurrent processing computers much of the clarity in this area has been lost. It remains true that an efficient computer system must be balanced, computer time remaining roughly equivalent to tape time; however, on a concurrent processing computer more than one program can be running at the same time. Consequently, some believe that it is enough that the computer system remain in balance. There is no necessity for each program to be in balance. If there is a heavily computer limited program, the system can be kept in balance by running it in conjunction with a heavily I/O-limited program.

This reasoning presumes that there are relatively fixed or well-predicted aspects of the computer center production schedule. The schedule would need to guarantee the ready availability of I/O-limited routines in a reasonable production sequence whenever one was compelled to operate a computer-limited run. Conversely, one would need to be able to supplement a required I/O-limited run with available computer-limited runs. In a computer installation engaged in several application systems, or even in several subsystems or runs within one system, this good fortune in schedule complement is infrequently encountered and seldom sustained as a recurring phenomenon over a significant period of time. Hence, there is little or no assurance that computer system balance for a complex of concurrent processes can be achieved in this way. The only reasonable approach seems to be to balance individually and to the utmost each tape-to-tape run. On the other hand, on-line I/O conversion runs may be very little demanding of computer time so that the rest of the processor power may be used for tape-to-tape processing.

On a concurrent processing computer a processing run is often executed in conjunction with one or more peripheral runs. To determine how significant the demand of a peripheral run on the computer is, consider a printer run. Presume a printer operating at 700 lines per minute. Also presume that 32 computer words of four characters each (128 characters) are printed on one line. Therefore, 700 times 32, or 22,400, words are printed per minute. Assuming a tape blocked at 500 words per block, 44.8 blocks are printed per minute (22,400 divided by 500). That is, 21,504 blocks per 8-hour shift are printed (44.8 times 60 times eight). Assume that a block is read in 0.020 second. Therefore, in an 8-hour day, a printer ties up the tape synchronizer 430.1 seconds, or 7.2 minutes. Presume that the printer run runs in three times tape time. Therefore, the printer's demand on the computer is 21.6 minutes. The other peripheral equipment, the card reader and punch and the paper tape reader and punch, make similar demands on the computer. The bulk of computer and synchronizer time is consumed by the processing runs. To use the computer and synchronizer to their maximum, processing runs should be balanced.

However, the prime consideration in the division of operation between runs is to develop the most efficient system. Computer to I/O balance is a run concept, not a system concept. Even though a balanced program is more desirable than an unbalanced one, it is not necessarily the case that the system containing the most balanced runs is the most desirable. When a system contains heavily computer-limited runs and heavily I/O-limited runs, or when a system consists of nothing but I/O-limited runs, this fact may be an indication that the system design can be improved. However, this is not necessarily the case. A system consisting of nothing but computer-limited runs may be more efficient than a comparable system made up of a greater number of runs, each of which is balanced. In the context of the preceding remarks concerning overall system efficiency, a discussion of those avenues that may be explored to bring a run more into computer to I/O balance is presented.

An I/O-limited run surrounded by computer-limited runs can be brought into balance by incorporating operations in it from the surrounding runs. A computer-limited run can be brought into balance by any one or a combination of several methods. Coding for the program can be linearized; that is, less iterative coding can be used. Such an approach requires more memory space for program storage and is applicable only if this space is available.

Another method for balancing a computer-limited run is to reduce the amount of field selection and indirect addressing to a minimum, since each such operation costs the program time. This approach requires an alteration in item design and a greater use of memory space. A third method is to effect improvements in the flow chart logic of the run. A final method is to transfer operations, originally designed to go into the current run, into surrounding runs. This approach is a possibility only when the surrounding runs are tape limited.

It is sometimes possible to eliminate a run by unloading the operations originally assigned to it into earlier and later runs. In collapsing runs in this manner be certain the tape handler and memory limitations placed on runs by hardware are complied with and the sequence of operations called for by the system is maintained. Run elimination is important on newer computers because of the relatively large amount of time consumed by setup-takedown time when contrasted to the running times associated with such equipment.

Runs should be designed so the division of work between runs creates runs with distinctive functions. That is, the run organization should manifest the characteristic that work of a similar nature is done in the same run and not scattered over several runs. For example, suppose a data processing operation calls for the validation, editing, sorting, and summarizing of a data file. One approach to run design for this operation is to have four runs: a validation run, an editing run, a sorting run, and a summarization run. Or it might be possible to combine the validation and editing functions into one run and have a three-run system: a validation and editing run, a sort run, and a summarization run. Again, it might be possible to summarize during the last pass of the sort and have a two-run system, one doing the validation and editing, the other the sorting and summarizing. Finally, it might be possible to accomplish the validation and editing during the first pass of the sort and have a system that performs the function of validation, editing, sorting, and summarization in one run.

All four of these approaches are acceptable as far as the principle stated at the beginning of the paragraph is concerned. The choice between these approaches is a function of the power of the computer on which the system is going to be run. The more powerful the computer, the more the consolidation of functions into one run can be pursued.

The principle enunciated here is to avoid design creating a three-run system (a validation run, a sorting run, and a summarization run) in which the editing function is distributed over all three runs, each performing a part of the editing.

Notice that this principle of keeping a clear distinction between the functions of different runs often leads to conclusions which are opposed to those reached from the principle that it is often possible to effect economies in system design by collapsing runs—allocating the operations of a given run to earlier and later runs with a consequent elimination of the given run. The idea of a three-run system with the editing function split over the three runs fits in with this latter principle.

There is no arguing with the principle of collapsing runs. It does effect system economies. The reason the principle of a clear functional distinction between runs can sometimes run counter to the principle of collapsing runs and still be a valid system design principle is because there are many goals in system design. Not all of these goals are compatible. One of these goals is system economy; another is to design a system easily susceptible to modification.

One characteristic of data processing systems is their vulnerability to change. No sooner is a system set up and in operation than it is decided that some other output would be desirable from the system, or a feature of the operating system from which the transaction data originates changes with the consequent necessity for corresponding change to the data processing system. One of the qualities of a good system is that it be easy to modify.

One feature of a system in which runs are functionally distinct is that it is more amenable to modification than a system in which functions are scattered over many runs and mixed together so that each performs small parts of many different functions. The reasons for this are as follows. Functionally distinct runs are more straightforward logically. They involve less condition testing to determine the classification of the current item and what action must be taken. There is less "left over" processing from previous runs and less "anticipated" processing for future ones. There is a greater uniformity in the data moving into and out of these runs. All these factors lead to programs that are less interdependent than otherwise. A change in one section of a program has fewer repercussions on other parts of the same program and on other programs in the same system. Consequently, the programs are more amenable to change.

Confine all operations dependent on a file to the same run. Such an approach avoids passing the file more than once. Similarly, all operations related to an internally stored table or set of program constants should be restricted to one run. This approach means the table or constant set has to be loaded into the computer for only one run instead of more. This perspective toward run layout not only increases system efficiency, but also segregates functions among runs to make the runs more amenable to modification.

Another factor influencing the number of operations to be incorporated in one run is memory space. The amount of memory space available for storing program steps places an upper limit on the number of operations that can be allocated to a run. The degree to which it is anticipated that the operations allocated to a run will change or expand in scope should also be taken into consideration in determining how many operations to assign to a run, again for memory space reasons. A run that has no memory space cannot be patched. For example, with respect to a payroll system, the run that has the handling of local income taxes as one of its functions should be designed so there is plenty of excess memory space when the program is loaded in the memory, because this type of taxation is on the increase. Many changes to this run in the form of additional processing can be anticipated.

In laying out runs the possibility of using library routines should be taken into consideration. A library routine has the advantage of being coded and debugged. Every library routine incorporated into the system means one more run in the system on which development effort and time do not have to be expended. Be willing to tolerate some inefficiencies in a system to be able to maximize the use of library routines.

If a sequence of operations, each involving the reading of input and the production of output, can be strung together without interruption on the computer, they should be considered as one run. This approach is recommended in the interests of minimizing the amount of necessary administrative control. For each run in the system certain procedures must be followed: an interrun locator must be executed; run numbers must be typed; labels must be checked; and so on. These are standard computer room controls, whose power comes from being followed in 100 percent of the cases. By considering a series of operations, each one of which makes a pass on data as one run, the necessity for conforming to these computer room procedures is avoided and flexibility as to how these operations are to be tied together is gained. For example, it is recognized that, even though a sort consists of a number of passes (each pass of which may require a complete new load of instructions), each pass should not be considered a run. The sort as a whole is considered one run. In this way the several passes of the sort are run as one continuous operation. The computer room controls between passes are fewer than those required between runs.

Any sequence of operations similar to a sort, where there is a multipassing of the same data or a multipassing of the same tape, is a candidate for designation as one run. As an illustration, a computer operation that consists of several passes, but which can be considered one run, is shown in Figure 8-3.

Another aspect of combining different operations into one run is con-

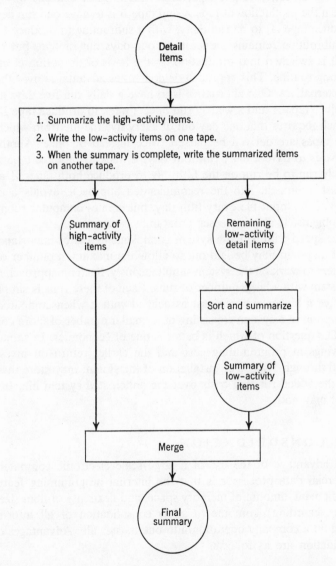

Fig. 8-3 Example of a Sequence of Operations that Can Be Considered To Be One Run

cerned with operations that belong to different operating cycles. For example, suppost a system incorporates a daily cycle during which a file is passed by a run to produce an output tape, tape A. Suppose also the system contains a weekly cycle during which this same file is passed to produce a different output tape, tape B. The most efficient way to accomplish the production of tape A and tape B is to have one run designed to produce tape A, to be run daily, with a subroutine to produce tape B. This subroutine remains inoperative four days out of five, but once a week it is switched into production on the basis of an option elected by the dating routine. This approach demonstrates advantages over the possible alternatives. One alternative is to have a daily run five days a week to produce tape A and a weekly run once a week to produce tape B. This approach requires that one day out of every five the file from which both output tapes are derived be passed twice instead of once. Another alternative is to have a daily run four days a week to produce tape A and a weekly run to be run on the fifth day to produce both tapes A and B. This last approach, like the recommended approach, avoids a double passing of the input file every fifth day, but creates computer room control problems. It also increases programmer cost.

If the speed with which a system is implemented is of importance, the runs of a system may be laid out to allow the maximum number of programmers to work on the system simultaneously. Such an approach results in a system with a large number of runs. Each of these runs is simple and may have a higher running cost associated with it when compared with the adoption of a system consisting of a smaller number of more complex runs. The question of which is better is one of economics. In some cases the savings in programming cost and the earlier return on investment realized through a speedier installation of the system may more than outweigh the added running costs over the anticipated system life. In other cases it may not.

FILE CONSOLIDATION

One advantage of the use of a large scale electronic computer as a commercial data processor is that the internal programming feature of the equipment, amount of memory space, and flexibility of item size (due to tape recording) combine to allow consolidation of all information bearing on a company operation into one master file. Advantages of this consolidation are as follows.

1. Master file consolidation changes the nature of the control over data required in a system. Consolidation calls for normalization of the

master file item design. Normalization means that, within the programs handling the master file, the control testing network which distinguishes one master item type from another is of increased complexity. However, the computer is the ideal device for handling controls—it is quick and accurate. The alternative to a consolidated master file is a group of specialized master files. Here normalization of item design is not a problem, since the item design is specialized to the file to which it belongs. However, another control problem comes into being: the synchronization and control of the maintenance of specialized files. Controls in this area are never completely automatic; some human handling is present. Consequently, accuracy is reduced. A consolidated master file represents an improvement over specialized files as far as control over data is concerned.

2. Master file consolidation reduces the profusion of process logic in a system. Specialized files often imply parallel streams of processing operations that can be collapsed into one if the files are consolidated.

3. A reduction in the duplication of information is realized. If there are two interrelated specialized master files, at least the key field of each item has to be duplicated. The duplication of fields may be more widespread. For example, an employee master file that contains everything but name and address for each employee and a separate name and address file must carry an employee number to match name and address with the proper item on the employee master file.

4. There is a reduction in the investment in tape inventory. Less duplication of information means less tape length as far as storage of master file information is concerned. Moreover, one file instead of many means fewer end of file tapes with unused portions on the ends.

5. Master file consolidation means less setup and takedown time. There are fewer tapes to be mounted and dismounted.

6. The number of tape handlers used by a run is reduced, thus freeing tape handlers for other purposes such as more complex runs with omnibus processing to simplify the total process chart. Or the overall tape handler requirements of the physical computer system can be reduced.

7. The number of input and output areas in the memory is reduced, resulting in the freeing of memory space for other purposes.

8. Programming costs are reduced. A system incorporating a consolidated master file requires fewer overall instructions coded when compared with a comparable specialized file system.

For example, one railroad has traditionally divided its traffic accounting into two operations—coal traffic accounting and accounting for all other traffic, known as merchandise traffic. When computerization of the traffic accounting system was first considered, the question arose, "Should this division of operation with the concomitant specialization of master files be perpetuated in the computer system, or should the coal and merchandise traffic information be consolidated into one master file?" Studies indicated that the system would be more economical if the master file were consolidated.

Transaction files can also be consolidated. Such consolidation provides the advantages of reducing tape inventories, complexity of controls over tape files, setup and takedown time, the number of tape handlers, and the number of input areas. Transaction file consolidation may also reduce the number of runs in the system.

However, an indiscriminate consolidation of transaction files should be avoided. In some cases the consolidation of different kinds of transactions onto one file is compatible with the method with which the run accepting the transaction file as input handles the transaction types. In other cases such consolidation creates so much work for the run in the form of distinguishing between transaction types, that it is more efficient to have the transactions enter in separate files by kind. In particular, there is no point in consolidating different transaction types into one file if the first thing the computer system must do is disperse these transactions by type for subsequent processing.

Consolidation of output files is a possibility. For example, suppose a tape has to be produced to drive a printer run for the production of some report. In those cases in which this output tape is a specialized, edited version of the master file it may pay to dispense with the production of the special tape and use the master file to drive the printer run. In this case the special output tape is "consolidated" with the master file. Such consolidation results in a reduction of tape inventory and the controls over that inventory, a reduction of the number of tape handlers and output areas used, and may result in the elimination of a run.

When a computer system permits on-line printer operations, especially for concurrent processing (multiprogrammed) computers, the computer logic permits selection of data from the consolidated file for printing. Many off-line printers have *data select, selective print* and other similarly labelled capacities. File consolidation requiring selective printing in a subsequent printer edit run would not be used in a computer confined to on-line printing and lacking concurrent processing capability.

Another case in which output file consolidation is a possibility is as follows. Again, assume that the output files are being produced for printing. (This assumption is for illustrative purposes. The output files produced could be used in a run to drive a punch or in any kind of output equipment run. They could be used as input to subsequent processing runs. The principles exemplified in these printer illustrations remain unchanged.) If production of special output tapes is economical, and if one run is to produce output for more than one purpose, it is probably more efficient to produce one output file with combined information for all purposes on it than it is to produce a special output tape for each purpose.

For example, suppose a run is to produce special output to print report A and special output to print report B. It is probably more efficient to produce one file from which both reports can be printed than it is to produce a separate file for each report to be printed. The savings are similar to those of the previous situation: reduction in tape inventory and control and reduction in the tape handlers and output areas used.

The output information can be combined on the output file in two ways. The item design for the file can be normalized to contain the data necessary for producing reports A and B. Or a specialized item design can be retained, one item design for report A and one for report B. However, instead of writing these specialized items on separate tapes, they are both written on the same tape. When there is a large overlap between the items to appear on report A and those to appear on report B the normalized item design approach is more desirable. Specialized item design becomes unattractive under these circumstances because of the high percentage of items that must be put on the tape for both the A report and the B report. Whenever such an instance occurs there is duplication of information at least as far as key is concerned and perhaps more so.

However, the less the degree of this overlap, the more desirable specialized item design becomes. If normalized item design is used where there is little overlap, the great percentage of items placed on the output file find their way to only one report, either A or B. However, they each have an item design that provides space to store information for both reports. Such a situation results in more waste of tape space than would be taken by the occasional duplication of information required by the specialized item design approach.

If normalized item design is adopted, each item is keyed as to whether it applies to one report or both. If the item belongs to only one report, it is keyed as to which report it belongs. The reports can be printed by passing the tape once for each report. There is one pass to print report A and one to print report B. On each pass the proper fields for printing are selected from the proper items on the basis of the report key.

With specialized item design, each item is keyed as to which report it is associated with, but no item is associated with more than one report. In this case there are two ways the reports can be printed. One is similar to the normalized item design approach: the tape is passed once for each report and the proper items are selected for printing on each pass. The other approach is to sort the items by report key. The file is then ordered by report, and all items belonging to the same report are grouped together on the file. The reports are printed with one pass of the tape. First the report associated with items grouped at the head of the file is printed, then the report associated with the next group, and so on until all the reports are printed. This approach to printing a consolidated output file is desirable if the items in the file have to be reordered anyway before the reports can be printed. The report keys can be weighted so the information for the most important report ends up at the beginning of the final output tape of the sort, the information for the next most important report appears next, and so on.

Up to this point discussion has been confined to the consolidation of files that are related to one another—consolidation of master files in a data processing area, consolidation of transaction files that feed into a common run, and consolidation of output files from a common run. However, there are occasions when consolidation of unrelated data on one file has savings to offer. It is not unusual in a computer data processing operation to encounter several small files of unrelated reference data, each file requiring only a fraction of a tape. A multiplicity of small files creates a multiplicity of problems not all of which are small. For example, operating problems are created because of excessive tape handling. Each file requires a maintenance routine which expands the run structure and probably requires a separate input stream for file corrections. This tends to expand the requirements for clerical support. The problems of label control, tape retention, and physical storage increase proportionately with the number of separate tape files. So does the dollar investment in tapes.

The consolidation of files of unrelated reference data is most practical in cases where there are two or more files of approximately the same length which can be keyed by a single series of numbers. For example, in a payroll application, conversion directories were needed to encode and decode the following kinds of data in the system.

1. Work descriptions for preprinting on employee timecards.
2. Occupation titles for posting to the employee file when an employee changes occupation.
3. Account codes for labor distribution.

Items 1 and 3, although used at different times and for different purposes in the system, were related. Item 2 was unrelated to either of the others.

The system required approximately 400 work descriptions, 330 occupation titles, and 400 accounts. This situation presented an opportunity for combining files. A block of numerical codes from 001 through 999 was alloted for keying this combined file. A file item format was established with one key and three compartments, one for each type of data to be coded.

The clerical support group was provided with one code list reflecting work distributions and accounts and another code listing reflecting occupational titles. Both lists were keyed to the three-digit codes in the 001 through 999 series. In the first instance the numbers were called *Work Description Codes*. In the second instance they were called *Occupational Codes*. However, in both instances they addressed the same file.

Each time this consolidated file was used for encoding or decoding purposes inapplicable data was passed. If decoding of work description codes were going on, inapplicable occupation code information was being passed. This passing of inappropriate data was the price paid to reap the benefits of reduced system run structure, reduced tape investment, and all the other advantages of consolidating unrelated data on one file. The price was little enough for the advantages gained.

There is no necessity to have a correspondence of keys between the consolidated sets of data. The principle of consolidating files of unrelated data is applicable even if the data types have different kinds of keys. The ultimate extension of the concept of consolidating unrelated kinds of data on one file is the creation of a single run that handles such a consolidated file and performs the different operations with respect to the different data types.

MINIMIZING THE PASSING OF THE MASTER FILE

The master file is usually the most voluminous file of a system. Every time the master file is passed the system running time increases due to the file volume. It is advantageous to minimize the number of passes of the master file. One method for minimizing the passing of the master file is to maximize the consolidation of the runs that pass this file. For example, if a system contains four runs, each of which requires a pass of the master file, and if memory space requirements permit the elimination of one of these runs by packing its operation into the other three, such run consolidation may be a good thing. Another way to minimize the number of times the master file is passed over a period of time is to lengthen the cycle of the system as much as possible. The more times a system is run on the computer in a given period of time, the more times its files will be run in this interval.

A third way to minimize the passing of the master file is to create specialized master files. For example, in insurance premium billing the only time the policyholder's name and address are used is when he is billed. One of the more efficient orders in which to keep the master policy file for billing is by agency. However, for all other processing in a premium billing application, agency order is not the most efficient order in which to keep the policy file. For example, keeping the file in mode of payment order—first weekly, then monthly, then quarterly and so on, and within this breakdown ordering the items by due date—is a more efficient sequence than agency order. In such a situation it may be efficient to create a policyholder name and address file distinct from the master policy file and keep the name and address file in agency order and the policy file in mode of payment/due-date order. Such specialization of master files reduces the size of the policy file, which must be sorted into agency order when billing is done.

In the preceding example, even if the name and address file and the policy file were not kept in different orders, the fact that the name and address fields of the policy information are used in only one run of the premium billing application, while the other information is used in many, might be sufficient justification for a separate name and address master file. One insurance company estimated that by eliminating name and address information from the master item they were able to escape passing 50 percent more tape through the computer during the application runs.

An example of a situation in which it is profitable to have a consolidated master file in one part of the system and an abbreviated master file in another is as follows. The application is payroll. The pay period is semimonthly. For semimonthly reports (labor distribution), quarterly reports (FICA tax), and annual reports (W2 form), it is efficient to have a consolidated employee master file. A lot of updated and accumulated information is necessary to prepare these reports. However, for each semimonthly pay period there are four distinct paydays for four different groups of employees. The mobility of the employees between groups is high. In many instances an employee belongs to more than one group (and consequently, gets paid on more than one payday) in one pay period. As a consequence, it is not feasible to keep four different employee master files, one for each employee group. The result is that the entire employee master file must be passed four times each pay period to develop gross pay for each employee.

The computations to develop gross pay require only a small part of the information on the employee master file. Consequently, an abbreviated employee master file containing only the data necessary to these computations is an integral part of this system. The abbreviated master file is passed four times each pay period to develop gross pay for the four paydays. The complete employee master file is then updated on the basis of the abbreviated file. It is the complete file that is used in the rest of the system. By adopting this approach a considerable amount of tape passing is avoided. It is estimated by the designers of this system that, if there were only two paydays per pay period instead of four, it would then be more economical to use only the complete master file. The time used to update the complete file on the basis of the abbreviated file would more than use the time saved with the abbreviated file for gross pay computation. That the break-even point happens to lie here, rather than at some other point, is a function of the relation of the size of the abbreviated master file to the size of the complete file.

This principle of creating specialized master files of smaller size for more frequent passing is in opposition to the principle of master file consolidation. If the use of specialized master files reduces overall system running time to the point where this approach must be considered, the advantages should outweigh the disadvantages the system will incur by not making use of a consolidated master file.

HANDLING EXCEPTIONS

A data processing system handles a variety of transaction types. There is a distribution of the frequency at which these types occur. Some types occur frequently. Others occur rarely.

A system should be biased so the most frequently occurring transaction types are handled the most economically. The less frequently a transaction type occurs, the less important is the economy with which it is handled. The system can be designed to handle the common transaction types with economy at the expense of increasing the cost of handling exceptional types. Processing the exceptional case can be expensive per case without being costly systemwise.

A similar argument holds for output produced by the system. For example, a line official in the data processing area under computerization may remember that three years ago some unusual type of information was required. The system must be designed so this information can be produced when necessary, but it does not have to have the ability to produce this information routinely at high speed. It can be provided as an exceptional, even relatively expensive, procedure.

A problem created by exceptional cases is that, if the exceptions are handled by the computer, the subroutines to handle these exceptions take memory space away from the program in which they are incorporated even though they are executed infrequently.

If the exceptional operation is associated with particular master file items, the robbing of memory space by coding, the purpose of which is to effect this exceptional operation, can be avoided by incorporating this coding on the master file contiguous to the items to which it is applicable. Then, when one of these peculiar master items is read into the memory, the coding designed to handle it is read into the input area with it. The rest of the time, when the subroutine is inoperative, it is not present in the memory. No memory space allocated to the program is used by this subroutine. This approach means that a special subroutine exists on the master file for each peculiar master item. There may be a different subroutine for each type of peculiarity. This fact results in a longer master file. There is a point at which the number of exceptional items becomes too large to make this approach practical.

This method was used to handle the pay of fifteen people being remunerated under an obsolete retirement plan. In this case, the approach has a particular attraction, because when the last of these people dies, the coding to handle their pay will disappear from the system with no modification to existing programs. This may sound overdone but, since the file items were required to be processed frequently enough, manual exception procedures were too costly.

When a data processing area is computerized not every operation in that area should necessarily be automated. Some procedures may have so low an incidence of occurrence that their incorporation into the automated computer system would encumber the system without providing any benefits. For example, if a company located in one state has a few employees who work part time in another state, which taxes the wages of nonresidents earned within its borders and which requires the employer of such employees to withhold part of the employee's wages for purposes of paying this tax, automation of the procedure for computing this withholding tax may be uneconomical. It may be more economical to hand compute these withholding taxes and feed the results of this computation into the computer system as transactions for the master file items involved.

Considerations to keep in mind when choosing between computer and manual handling of exceptions are as follows.

1. Manual exception procedures take a small part of a clerk's time. The procedure never becomes standard. The chances that it will become second nature to the clerk are low. The odds are more likely that the clerk will never completely learn the procedure and will have to make frequent reference to a procedure manual, although a good work form might help.

2. Even if the exception is handled manually, some communication concerning the exception is generally required with the computer system. Relegation of a procedure to a manual subsystem only partially frees the computer system from concern with it.

3. As time passes, clerical costs rise, and computer costs decline. What is not economical to do on the computer today may be economical tomorrow.

4. The incremental cost of adding another operation to the computer part of a system is low. The incremental cost of adding another operation to the manual part is not.

5. Economies are realized in standardization and control by handling the operation on the computer.

Because of these facts the benefit of doubt should be given to handling exceptions on the computer. If there is a question as to whether an exception should be handled manually or on the computer, that doubt should convince the system designer to put the procedure on the computer.

One exception type that becomes difficult for a computer to handle is exemplified as follows. Consider a utility billing system. One of the possibilities in such a system is for an account to have its meter changed in the middle of the billing period. The billing system must be able to turn out a bill that divides an account's consumption and charge between two meter numbers. Perhaps the system can be built to handle two meter changes (three meter numbers) in a billing period, a less likely but still possible occurrence. However, the attempt to handle three meter changes in one period, an extremely unlikely occurrence, might break the system's back. Nevertheless, the system cannot be built on the arbitrary assumption that no more than two meter changes can occur during a billing period. Three meter changes in one period can and do occur. If the system could be built to handle three meter changes, it could not assume that four changes could not occur, and so on.

The solution to this type of problem follows. Suppose it is at three meter changes that it becomes difficult for the computer to handle the procedure without sacrificing the efficiency with which it handles more normal cases. Then the system should be designed so that one or two meter changes during a billing period are handled automatically on the computer. However, if three or more meter changes occur in one period, the computer should toss all transactions and related master information for the account out for printing. The account can be billed manually. Adjustments can be fed in during the next cycle to bring the master item of the account up-to-date.

PROVIDING FOR FUTURE MODIFICATION

A data processing system is subject to change. One system design goal is to make the system malleable. Not only should anticipated change be provided for, but general system design principles for making the system responsive to modification also should be followed.

Straightforward runs make for easy modification. This advice is particularly applicable in the case of runs that create statistical information or otherwise mark the beginning of a report creating process. It is in the output desired that the most frequent changes in data processing systems occur. Some new statistic is desired. A change in the method of summarization is wanted. A rearrangement of the form of the output is wished. The more flexible the design of the *output producing end* of the system, the easier it is to modify the system when the requests for changes occur.

Modification and extension of a system on the *output side* are simpler to solve than such changes on the *input side*. At most, changes on the output side require a forms revision and a modification of the runs producing the output reports. Changes on the input side are further reaching in their effects. The form of source documents must be changed. The impact on run structure is more wholesale. Clerical procedures are involved in the change. Avoid the necessity for such comprehensive change. Design the input side of the system in as all embracing a fashion as possible; that is, to capture as much detail as practical on the input side. The system should gather up and incorporate not only the source data presently needed, but also whatever future source data will be needed.

SYSTEM-TO-SYSTEM INTEGRATION

The system the designer is working on is only a part of his company's data processing operation. It should be designed to integrate with other systems in operation and with systems the company plans for the future. This integration has two purposes: One is to eliminate overlap between systems; the other is to avoid gaps between systems where neither system handles a necessary operation. For example, a payroll incorporating an employee stock-purchase plan requires an integration between the payroll system and the stockholder records system. In particular, the compatibility of keys and other pertinent fields and a coordination of the cycling of the involved systems must be provided for.

System-to-system integration may take several forms. At a primary level, it is found in the common conventions and standards used in every aspect of data processing—operating procedures, programming, and system design. Further, it is found in coordination of input collection to serve two systems, common design of code structure for fields, compatable item and block design, cooperative design of master file structure, sharing of use of these files, and so on.

There is even a possibility of system to system integration across company lines. For example, in some cases, the federal and local governments will accept magnetic tapes or punched cards produced in a prescribed format in lieu of other reporting. These serve as input to a data processing system used by the government. They are produced as a normal output from a payroll system, as for W-2 and social security tax reports; or a stockholder record system, as for form 1099, dividend payments reports.

SORTING

While the ordering of data is often a prerequisite for efficient data processing, a sort produces nothing but this ordering. It performs no transformation, only movement, of data. The fundamental system design principle with respect to sorting is to design systems so sorting is minimized. Reference here is to external sorting which is a relatively costly of setup and takedown time and of computer running time. If a file of data is small enough to be internally sorted, this sorting may well be indulged in for the simplification of subsequent processing it provides.

An uncritical adherence to this principle may create as many problems as it solves. Particularly with respect to small files, it may be better to introduce a sort to simplify a following run, such as a summary, than to design complicated runs that avoid the preceding sort, but which are difficult to modify when change becomes necessary. Some techniques for avoiding sorting follow.

Many values required for data processing can be looked up in a table or computed from a formula. An example of such values is logarithms. If the table of values to be used is small enough to fit in the memory, no problem is involved. The file of arguments on which the table of values is entered is not required to be in argument order. Instead, the argument items are read one by one, the internally stored table is entered randomly, and the proper values are assigned to the problem arguments.

However, if the table is not small enough to fit in the memory and the table lookup approach is used, the only efficient approach is to have both the table file and the problem argument file in argument order and to match merge the argument file against the table file. The table file can be initially created and thereafter kept in argument order by the system, but unless the problem argument file comes to the table lookup operation in argument order, this approach requires a sort of the argument file.

An alternative to this table lookup approach, feasible when the values desired can be computed by formula, is to abandon the table file and compute the value for each argument as it is read. This latter approach allows the arguments to be read in random order and eliminates the necessity for a preceding sort. It should be used if the function is computationally short. If the computation is complex and the file of detail items long, this procedure may be very costly.

Allied to the problem of looking up values for a series of arguments in a table is the summarization of a file of detail items under a number of headings. The same principles apply. If possible, the summarization table should be stored in the memory and the summarization performed internally. Such an approach allows the detail items to be fed into the summary run in an order independent of the headings under which the data is to be summarized. The alternative to such an approach requires sorting the detail file into heading order and the subsequent summary of the items one heading at a time. The internal summary approach avoids this sorting of the detail file into heading order. If the summary table does not fit in the memory, perhaps some data reduction technique can be used to reduce the volume of data fed into the presummary sort.

The principle of data reduction is to do as much of the summarization as possible before the sort begins or at least before the sort ends. For example, during each pass of a sort more and more of the detail items that are going to be summarized under one heading are grouped together in the lengthening strings of data. If during each pass the sort not only continues the sorting process, but also summarizes into one summary item all detail items found grouped together, the volume of data that the sort is going to handle with each subsequent pass is going to be reduced. This device is a data reduction technique.

More sophisticated data reduction techniques depend on bias in the detail data. For example, one company desired to produce monthly summary statistics on the distribution of its employee man hours over the range of job types worked on during that month. The detail data was made up of a series of items, each item describing the type of job an employee worked on during one day. (For purposes of simplicity, assume that an employee could not work on more than one type of job a day.) The data came in employee order. Consequently, all the items for one man appeared on the file together, then all the items for the next man, and so on. The presumption on the part of the designer was that a man would tend to work in the same work category from day to day and that, over a month's time, the number of different types of jobs on which the man worked would be small. Consequently, the system was designed in the following manner. A summary was carried out on all items pertaining to one man. These summary items were written on an output tape. Then a similar summary was performed for the next man, and so on. Only after this man-by-man summary had been completed were the items fed into the sort. It is estimated that this technique reduced the volume of the data which would otherwise have been fed into the sort ten and one-half times.

Another example of a data reduction technique utilized in the summarization of hours worked categorized by work type follows. In this case the data to be summarized came from four distinct previous cycles of processing. Consequently, the major data order was by cycle. Within each cycle group the data was ordered by department. Thus, if there were four departments, A, B, C, and D, there would be a group of items from department A, a group from department B, from C, and finally from D. This batch of data would be that generated by the first cycle of previous processing. There would then follow another batch of items grouped in order according to departments A, B, C, and D that represented the data generated during the cycle just previous to the one which generated the first batch. And so on for two more data batches.

There was a large number of work types, but indications were that the number of types for any one department was limited. Consequently, it was decided to partially summarize the data before it was fed into the sort. The presort summary run had space to summarize 128 different work classes at once. (The number of table entries was chosen as a perfect power of two. This choice optimized the efficiency of the log 2 lookup, the technique chosen for entry into the table.) Consequently, a 128-place table was set up in the memory. The first 128 different work codes that appeared on the detail tape became the arguments for the table. The work codes were numerical. The summary table arguments were arranged in ascending order. As long as no more than 128 different work codes appeared on the detail tape the table could handle the summary. However, when a work code appeared on the detail tape that did not match any of the current 128 table arguments, some action had to be taken. The nonfitting work code would be bracketed between two adjacent current table arguments. It was decided that the new work code would replace the higher of these two arguments, the summary which had been kept on the replaced work code being put out on an output tape. This approach cut the volume of the data to be sorted to about half of its input volume.

However, the method of argument replacement froze the higher-ranking work codes in the bottom of the table. As the summary progressed the table arguments became more and more fixed, with the result that the effectiveness of the presort summary correspondingly diminished. Consequently, it was decided that when one cycle of data had been processed the table would be cleared out and the process would begin anew. This change caused a reduction in volume by a factor of five from the volume of data that would have been fed into the sort had no data reduction technique been used.

If it is known that all the high-activity detail items can be summarized in an internally stored table, and the number of classifications according to which the summary is to take place is only slightly larger than the number of arguments in the table, the following data reduction technique can be used. Pass over the detail items. During this pass summarize the high-activity items in the internally stored table. Write the low activity items on a scratch tape. When the pass on the original data is complete, write on a final output tape those summary items from the table that precede all low activity items in the final summary. Then read the scratch tape backward. Summarize the low activity items in the space vacated in the memory by the summary items written on the output tape. When this summary is complete, write the summary items remaining in the memory on the output tape. All items are written on the output tape in the order they are to appear in the summary. The criterion as to whether this technique is applicable is whether there will be enough room in the memory to summarize the low-activity items after the initial group of summarized high-activity items have been written on the output tape.

If the high-activity detail items can be summarized in a table but the number of classifications exceeds the number of arguments by an amount that makes this approach impossible, the following technique can be used. Pass over the detail items, summarize the high-activity items, and write the low-activity items on a scratch tape. Then write the summary items in sequence on a second scratch tape. Sort and summarize the low-activity items, and then merge the output of this summary with the summary tape produced by the presort summary. A process chart of this technique is shown in Figure 8-3.

A dispersion of a detail tape according to some significant criterion may bring detail data into such an order that data reduction becomes a possibility when the original order of the data prohibited such an approach. The decision as to whether to disperse depends on whether the consequent data reduction that the dispersion allows saves more time than is expended in the dispersion.

The recognition that data reduction is a possibility in a system may have an influence on the organization of the system. For example, it may be a toss-up whether the master file is to be ordered one way or another. If data reduction is possible with one master file order but not with the other, the decision may be made to order the file in the way congenial to data reduction. Master file order affects the way the rest of the system is organized.

If a transaction file is to be run against a long file, *A*, and a short file, *B*, the creation of some redundancy in the *B* file sometimes reduces the number of transaction file sorts. For example, one railway company classifies its coal traffic into seven types. There is anthracite, coke, and bituminous traffic. Bituminous traffic is subdivided into all rail, lake, tidewater, river tipple, and lake coal delivered to connections. For each carload of coal handled by this railway a transaction item, called a *coal waybill item,* is entered into the freight accounting system. Each waybill item contains a *type of traffic field* and a *shipper field,* which identifies the company shipping the coal. This identification is given in terms of a *patron code.*

Each month the waybill items are used to update an *A* file, which is used to produce a report to company management on performance. The major breakdown of this report is by coal traffic type. Within each traffic type the report is subdivided by shipper. Consequently, the major order of the *A* file is by traffic type, the minor order by shipper. Each month the waybill file is sorted to this order to accomplish the updating of the *A* file.

The *A* file is an *active* file. That is, it is purged periodically. Consequently, it does not contain all the possible combinations of type and shipper. Therefore, there are mismatches between the waybill and *A* files. The number of such mismatches is about 3000 per cycle. They are written on a mismatch file which enters a subsystem of runs the purpose of which is to fabricate *A* items corresponding to the items on the mismatch file. These fabricated items are subsequently to be merged into the *A* file.

One of the steps in this fabrication system is to run the mismatch file against a *shipper file* to validate the patron code in the shipper field of each mismatch item. This shipper file consists of a list of coal shippers patronizing the railroad involved. Each shipper is identified by patron code. There are about 200 shippers on this file. One approach to this validation of the shipper field of mismatched waybill items is shown in Figure 8-4, where the shipper file is in order by shipper, keeping the file at a minimum size. Consequently, the time spent maintaining the shipper file is minimized. However, the system requires two sorts of the mismatched waybill file: one to put it in shipper order for matching against the shipper file, and one to return it to its original order, major by type and minor by shipper. This second sort is done after the validation process and is required to get the items in order for subsequent merging with the *A* file.

By increasing the shipper file length six more times so the shipper list is repeated seven times on the file, once for each traffic type, the system shown in Figure 8-5 evolves. The system involves a longer

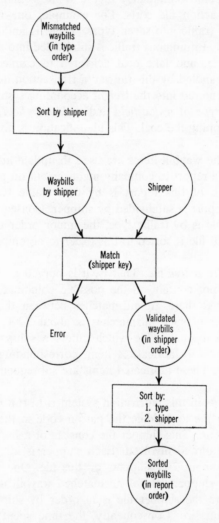

Fig. 8-4 One Approach to Validation of the Shipper Field

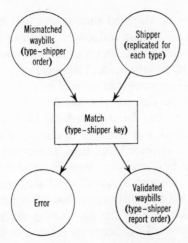

Fig. 8-5 Another Approach to Validation of the Shipper Field

shipper file and requires a more complicated maintenance procedure for that file. However, since the file was small to begin with, the resulting inefficiency is slight. The advantage of the system is that two sorts of 3000 items each have been eliminated. The mismatched waybill file does not have to be sorted before it is matched against the shipper file, because for each classification of shippers by traffic type on the waybill file there is a corresponding list of shippers on the shipper file. Consequently, the mismatched waybill file does not have to be sorted after the validation process; it is already in order for merging with the A file.

It is sometimes possible to substitute a dispersion for a sort. For example, in one railroad application each item of a file contained a field consisting of an ICC code. It was necessary to look each of these codes up in a table to determine the associated description for printing purposes. The codes appeared on the file in random order. The table was too large to fit in the memory all at once. However, the table could be divided into a small number of segments each one of which could fit in the memory. Rather than sort the file on ICC code and match merge the sorted file against the entire table, the file was dispersed on the basis of the way the table was segmented. The first table segment was then read into the memory. The group of dispersed file items associated with this table segment was read in one by one in random order and looked up internally in the table segment in the memory. Then the second table segment was read in. The group of items associated with this second segment was run against it, and so on until the lookup was complete. The dispersion approach to this decoding operation involved fewer passes of the information to be decoded than a sort and match would have.

In some cases it is possible to reduce the length of a sort by preceding it with a dispersion which groups items so strings created by the first pass are longer than would be otherwise. This increase in string length must result in a savings of sort time that more than compensates for the time spent in doing the dispersion for this approach to be practical.

In other cases items can be siphoned off by a dispersion so fewer items remain to be sorted. For example, at one installation it was desired to arrange a stockholder record file, kept in account number sequence, by postal district for bulk mailing purposes. The system designer had available to him a statistical distribution of accounts by bulk mailing district. It was felt that this distribution would not change significantly over the years. On the basis of the distribution the system designer set up the system to siphon off the accounts located in the more populated districts by a series of dispersions, which left a minimum of items to be sorted. (This is population by stockholder accounts, not by persons.) More accounts were located in New York City than in any other district. Consequently, all New York City accounts were dispersed onto one tape. These accounts were passed only twice (once to disperse them and once to collect them and all other dispersed items on a final output tape). The accounts in the six next most populated districts were dispersed onto another tape, which become input to a subsequent six-way dispersion. These accounts were passed three times. Accounts in the next 49 districts were dispersed to a third tape, which was subsequently acted on by a series of two seven-way dispersions, and so on. At the point at which dispersion became more expensive than sorting, dispersion was dispensed with. The residual items which had been collected on one tape during the initial dispersion were then sorted. In determining the breakeven point between dispersion and sorting take tape mounting and dismounting time into consideration.

In investigating the possibility of dispersion as a substitute for sorting do not be fooled by the size of the key on which to sort. In some cases the number of key possibilities is small, even though the key size is large. It is the number of possibilities, not key size, that determines dispersion feasibility.

A system should be designed so, when a sort is required, the requirement can be handled by a canned (library) sort. Such an approach saves programming time and guarantees a high-quality sort. A significant part of sorting time is consumed by mounting and dismounting scratch tapes. Because of this fact, of two sorts identical in all respects except for power of collation, the one with the lower power may have a shorter time, even though it requires more passes. Less scratch tapes to mount and dismount make the difference. This will almost always be the prevailing consideration in sorting relatively short files, where short refers to tape length not to file volume.

MERGING

The objective in merging is to keep the number of passes at a minimum. One factor in this minimization is the power of the merge. The higher the power, the fewer the passes. For example, if there are four tapes to be merged and a two-way merge is the maximum power possible, eight tape passes are required to complete the merge. If a four-way merge is possible, four tape passes are all that is necessary.

This consideration is usually of chief practical import. However, it is not strictly correct in that it ignores other factors which may affect the efficiency or feasibility of a merge. For example, if the items to be merged are short in character length and the power of the merge is set very high, the merge run may possibly become computer limited rather than I/O limited as is commonly the case. This is because so many more items have to be merged per I/O cycle when the items are small and there are more of them delivered to the computer in an I/O cycle. In general, for each item size, there is an upper limit on the power of merge which can be used before computer limiting replaces I/O limiting. Of course, the larger and more complex the key on which the merge comparisons must be made, that is, the more computer processing required by the item, the lower this upper limit will be. Thus, the object is still to minimize overall processing time, and this can be done through minimizing tape passes only to the extent to which all runs are tape limited. When the merge power is high, computer time may have to be considered instead of tape time. A quick "rule of thumb" is this: large-sized items can afford high-power merges, small items cannot.

The equipment configuration may limit what can be accomplished in efforts to optimize merge design. Merge power may be limited by availability of tape handlers or input/output area in memory.

The manner of merging is also a factor in minimizing the number of passes. For example, consider merging 12 tapes with a three-way merge the maximum possible. One approach is shown in Figure 8-6.

This approach consists of four three-way merges producing four ordered groups of three tapes each. Three groups are merged to form one ordered group of nine tapes, which is then merged with the fourth three-tape group to form one ordered file of 12 tapes. The number of

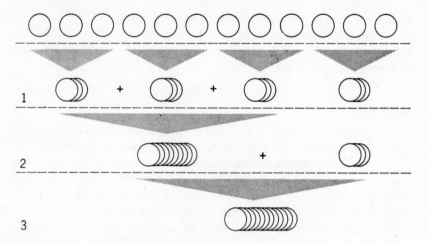

Fig. 8-6 Possible Merging Approach

passes is 33. However, by merging as shown in Figure 8-7, only 29 passes are involved.

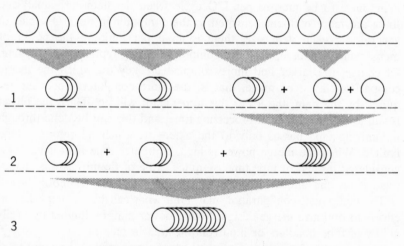

Fig. 8-7 Optimum Merging Approach

The algorithm for expressing optimum merging technique is as follows. Given k tapes and a b-way merge as a maximum, find n such that

$$b^{n-1} < k \leq b^n$$

Form b groups, $G_1, G_2, G_3, \ldots, G_b$, each consisting of b^{n-2} tapes. Add the remaining tapes to the groups according to the following rules.

1. No group may contain more than b^{n-1} tapes.
2. Bring G_1 to its maximum first, then G_2, then G_3, and so on.

Applying the algorithm to the preceding 12 reels:

$$k = 12$$
$$b = 3$$
$$3^{n-1} < 12 \le 3^n$$
$$n = 3$$
$$b^{n-2} = 3$$

The groups are

	Initially	Finally	
G_1	3	6	(maximum $G = 9$)
G_2	3	3	
G_3	3	3	

These are taken as new k's. G_2 and G_3 result from three-way merges of single reels. G_1 is derived using the algorithm with k equal to six to give

$$k = 6$$
$$b = 3$$
$$3^{n-1} < 6 \le 3^n$$
$$n = 2$$
$$b^{n-2} = 1$$

	Initially	Finally	
G_1	1	3	(maximum $G = 3$)
G_2	1	2	
G_3	1	1	

The six reels are formed by a three-way merge and a two-way merge of single reels, and then a three-way merge of the three-reel string, the two-reel string, and the single reel.

As remarked in connection with sorts, the designer should be influenced by the availability of prefabricated library routines in the selection of merge runs and run patterns. Also, he should seek combination of merging with other functions. These will have a bearing on the number of tape handlers, amount of I/O area, and computer-I/O balance factors to be considered in the merge phase.

TIME ESTIMATING

The purpose of estimating running time for a run, series of runs, or a system is twofold.

1. The estimate serves as a basis for comparing alternative approaches to a system design problem.
2. The estimate serves as a first determination of the computer time needed by the system for scheduling purposes.

Timing is first considered here for the processing run. A processing run is one that has only tape input and output. If a series of processing runs is to be timed, each run in the series is timed. The time for the series is then the aggregate time for all the runs in the series. A system is timed in a similar manner with due regard for the number of times a run is repeated over a given time span because of cycling. For example, if an annual system time is being developed, the time for the runs constituting the monthly cycle is counted twelve times.

Timing a tape-to-tape processing run is done as follows. A unit of data volume is decided on. For example, in a run updating a master file on the basis of a single transaction file representing 20 percent activity, the unit of five master items and one transaction item might be fixed on.

The method of selecting the unit of data volume exemplified assumes that master file activity constituted by the transaction file is evenly distributed over the master file. Such may not be the case. The degree to which the actual situation departs from the assumed situation should be determined so the degree of confidence in the resulting time estimate can be stated, and if necessary, the estimate can be altered accordingly.

After a unit of data volume has been decided on, the next step in timing a run is to determine the running time for the data volume unit. This time figure is used to extend data volume expressed in data units to arrive at a running time for the run. This method of arriving at a running time presumes that time can be expressed as a function of the data volumes handled by the operation to be timed. The applicability of this presumption varies from case to case. This applicability should be determined so confidence in the estimates arrived at can be expressed.

Running time for the data unit depends on the equipment being used. If tape read-write is unbuffered, running time is the sum of processing time for the data unit plus reading and writing time for the unit. To the extent that tape reading and writing can occur simultaneously or can occur simultaneously with processing, the running time is reduced by this overlap. For example, if tape reading, tape writing, and processing can be done simultaneously, running time is the larger of reading, writing, and processing time. (This statement needs qualification for variations in file activity, which will be made subsequently.) If tape reading or writing, but not both, can occur simultaneously with processing, running time is the greater of processing time and the sum of read and write time. In runs involving several inputs and outputs, the number of buffered channels available in the computer system and their bidirectionality have an influence on the amount of overlap possible. In general, all the considerations described in the chapter on blocking have an influence on timing. In the following discussion concern is with a computing system which permits simultaneous read, write, and compute. Appropriate modification of the discussion along the lines indicated is left to the reader.

As for the computer permitting simultaneous read-write-compute, determine whether the run is computer or tape limited. If the run is computer limited, running time for the data unit is the time it takes to process this unit of data internally in the computer. If the run is tape limited, running time for the data unit is the time it takes to pass this data on tape. These times are, respectively, computer time and tape time.

To determine whether the run is computer or tape limited, computer and tape time for the data unit must be developed and compared. If computer time for the data unit exceeds tape time, the run is computer limited. If not, the run is tape limited.

A tape limited run can be input limited or output limited. If input data volume exceeds output data volume, the run is input limited. If not, it is output limited. For example, consider a tape limited run whose inputs are a master file and a transaction file, whose outputs are an updated master file and a report file, where the volume and item size of the master and updated master files are identical, and where the item size of the transaction file is the same as the item size of the report file. If the data volume of the transaction file exceeds the data volume of the report file, the run is input limited; if not, it is output limited. If a run is input limited, tape time is the time to pass the input data. If it is output limited, tape time is the time to pass the output data.

A run may be computer limited at one time and tape limited at another. In such a case this split of time is reflected in the data unit. For example, presume a run in which a master file is updated by a single transaction file made up of two item types, A and B. When transaction type A is processed, the run is computer limited. When type B is processed, the run is tape limited. Type A represents ten percent activity; type B, 20 percent. Finally, presume that inactive master items are processed in tape time. In such an instance a data unit of ten master items, one type A transaction item, and two type B transaction items might be applicable. That part of the data unit comprised of the A transaction item and the master item on which it acts is timed in terms of computer time. The rest of the data unit is timed in terms of tape time. Running time for the data unit is the sum of the time for these two parts.

Suppose that tape time in milliseconds for an item is determined by the following formula:

$$T = 0.030(x + 1) + 7.450x/w$$

where T is tape time for the item, x the number of words in the item, and w the number of words in a block. (The formula for a character-oriented computer would be similar except that it would be expressed in characters rather than words.) For example, tape time for a data unit of one updated master item being written from the computer, where the updated master file has a block size of 500 words and an item size of 50 words, is 2.275 milliseconds.

If the data unit consists of two updated master items and one report item 32 words in size written on a report tape blocked at 480 words, tape time for the report item is 1.467 milliseconds. Tape time for the data unit is 2(2.275) plus 1.467, or 6.017 milliseconds.

Computer time is estimated as follows. A time is determined for main chain processing. To this time is added the following.

1. The time to transfer the data unit between the tape synchronizer and memory
2. Executive routine time allocatable to the data unit for those computing systems in which such a routine is called into play for I/O handling
3. The time required by the block handling subroutine to handle the data unit
4. The time required by the item advance subroutine to handle the data unit

The time in milliseconds to transfer an item between the synchronizer and memory might be determined by the following:

$$A = 0.004(x + 1) + 0.016x/w$$

where A is the time to transfer an item between the synchronizer and memory.

The time in milliseconds required by the executive routine to handle an item might be determined by the following:

$$I = 2x/w$$

If an item is only read or only written, these formulas give proper times for synchronizer and executive time. If the item is both read and written, the times developed from the formulas must be doubled to arrive at synchronizer and executive time.

For example, the sum of synchronizer and executive time for a data unit of one updated master item (block size 500 words, item size 50 words), where the item must be both read from the master file and written on the updated master file, is $2(0.206 + 0.200)$, or 0.812 millisecond. If the data unit consists of two updated master items and one report item (block size 480 words, item size 32 words), synchronizer and executive time for the report item is 0.133 plus 0.128, or 0.261 millisecond. Synchronizer and executive time for the data unit is $2(0.812)$ plus 0.261, or 1.885 milliseconds.

The time required by the block handling subroutine and the time required by the item advance subroutine to handle an item depend on the input-output technique used. For example, block-read block handling and item advance time, respectively, might be

$$H = 0.432x/w$$
$$D = 0.048$$

For block write, block and advance time might be

$$H = 0.440x/w$$
$$D = 0.048$$

For the input side of blockread-gatherwrite, block and advance time might be

$$H = 0.500x/w$$
$$D = 0.196$$

For the output side of blockread-gatherwrite, block and advance time might be

$$H = 0.560x/w$$
$$D = 0.196$$

For example, the sum of block and advance time for a data unit of one updated master item (block size 500 words, item size 50 words), where blockread-gatherwrite is used to both read the item from the master file and write the item on the updated master file, is 0.050 plus 0.156 plus 0.056 plus 0.196, or 0.458 millisecond. If the data unit consists of two updated master items and one report item (block size 480 words, item size 32 words) written with a block write, block and advance time for the report item is 0.029 plus 0.048, or 0.077 millisecond. Block and advance time for the data unit is 2(0.458) plus 0.077, or 0.993 millisecond.

The most accurate way to time the main chain is to code it. If a more approximate estimate is satisfactory, the number of instructions in the chain is estimated. The average instruction execution time for the computer involved, say 0.014 millisecond, is then used to extend this number to a time figure.

For example, time the run in Figure 8-8. The chart in Figure 8-9 gives statistics on the run in Figure 8-8.

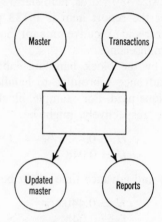

Fig. 8-8   A Run

File	Block Size	Item Size	Number of Items	Number of Instructions to Process an Item	Input-Output Technique
Updated Master	500	50	10,000 ⎫	50	Block read-gatherwrite
Master	500	50	10,000 ⎭		
Transactions	500	10	1000	200	Block read
Reports	480	32	5000	350	Block write

Fig. 8-9   Run Statistics

1. Data unit

   10 master items
   2 transaction items
   5 report items

2. Distribution of items in data unit

Master	Transaction	Report
X	X	X
X		
X		X
X		
X		X
X	X	
X		X
X		
X		X
X		

3. There is more output than input
4. Tape time for the master item

$$T = 0.030(50 + 1) + \frac{7.450(50)}{500} = 2.275$$

5. Tape time for a master item and a report item

$$T = 2.275 + 0.030(32 + 1) + \frac{7.450(32)}{480} = 3.742$$

6. Computer time allocated by cause for a master item

Synchronizer

$$2\left[0.004(50 + 1) + \frac{0.016(50)}{500}\right] = 0.411$$

Executive

$$2\left[\frac{500}{2(50)}\right] = \qquad\qquad 0.400$$

Block

$$\frac{0.500(50)}{500} + \frac{0.560(50)}{500} = \qquad 0.106$$

Advance

$$0.156 + 0.196 = \qquad\qquad 0.352$$

Processing

$$0.014(50) = \qquad\qquad \frac{0.700}{1.969}$$

7. Computer time for a master item and a report item

Synchronizer

$$0.411 + 0.004(32 + 1) + \frac{0.016(32)}{480} = 0.544$$

Executive

$$0.400 + \frac{2.000(32)}{480} = \qquad 0.528$$

Block

$$0.106 + \frac{0.440(32)}{480} = \qquad 0.135$$

Advance

$$0.352 + 0.048 = \qquad 0.400$$

Processing

$$0.700 + 0.014(350) = \qquad \underline{5.600}$$
$$7.207$$

8. Computer time for a master item and a transaction item

Synchronizer

$$0.411 + 0.004(10 + 1) + \frac{0.016(10)}{500} = 0.775$$

Executive

$$0.400 + \frac{2.000(10)}{500} = \qquad 0.440$$

Block

$$0.106 + \frac{0.432(10)}{500} = \qquad 0.115$$

Advance

$$0.352 + 0.048 = \qquad 0.400$$

Processing

$$0.700 + 0.014(200) = \qquad \underline{3.500}$$
$$5.230$$

9. Computer time for a master item, report item, and a transaction item $1.969 + 5.238 + 3.261 = 10.468$.
10. Running time for a master item is tape time—2.275.
11. Running time for a master item and a report item is computer time—7.207
12. Running time for a master item and a transaction item is computer time—5.230.
13. Running time for a master item, report item, and a transaction item is computer time—10.468.
14. Data unit time

$$4(2.275) = \qquad 9.100$$
$$4(7.207) = \qquad 28.828$$
$$5.230$$
$$10.468$$
$$\overline{53.626}$$

15. Number of data units in data

$$\frac{10,000}{10} = 1000$$

16. Running time $53.626 \times 1000 = 53.6$ seconds

Besides running time, time estimation must also take into consideration tape rewind, setup, and takedown time. These times can be added to running time to the extent that these operations cannot be overlapped by the running of the current run or prior or succeeding runs. For example, if a run processes a two tape file using *tape handler swap,* only the rewinding and dismounting of the second tape and the mounting of the first tape represent an increase over running time. The first tape can be rewound and dismounted and the second tape mounted during running time if a "swap" tape handler is provided for mounting the second tape reel while the first is being processed.

Another limit on the extent to which rewind, setup, and takedown time represent an increment over running time is the extent to which these operations are done in parallel. For example, if a run has two inputs, and if at the end of the run these two inputs are rewound simultaneously, rewind time is not the sum of the time to rewind each of the two tapes but is the time to rewind the longer of the two. The rewind of the shorter tape is overlapped by the rewind of the longer. Simultaneous rewind capability is common in some degree to virtually every tape-handling computer.

Rewind time is determined essentially by the product of rewind speed and the length of tape to be rewound. For example, in the run in Figure 8-8, the updated master file is the last file to be rewound. It is also as long as the master file and longer than the reports or transaction file. Rewind time for the run is rewind time for the updated master file. In Figure 8-8, 15.069 milliseconds is a plausible figure for the rewind time of one block of the updated master file; on which there are 200 blocks. Rewind time is 15.069(200), or 3013.8 milliseconds, or 3 seconds.

In addition to running time and rewind time, time to remove reels from tape handlers and mount other reels must be considered to the extent that these operations cannot be overlapped with other operations of the current, prior, or succeeding runs. Mount-dismount time is a function of tape handler design and the experience and adeptness of the operator. It ranges from fifteen seconds to several minutes. Since there are usually several tapes to be mounted or dismounted between two runs, the time required for manual tape handling may be reduced by use of more than one operator for tape tending.

Up to this point, timing only of tape-to-tape processing has been covered. Timing of peripheral operations is dependent on the type of peripheral equipment involved as well as the computer hardware organization. The simplest case is that of off-line peripheral equipment. Virtually all such equipment have a rated speed which can be achieved in ordinary circumstances. However, many have plugboard and other program control facilities. Extensive use of these facilities may slow down the item processing rate. That is, the off-line peripheral may be viewed as a special purpose computer which can become computer limited under heavy programming.

The peripheral unit may have more than one rated speed depending on the way in which it is used. For example, a line printer will produce more lines per minute printing single space than when required to multispace between lines. In some printers, irregular space patterns can be more time consuming than fixed multispacing.

In timing all peripheral operations off-line and on-line, allowance must be made for the manual operations involved. Forms must be set up and taken away from a printer. Cards must be loaded into input hoppers and removed from output stackers. Reels must be mounted or strips fed into perforated tape units. And so on.

As for on-line peripheral operations, the timing problem is different for concurrent processing computers from what it is for nonconcurrent processors. On a nonconcurrent processor, the timing considerations are very similar to those discussed previously with respect to timing tape-to-tape runs. Are the channels servicing the peripherals buffered? If not, running time is the sum of operating time for each of the unbuffered peripherals plus computer time. If so, running time is the largest of the operating times of the peripherals involved, if the run is peripheral limited, or computer time if computer limited. For example, on a completely unbuffered computer, if a run involves tape input and output, card input, and printer output, running time is the sum of tape read time, tape write time, card read time, printer time, and computer time. On a fully buffered computer, running time is the largest of these times. As pointed out previously with respect to timing tape-to-tape runs, this generalization is subject to qualification as far as activity on the files involved is concerned. This activity may cause the run to be computer bound at one point, printer bound at another, and so on.

On a concurrent processing computer with on-line peripherals, development of elapsed time to perform a particular peripheral operation, such as card-to-magnetic tape or magnetic tape-to-paper tape conversion, is identical to development of elapsed time for such operation on a special purpose off-line peripheral. This time is determined by the rated speed of the peripheral unit subject to the qualification that, if enough processing is combined with the conversion operation, the process may become computer bound.

However, an on-line peripheral operation also makes a demand on the overall hardware in terms of access to memory and utilization of the tape synchronizer for data transfer, and in terms of use of the control and arithmetic units for instruction execution. Consequently, running a tape-to-tape program concurrently with several peripheral programs may allow each peripheral to operate at top speed, but it will cause the tape-to-tape run to dwell on the computer for a longer time than would be the case if the tape-to-tape run were nonconcurrent. Generally, it is possible to develop a percentage figure for each type of peripheral program. This prcentage represents the increase in dwell time over running time of a tape-to-tape program when run concurrently with such a peripheral program. Thus, in timing peripheral runs for a concurrent processing computer, one develops not only an estimate of elapsed time for peripheral occupancy, but also the extent to which running time of concurrent tape-to-tape processing is penalized. The timing considerations discussed here apply equally well to random access computers, if the drums, discs, or other bulk storage involved are looked upon as on-line peripheral units.

TABLE LOOK-UP

There are three types of internal table lookup: function table lookup, sequential table lookup, and log 2 lookup. In sequential table lookup the table arguments can be arranged in any way desired. The problem argument is run against the table arguments by starting at the top of the table and moving down the arguments sequentially until a match is found.

In log 2 lookup the table arguments must be arranged in ascending or descending order. The table arguments are divided in half. A comparison of the problem key against a middle table argument then determines in which half of the table the problem argument lies. This half is then halved. As a result, a second comparison determines in which quarter of the table the problem argument lies. And so on, until the choice is narrowed down to two table arguments, at which point a comparison determines which of the two remaining entries is appropriate to the problem argument.

The name of log 2 table lookup arises from the following fact. Let A be the number of entries in the table. The number of comparisons required for one complete lookup is the logarithm of A to the base two, if A is a power of two. The number of comparisons is one plus the integral part of $\log_2 A$, if A is not a power of two.

In function table lookup the address of the table entry is related to the argument by some closed mathematical function. Thus, a problem argument is related to an element of the table by computational operations on the problem key which generates the address in memory of the corresponding table item.

If applicable, function table lookup is the most desirable table lookup technique in terms of both coding space and execution time. If function table lookup is not applicable, a choice must be made between sequential and log 2 lookup. Factors to take into consideration in making a choice are as follows.

1. If all table arguments are equally likely to be called for by the problem key, log 2 involves a smaller average number of comparisons per lookup.
2. Sequential lookup takes less coding space and execution time per comparison.
3. If the frequency of occurrence of problem key is highly biased and if table arguments are arranged in descending order by frequency of occurrence of problem key, the average number of comparisons per sequential lookup can be reduced from that achieved by a random arrangement of table arguments. If such a frequency distribution of arguments is not available when the system is designed, the arrangement of arguments in the table can initially be set up randomly. Then during parallel running and subsequent production, transaction files of problem arguments introduced into the system can be analyzed by a specially prepared program to generate this frequency distribution. Table arguments and entries can then be rearranged in the production run to conform with the distribution.

Perhaps the optimum solution to the choice between sequential and log 2 lookup is to do a sequential lookup on the more frequently occurring arguments and then switch to log 2 for the remainder of the lookup. However, such an approach cannot be chosen arbitrarily. The sophistication of the programmer, who is to program the run containing the lookup, may influence the choice of method.

Regardless of the method selected, when a run is designed to incorporate table look-up it must be so planned that change and addition to the table arguments and entries can be accommodated. Tables commonly represent classifications. In data processing areas classifications are forever changing.

ELIMINATION OF INTERLOCK

When the computer is ready to process a block before the block is completely read, the computer must wait until the read phase is complete before operating on the block. This situation is referred to as read interlock. In a concurrent processing computer, the computer can turn to the execution of some other program until read interlock is completed. However, if read interlock occurs on a processing run and all other programs in the computer are peripheral runs, there may be nothing to be done in the peripheral runs. The computer is then truly interlocked. It is unable to do anything until interlock disappears on one of the programs.

Most multiple input techniques initiate the read of a block only when a block of data in the memory is exhausted. Consequently, reads are unevenly spaced. If a large number of items from several blocks are processed before a block is exhausted, processing may continue unaccompanied by a read. If following initiation of a read, only one item is processed before another block is exhausted, read interlock may occur. Consequently, even in a run where total read time is equal to total computer time, running time may exceed this figure by a considerable amount due to intermittent read interlock. In such a situation even spacing of read operations will eliminate read interlock.

Under certain conditions the output operation of a run can be used to space read operations evenly. The conditions are as follows:

1. Only items read are written.
2. All items read are written.
3. No item contracts or expands.
4. There is only one output file.
5. All blocks are the same size.

Sorts and merges are examples of such runs. Under such conditions reads can be evenly spaced by following these rules.

1. A read is initiated only when a write is initiated.
2. A read is initiated whenever a write is initiated.

To follow these rules the input area must be large enough to guarantee that

1. There is always enough input to be processed.
2. There is always room to initiate a read when such an initiation is called for.

To make this guarantee for n input files, the input area must be $n^2 + n$ times the block size if standby is used. Another input method, preselected standby, requires only $2n - 1$ block areas of input space. Other methods require a number of block areas falling between these limits. For a discussion of this subject see Margaret M. Deutsch, "Preselected Standby for Multiple Input," *Univac Review,* (Spring 1958), Vol. 1, No. 1, p. 22.

If the conditions for using the output operation to space reads is not met, some other technique is necessary. Even if no regulation of the initiation of reads is made, the more standby area there is available to a run, the less chance there is for read interlock.

Write interlock is analogous to read interlock except that it arises when it is the completion of a write operation for which the computer is waiting. Write interlock can sometimes be avoided by providing backup storage to output areas, areas analogous to standby areas on the input side. Backup storage is most useful in runs where there are many outputs and only one input, such as editing and dispersion runs. Under such circumstances it may be possible to evenly space the initiation of write instructions on the basis of the input operation.

CONSOLE USE

The console typewriter has a low operating speed when compared with that of the computer. Consequently, excessive use of the typewriter generally slows down the computer. Use of the typewriter should be restricted to two purposes.

1. When communication is necessary between the computer and operator. For example, if the operator has mounted an incorrect tape, the computer must tell him so. To minimize this type of typewriter use a set of codes may be adopted for abbreviating this communication.

2. When printing of operational control totals that must be checked manually before the system continues. However, if this check involves more than the comparison of a number printed by the computer with an independently developed figure, the check should not be done manually but should be done by program. Too much time is wasted during a complicated manual control check. Perhaps the check of all operational control totals should be done by program. This will enable the routine to designate action to be taken—interrupt run sequence, continue cycle, and so forth.

The typewriter is sometimes used to record error items. This is a misuse of the equipment. It takes a long while to print enough information to document an error. The run may have to wait until the printout is complete before it can continue. Moreover, error information mixed in with the other information appearing on the typewriter hardcopy is difficult to decipher for corrective purposes. Write error information on a tape.

For economy of computer use and for internal control of application output, operator intervention into the computer system should also be minimized. Options that must be elected from cycle to cycle, such as whether a certain subroutine should be active, should be specified in design and built into programming. It should not be controllable by the operator.

The operator should not be used to enter data of any volume into the computer via his console keyboard. None of this keyboarding will be verified for operator accuracy unless the program is also provided a routine for accepting two keyboardings of the same data and comparing them. The typewriter copy of the console keyboarding is often difficult to proofread and is a poor means of validating data entry.

TAPE HANDLER ALLOCATION

Minimize the number of tape handlers used by a run to minimize reel setup and takedown time. For the same reason, and also for run-to-run integration, start tape rewinds as early as possible. For tape-to-tape processing, assign at least two tape handlers to a multireel file. This technique allows the computer to be reading one tape in a file while a previous tape is being rewound and dismounted and a subsequent tape is being mounted. Similarly, with a multitape output file, a tape can be written while a previously written tape is being rewound and dismounted and a blank tape is being mounted to be written on next. If the time to rewind, dismount, and mount a tape is not much less than the time to read or write a tape, it may pay to allocate three tape handlers to a multitape file to avoid a situation in which the computer finishes reading or writing a tape and there is no subsequent tape yet available to continue the tape operation.

For runs involving extensive use of on-line peripheral equipment, as in conversion runs, the time to rewind, mount, and dismount reels tends to be a small fraction of the total running time. Hence, computer efficiency is not seriously affected if only one tape handler is assigned to each file. Such an approach frees a larger number of tape handlers for tape-to-tape runs if a concurrent processing computer is used, or it may make possible a reduction in tape handler complement.

PROGRAMMING CONVENTIONS

Independent programming conventions should not be established. Use standardized conventions. Similarly, when using automatic coding techniques the coding generated should conform to the conventions set up at the computer installation. Only in this way is there a guarantee that the output of a run is acceptable as input to a run designed by some other designer. Moreover, operator performance is improved if the operator has only one set of conventions to which to conform for all runs.

Beyond these considerations, any effort to exploit the availability of library routines and of interinstallation exchange of programs requires fixed standards in programming and documentation. In particular, it has become common for the manufacturer to provide an extensive executive routine structure for intimate control of hardware operation and supervisory routines systems for reducing and simplifying operator-computer intercommunications. The programmer's own coding must communicate with the manufacturer's software package. The software expects to find certain standard conventions used in the programmer's own coding. This is a most compelling reason for suppressing individual tastes in the matter.

NUMBERING RUNS

When the computerization of a data processing area reaches the process chart stage, a series of run numbers is assigned to the application. The run numbers are used to identify the runs in a system. Runs should be numbered in the sequence they are to be run for two reasons:

1. It makes the process chart easier to read.
2. Routines are arranged on the master instruction tape in run number order. Having runs numbered in the sequence they are run minimizes the hopping around done on the master instruction tape to locate the next run to be executed.

When the process chart has reached the stage of development where run numbers are to be assigned, leave gaps in the number assignment. The first process chart is not the last one. Runs are eliminated and inserted many times before the form of the process chart is fixed. Gaps in the initial run number assignment allow the numbering of inserted runs without destruction of the run number sequence. One technique for determining the initial size of this gap is to divide the number of runs in the current process chart into the number of run numbers allotted to the system. The quotient is the gap to be left between assigned run numbers.

For ease of reference to the process chart, like run numbers are assigned to runs with similar functions. For example, in a system using specialized master files there may be parallel streams of processing, the corresponding runs of which are essentially the same. In such a case assigning like run numbers to corresponding runs in the two processing streams aids reference between the two. Thus, corresponding runs could be assigned corresponding low-order digits. Similarly, run numbers of daily runs could start with one; of weekly runs with a two; of monthly runs with a three; and so on.

One problem, which must be faced in connection with numbering runs, is the existence in the process chart of optional runs and alternative runs. The process chart may be designed to provide some runs for transactions not expected to occur each cycle. Often, the system design will provide additionally for bypassing these runs in any cycle for which the class of transactions does not occur. The runs for processing the special class are then optional, and the process charting associated with them is often done with dotted lines.

In another common instance of variability in the process chart, the system is designed to use one set of runs or another depending on the nature of the cycle, the volume of data, or some other criteria. For example, on the last day of the week, a set of daily runs may be replaced by another set which integrates daily and weekly processing. Another common example is associated with sorting runs for files with considerable variation in input volume. The pattern of merging runs, as discussed in an earlier section, will be varied with the volume range occurring each running of the sort.

Good control calls for full cognizance of the optional and alternative forms of the process chart and numbering all the runs which can exist in it in accordance with the standard run-numbering procedures. The problem usually begins with careless charting which neglects to show all possible branchings within the process chart.

FILE RETENTION

There are two factors to be considered in setting up the file retention schedule, system requirements, and regeneration requirements. An example of a system requirement is a company legally required to retain records for a period of time. The most efficient method of retention may be on magnetic tape or other machine form for ready retrieval.

With respect to regeneration requirements there are three types of files: cycle files, such as master and transaction files, that are used in one cycle to create tapes which are input to the succeeding cycle; intermediate files, which are outputs of runs in one cycle used only as inputs to succeeding runs in the same cycle and are then no longer needed; and peripheral files, which are produced to be used in creating card, paper tape, or hardcopy output and are then never used again. Cycle files are referred to by generation. Consider two cycles, A and B, where cycle B succeeds cycle A. The cycle files that are input to cycle A are called parent files with respect to the cycle files produced by cycle A and grandparent files with respect to the cycle files produced by cycle B. The cycle files produced by cycle A are input to cycle B and constitute part of the parent generation with respect to the cycle files produced by cycle B.

For regeneration of an unreadable file, parent files are a necessity. For example, if a cycle file produced by cycle A is unreadable when used as input to cycle B, cycle A must be rerun to regenerate the unreadable file. The input to cycle A is necessary for this rerun. Grandparent files are also retained in case a parent file is found unreadable during regeneration. When a cycle file becomes a great grandparent it is released.

An intermediate file is looked upon as being the parent of all output files of every succeeding run into which it becomes input. Consequently, it is retained, at a minimum, until all such output files have in turn proved to produce valid output files from every further run in which they have become inputs. Since this requires following the course of physical files down all the branchings of a complex process chart to determine when each one of the grandchildren of the intermediate file exists, it is usually simpler to preserve all intermediate files until the cycle output is accepted. A peripheral file is retained until the output has had a chance to reach its destination to be reviewed. Then if no complaint on the output is forthcoming, the file is released.

Random access computers and on-line peripheral operations present some special problems of file retention stemming not only from the need to preserve ability for regeneration, but also from the need to establish audit trails. Often, input is presented as keyboard entries, paper tape or punched card decks. A magnetic tape copy of all input often is made concurrently with the posting of the input data to the random access file. Hence, the file used in regeneration will not necessarily be in the original medium but will be its magnetic tape counterpart. Also, the random access file itself will be periodically dumped onto magnetic tape or punched cards for *security copy* as well as for possible regeneration needs. Unreliability of early disc file devices encouraged this procedure. However, in general, the practice is valid. No equipment is 100 percent safe from error or breakdown.

SPECIAL RUNS

In a production system when something has to be done to a file as an entity that is not provided for in the system, a special run or series of runs is created to do the job. An example is an across the board percentage wage-rate change where it is more economical to create a special run, applying the percentage to each rate in the file, than to create a change item for each such rate in the payroll master file and feed these changes into the normal file maintenance operation of the system. Another example is a special summary report.

These special runs are characteristically created on an exception, often on a crash basis, and require a close cooperation between system designer, programmer, and computer operating staff. As a result these runs are often created without a concurrent development of documentation and operating control. They have no run number, run description, or operating instructions. When the purpose of the run has been fulfilled the coding and rudimentary logical analysis are filed away.

Such procedure should not be allowed. Special runs should be documented and incorporated into the controls of the system. The need for special runs recurs. If no documentation was made, much of the effort that went into the development of the special run is lost in the difficulty of reconstructing what the run is and how it is used when the need for it recurs.

BREAKDOWN PROCEDURE

A system must have an alternative to be followed when the system breaks down. For example, if communication of clockcard information from the field to the computer breaks down, there must be some provision for meeting the payroll. Perhaps clockcards from the last pay period or standardized clockcards can be used. Such an arbitrary approach to breakdown procedure can be made to any kind of payment system in which a deadline is involved.

SYSTEM REVIEW

It does no harm for one system designer to look at another's work, perhaps to discover errors, omissions, and opportunities for improvement that have been overlooked. A proposed system should be reviewed by the customers served before it is frozen so that when in production it will satisfy their needs. It is expensive to alter a going system. The alteration can be avoided by getting prior agreement to the proposed system by all concerned. Detailed guidance to the customer of the computer application design for discharge of his review responsibilities and, incidentally, to the system designer for enlisting the customer's support can be found in *Electronic Data-Processing for the Line Official,* Sperry Rand Corporation, UNIVAC Division publication UT-2448.

Additionally, the system designer should review the design with other computer technical personnel. The programming staff should have an opportunity to judge the complexity of the programs demanded and even their feasibility. The staff for the computer center and supporting services should have an opportunity to judge the difficulty of operating procedures incorporated in the design. The system must be reviewed for the timing and control requirements imposed and other aspects of operability.

If the system application is an accounting or management control system of some significance, the company may oblige the system designer to review the design for its audit and control aspects with an internal audit staff or public auditors retained by the company. Again, the UNIVAC publication referred to should be of assistance to these reviewers and to the system designer in minimizing his review problems.

PART TWO

The Documents

9

SOURCE DOCUMENT
CONSIDERATIONS

FORM DESIGN

A source document is the initial form on which transaction data is transcribed. Its purpose is to introduce new information into the system. Observations of any phenomena of the business such as hours worked and quantity ordered are legitimate entries on source documents. If an information source generates nothing but an endless succession of A's, the information does not have to be introduced into the system. It can be generated in the system. Whatever information can be predicted in the system need not be gathered and introduced into the system.

Situations exist in which it is less expensive to gather redundant information on a source document than it is to generate the information in the system. On a clockcard it is less expensive to have a field to check if a man works a standard work week than it is to have a computer investigate the medical absence, personal absence, and other nonstandard work fields, determine that all such fields are zero, and conclude that the man worked a standard work week.

After determining what data the source document must ask for, it is necessary to determine the document format. In form design the foremost consideration is to design the form so it is easy to fill out. The result will be that the form is filled out: (1) quickly, (2) accurately, (3) completely, and (4) inexpensively.

Methods for designing easily completed forms are as follows.

1. Minimize the amount of recording that must be done. Methods for such minimization are as follows.

    a. Similar forms should be consolidated. By form consolidation it is possible to fill out portions of the forms at once rather than copy information at different times on more than one form.

    b. As much information as possible should be preprinted. This eliminates recording of standardized information. For example, dollar signs can be preprinted.

177

c. Exhaustive multiple choice should be used to avoid ambiguity or omission of data. If one of the questions is to determine which diseases the applicant has had, it is better to present the question in the following format rather than ask, "List all the diseases you have had."

CHECK ALL THE DISEASES YOU HAVE HAD

☐ Cholera ☐ Kidney
☐ Diptheria ☐ Measles
☐ Heart ☐ Pneumonia

In this type of presentation the applicant's memory is jogged. His effort in filling out the form is minimized. There is uniformity to the answers. This uniformity results in answers presented in the same order and without the need for interpretation.

d. Make the amount of information the respondent must fill in as short as possible.

e. Consideration should be given to the space needed to transcribe the data requested. Box design frees the most space for entries. An example of box design is shown in Figure 9-1. Provision for writing on the back of the form for continuation of data

Fig. 9-1 Example of Box Design

MO	DAY	YR

is undesirable. When additional information is sometimes written on the back of the form each form must be turned over to ascertain if there is additional information on the back. This is an additional and time consuming step. It is also possible for information written on the back of a form to go undetected if personnel forget to check the back of the form.

2. Arrange the fields on the form so the respondent can work through the form straightforwardly. Methods are as follows.

a. Arrange the form to be filled out from left to right and from top to bottom. This is the way the respondent reads and writes.

b. Cluster the area in which information is to be inserted. Don't scatter points of insertion over the form.

c. Sequence fields to follow work flow. For example, the income tax long form is designed so information is requested in the order it is developed in the most common tax calculation.

d. Arrange information requests in familiar sequences. For example, address is usually requested in the order, number, street, city, zone, state.

e. Arrange fields so those always filled in are at the left of the form, those usually filled in in the middle of the form, and those seldom filled in at the right of the form. An example of this is shown in Figure 9-2. The fields always filled in (invoice number, requisition number, shipping date) are to the left of the form. Billing number and contract number are filled in 60 percent of the time and are in the middle of the form. The serial number is used only 30 percent of the time and is to the right of the other items. The advantage of this format is that most respondents work across this line only as far as they have information to record. It is not necessary to fill in a field on the left and then jump to the right to fill in the next field with the fields between left blank.

f. Arrange fields in related documents in the same order. Advantages are:

(1) The field sequence is fixed in the respondent's mind.

(2) The recording from one form to another or comparing two forms is more straightforward.

3. Make the instructions for filling out the form useful. Methods are:

a. If possible, combine the instructions with the questions. Blank spaces to be filled with information should be clearly labeled to avoid misinterpretation when being filled out. Consider the example of blanks correctly and incorrectly labeled shown in Figure 9-3.

The query, "date," does not specify whether "month, day, year" or "day, month, year" is desired, and does not indicate whether month is to be spelled out or shown by a number. The labeled box design specifies both.

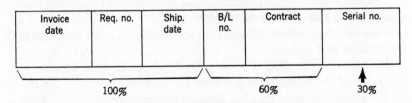

Fig. 9-2   Example of Field Arrangement

Fig. 9-3   Example of Labeling

DATE —————————————

INCORRECT

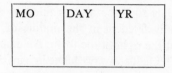

MO	DAY	YR

CORRECT

b. If the questions and instructions take up more than one side of a sheet of paper, put the questions on one side, the instructions on the other. The advantage is that, after the form is filled out, the answers are on one side of the form. The completed form does not have to be turned over to be read. Flipping the form over for instructions is awkward for the respondent. If the paper cost is not too significant a consideration, the form can be two-part, hinged and perforated with the instructions on one sheet facing the questions on the other. Since most people are right-handed, use the left sheet for instructions so the writing arm will not obscure them. The instruction sheet can be torn off after use and retained by the applicant, while the question sheet alone is delivered for further processing.

c. If the questions and instructions take up several sheets of paper, make a question and answer form and a separate instruction booklet. Advantages are:

1) After the form is filled out only the form has to be handled.

2) The instruction booklet can be used over again.

d. If the instructions are separate from the questions, number the questions and key instructions to the questions.

A second consideration in form design is the filing of the form. Standardized form sizes should be selected for filing ease. Binders and file cabinets for off-standard size material are more expensive than standard size binders and cabinets.

If a form is to be filed in a file cabinet, place the form identification at the top of the form. Then it is easy for someone searching the file to see the identification as they fan through the contents of the file drawer. If the form is to be bound on the left side in a binder, place the identification in the upper right-hand corner. If the form is to be bound on the top in a binder, place the identification at the bottom. File forms loosely. This frees more space on the form. No space has to be allocated to margins.

A third consideration is the operation to follow the completion of the form. For example, if after a form is filled out the information is to be keypunched on cards, the form should be designed to facilitate keypunching. This is a secondary consideration. The first consideration is to make the form easy to complete.

When possible avoid the use of handwriting in form completion. It is often illegible. If a typewriter or other transcribing machine is used to fill out the form, design the form for ease of machine use. Suppose a typewriter is used: The horizontal lines of the form should conform to the spacing provided by the carriage return lever. This eliminates the need for the typist to make fine adjustments to align the type with each line.

Horizontal lines should have the same ratchet spacing throughout the form. Make the form all single space or all double space. The availability of selective line finders for repetitive form typing is a consideration in choice of spacing. The left- and right-hand margins of forms should be standardized to eliminate the need of resetting the margin controls each time a different form is prepared. Standardize tab stops in a form. The box design of forms facilitates this standardization. Design the form so it can be filled in by typing directly across the form. Avoid a design that requires the typist to back up.

Minimize the number of skips required to fill out the form. Box design aids in this minimization. Box dimensions should reflect the characters per inch of the particular typewriters used. Minimize the number of carriage returns required and do not use cross rules between fields. For example, do not separate dollars and cents with a line. Let the typist type the decimal point. Cross rules slow typing and impair the appearance of the completed form.

If the source document has to be encoded before keypunching, leave room for the editor to write the codes.

Figure 9-4 shows an example of poor form design. The form has the following faults.

1. The entries for "our order no., ship via, inv. date, cust. ord. no., and cust. req. no." are not standardized for tab stops.
2. These entries are not standardized for platen ratchet spacing. Some require single space, others double space.
3. The entries for "inv. no." and "terms" can be preprinted.
4. There is waste space on the top, bottom, and right of the form.
5. The information to be entered is scattered over the form.
6. The typist must tab to type the "sold to" address.

7. The typist must backup to type the "ship to" address after typing the "sold to" address.
8. "Quan. ord." and "description" are filled out at one typing; "quan. shipped," "price," and "amount" at another. The column order requires skips in both operations.
9. The "description" column is not wide enough.

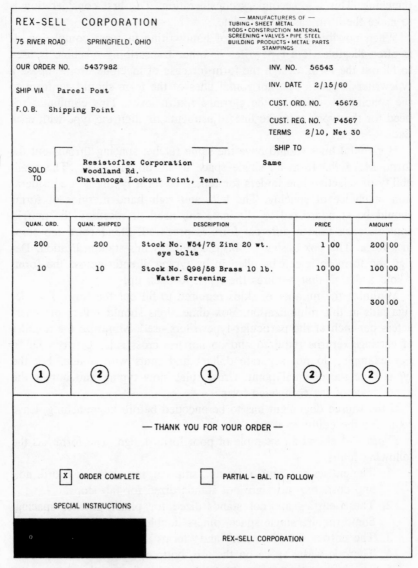

REX-SELL CORPORATION		— MANUFACTURERS OF — TUBING • SHEET METAL RODS • CONSTRUCTION MATERIAL SCREENING • VALVES • PIPE STEEL BUILDING PRODUCTS • METAL PARTS STAMPINGS
75 RIVER ROAD SPRINGFIELD, OHIO		

OUR ORDER NO.   5437982   INV. NO.   56543

SHIP VIA   Parcel Post   INV. DATE   2/15/60

F.O.B.   Shipping Point   CUST. ORD. NO.   45675

CUST. REG. NO.   P4567

TERMS   2/10, Net 30

SHIP TO

SOLD TO   Resistoflex Corporation   Same
Woodland Rd.
Chatanooga Lookout Point, Tenn.

QUAN. ORD.	QUAN. SHIPPED	DESCRIPTION	PRICE	AMOUNT
200	200	Stock No. W54/76 Zinc 20 wt. eye bolts	1 00	200 00
10	10	Stock No. Q98/58 Brass 10 lb. Water Screening	10 00	100 00
				300 00
①	②	①	②	②

— THANK YOU FOR YOUR ORDER —

[X] ORDER COMPLETE   [ ] PARTIAL - BAL. TO FOLLOW

SPECIAL INSTRUCTIONS

REX-SELL CORPORATION

Fig. 9-4   Example of Poor Form Design

10. The form requires all shipped quantities to be recorded. A better, exception procedure would be to record only backorder quantities.
11. Dollars and cents are separated by a line.
12. The blacked out area is ugly and will not hide confidential information.

An example of good form design is shown in Figure 9-5.

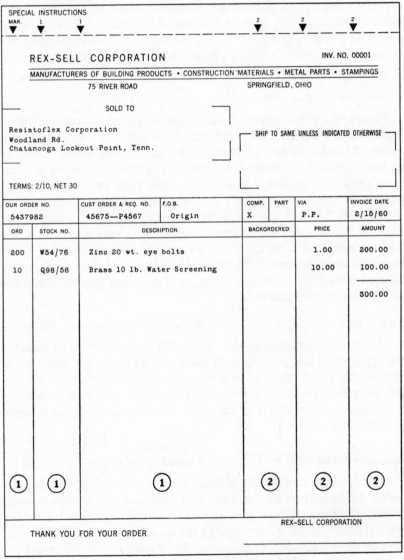

Fig. 9-5 Example of Good Form Design

AUTOMATIC ENCODING OF INFORMATION

Information can be in the *clear* (in English) or *coded* (in an abbreviated form comprehensible only when interpreted with reference to a key). In the latter case information generally is originated in the clear and encoded in a later step. Encoding must be verified to ensure an accurate transcription of clear information to coded information. Automatic encoding is the origination of coded information directly, eliminating the encoding and verification steps. Where automatic encoding can be applied, cost savings can be effected. Methods of automatic encoding are as follows.

Rubber stamps and plates.

Stamps and plates can be made to encode addresses, routing, membership names and addresses, and other information of a semipermanent nature. Through the use of stamps and plates it is no longer necessary to transcribe this information by handwriting. Perhaps the most common application of this nature is the credit card or charge plate to register the name, address, and account number of a customer making a purchase. Through the use of such devices the sales person is not required to write this information longhand; the information is neatly written, and there is no chance of an error by the sales person. However, the most important benefit is the savings of time and money effected through the automatic encoding of customer information in the form of an account number.

Forms with both clear and coded information presented

This form is organized so the person filling out the form by marking the appropriate box provides both the clear and the coded information. Because the coded information is provided alongside the clear information there is no need for reference to coding directories. As the encoding is automatic the possibility of encoding error is eliminated. An example is shown in Figure 9-6.

Multipart forms with both clear and coded information

With this type of form the original is in the clear while the copy is coded. As the parts of the form are bound together with carbon between copies, alignment of the copies is assured. Information circled on the original circles coded information on the copy. By checking the correctness of the information in the clear, the correctness of the coded information is assured. An example is shown in Figure 9-7.

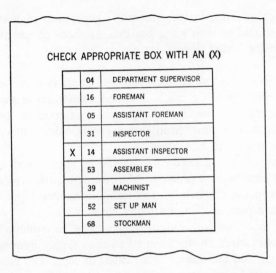

	04	DEPARTMENT SUPERVISOR
	16	FOREMAN
	05	ASSISTANT FOREMAN
	31	INSPECTOR
X	14	ASSISTANT INSPECTOR
	53	ASSEMBLER
	39	MACHINIST
	52	SET UP MAN
	68	STOCKMAN

CHECK APPROPRIATE BOX WITH AN (X)

Fig. 9-6   Example of Form with Clear and Coded Information

AUTOMATIC GENERATION OF MACHINE CODED DOCUMENTS

Automatic generation of machine coded documents is the transcription of source information directly into format suitable for introduction into the computer. The advantages of automatic generation of machine coded documents include:

1. Elimination of the transcription to machine code in a separate step.
2. The possibility for the provision of automatic encoding.

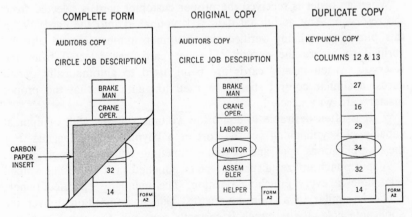

Fig. 9-7   Example of Multipart Form with Clear and Coded Information

SOURCE DOCUMENT CONSIDERATIONS   185

As transcription is expensive, automatic generation of machine coded documents should be used when possible. Methods of automatic generation of machine coded documents are as follows.

1. Office machines can be equipped with paper tape or card punching equipment which produce machine coded documents at the same time other documents are prepared for purposes external to the computer. Such devices may be attached to cash registers, adding machines, bookkeeping machines, and tabulators.

2. The use of mark-sensed cards should be approached with caution. Accuracy is sometimes a problem. Mark-sensed cards are effective as a means of reducing the cost of generating computer input, when used by responsible personnel in controlled circumstances.

3. Office machines with output punches can be equipped with input readers. Master cards or tapes can be used to supply information to the office machine and the output detail cards or tape. The master card or tape can be used similarly to control keypunching on a keypunch not necessarily attached to an office machine.

4. In the duplication of cards using gang punching the standard information a card may contain is reproduced in many cards. Variable information is punched later. For example, in order-processing a reservoir of customer cards can be maintained. This reservoir contains several cards for each customer. The cards for one customer have gang punched in them the customer number, name, address, and other required information about the customer. Enough of this key information is interpreted on the card to make it readily identifiable. Sales analysis data such as class of trade and geographical area can also be gang punched in the cards.

When an order is received the proper customer card is selected from the reservoir. Any additional data is keypunched into the card. When this punching is being verified the customer number should also be verified to assure the correct customer card was selected from the reservoir. When master cards are being used to automatically punch cards, a similar control should be used to guarantee that the proper master card was selected.

5. It is often desirable to equip low volume stations with equipment capable of keypunching yet the cost of a keypunch is unfeasible. For these applications spot and portable punching equipment is available.

A spot punch utilizes a special type of punched card which has a small pilot hole in every punching position. The manually operated punch, which is similar to a train conductor's punch, is positioned over the applicable hole. If the punch is correctly centered, the punch is made.

If the punch is not aligned with the pilot hole, the punch jams and does not perforate the card.

The portable electric punch is keyboard controlled and has only numeric keys. If it is desired to punch alphabetics using the portable electric punch, the applicable numeric keys which comprise the alphabetic code are depressed simultaneously.

Punching done using either of these devices is slower than standard keypunching. However, there are applications where limited punching is sufficient. In applications for the spot or portable punch, machine gang punching is usually applied prior to any subsequent punching. An example of an application is stock control in a warehouse. Quantities received can be spot punched into gang punched cards for each item carried in the warehouse.

6. The computer can be used to predict transaction information. For example, in one payroll system where pay is based on the type of work performed, the computer predicts the work a man will do on a given day on the basis of a work history. The computer prints this prediction on a card and punches the man's identification number in it. If the man works as predicted, the card is turned in, and the computer senses the identification number and uses its prediction, which it has recorded on tape, to compute the man's pay. No keypunching is necessary.

7. Mechanical encoders are designed for specific applications such as airline reservations. When a clerk gets a request for a seat on a specific flight on a specified day he sets this information by selecting the appropriate precoded matrix, somewhat like an enlarged charge plate or credit card, and inserting it into a mechanical encoder. Once the information has been preset he pushes a release key. This information is fed into the computer. The computer ascertains if there is space available, and if there is, returns a yes answer to the mechanical encoding device. The reservations clerk can give the customer an almost immediate answer for an inquiry. Banks use the same principle with mechanical encoders being used to update customer savings or special checking accounts. The mechanical encoding device allows direct query of the computer and the return of information from the computer.

ENCODING

There are two choices for information recording. They are information:

1. In the clear
2. In coded form

If code is chosen, there must be a reason for the code. For example, code may allow a more meaningful sequence in sorting than would data in the clear. If it is desired to order employee information by department, it is desirable to identify employees with identification numbers whose first digits indicate the department in which the employee works.

Evaluation of the choice for code is particularly important when the information must be represented in clear form at some later point in the system. For information that is encoded and later presented in clear format the following costs are incurred.

1. Cost of establishing code
2. Encoding costs
3. Validation costs
4. Run to decode the codes against a reference file
5. Maintenance system for the reference file
6. Maintenance of field coding directories

These costs must be compared with the cost of transcribing the message and processing it in the clear all through the system. One solution is a compromise where information is recorded in a combination clear and coded form. This system is used by the airlines. For example, BAL-Baltimore, BOS-Boston, BUF-Buffalo, CHI-Chicago, CLE-Cleveland. By using standard abbreviations on tickets, reservations, and baggage the airlines save the cost of writing the name out. Yet from the abbreviation it is clear what the desired location is.

There are certain characteristics a code should incorporate. These characteristics include:

Flexibility

Code must provide for an expansion of entries within categories. There are two types of expansion:

1. Tailend
2. Interspersed

It is sometimes vital that entries be in sequence, which calls for interspersed additions. At other times sequence of entries is immaterial. To provide tail-end expansion it is necessary only that the addition of new entries to the end of the list in any category be possible.

Interspersion can be provided by leaving gaps or providing suffixes. If gaps are not set up originally, they have to be set up when the assigning of suffixes begins. Code assignment requires judgement as to what assignment leaves the best possible distribution of codes unassigned. One way to set up gaps is to divide the number of cases into the number of possible codes. This might be a better starting point than finishing point when determining gaps.

Scope

The design of a code should cover all uses to which the code will be put. For example, material codes, sales codes, and accounting codes have interrelationships. They should not be designed by the manufacturing, sales, and accounting departments independently but by a central group to ensure uniformity of the code throughout the company. A code system should also allow for future expansion of its categories.

Operation

The code selected must be adequate for all operations it is used for. For example, if eighty-column punched card equipment is used, 47 different characters are available for assignment in the code. Yet, alphabetics are more expensive to keypunch than numerics.

Convenience

A code should be easy to:

1. Assign   3. Transcribe
2. Write   4. Check

Any time a coding system is instituted consideration must be given to the benefits as opposed to the job required to get the system in operation. If a previous coding system was used, it may be difficult to get employees acclimated to a new system. There are situations when no choice is possible. An instance is ICC commodity codes which have been fixed by the government.

The code should include the least number of digits consistent with the job and should be simple to use. This results in minimization of the need for reference directories. Coding systems should contain a fixed number of digits to simplify the writing, transcribing, and checking of the code.

The frequency distribution of cases should be considered so the simpler and more easily remembered codes can be assigned to the most used cases. The more convenient a code is to use, the greater the speed and accuracy in the code's use.

Uniqueness

A code must distinguish each case from all other cases. With the airline code if two or more airports had the same code, there would be mixups in baggage handling and ticket distribution.

Classification

A coding system should facilitate classification of like items. Items should be coded for what they are or are used for rather than by brand name or current nomenclature. For example, Tufnol Kite, Bakelite B152/1, Texolex ZA, and Pirtoid MP.31 are different trade names for the same plastic resin bonded paper tube.

In one company it was discovered that interchangeable parts were classified under eight different names: pin, pivot, spigot, axle, stub, bolt, swivel, and stud. This resulted in duplication, overlap, and superfluity. To avoid this situation items should be classified according to those characteristics that are permanent. In this manner the classification remains meaningful.

A proper coding system facilitates comparison between proposed new items and existing items so duplication, overlap, and superfluity are avoided.

Identification

The code should facilitate visual identification of an item. In the case of the airline code, identification of the destination of baggage is possible due to the ease of identification of this code.

TYPES OF CODING SYSTEMS

SEQUENCE CODE

One of the simplest codes is the sequence code. It is a numerical listing of items starting with one and continuing in number until there are no more items. An example of a sequence code is shown here.

1. California
2. Florida
3. Maine
4. New York
.
.
.
20. Vermont

The sequence code does not provide for grouping of data and is therefore limited in application. It does, however, provide the most practical method of listing not more than twenty or thirty items, subject to the provision that there will seldom be a need for group classification of the list.

Sequence codes are sometimes used in situations where other forms of code would be more applicable. A situation such as this exists where no provision has been made to have groupings in the code and where such divisions are necessary.

The most general use of sequence codes is in subdivisions of some other coding method. Consider:

Case 1

2015 (Binders)—5 × 7—3 (ring)—11 (black)—1 (plain)
2015 (Binders)—5 × 7—3 (ring)—11 (black)—2 (embossed)
2015 (Binders)—5 × 7—3 (ring)—12 (red) —1 (plain)
2015 (Binders)—5 × 7—3 (ring)—12 (red) —2 (embossed)

Case 2

2015 (Binders)—(Type) 1
2015 (Binders)—(Type) 2
2015 (Binders)—(Type) 3
2015 (Binders)—(Type) 4

In Case 1 six digits are used to describe size, number of rings, color, and cover type. In Case 2 one digit describes the size, amount of rings, color, and cover type. This type of coding is used to avoid overcoding and allows for quicker identification than a more complicated code might provide. In addition, the sequential listing of items lessens the possibility of overlooking an item.

BLOCK CODES

The basis of the block code is that blocks of numbers are used to represent classifications. No delineation is made by tens, hundreds, or thousands digit positions. Delineation is based on the divisions as assigned by the code originator. Division does not have to be standard as to the number of items in a block.

1–5 Light Bulbs

1. 40 Watt Bulbs
2. 60 Watt Bulbs
3. 100 Watt Bulbs
4. Threeway Bulbs
5.

6–13 Fuses

6. 15 Amp Fuses
7. 20 Amp Fuses
8. 25 Amp Fuses
9. 30 Amp Fuses
10. 15 Amp Slow Blow Fuses
11. 20 Amp Slow Blow Fuses
12. 25 Amp Slow Blow Fuses
13. 30 Amp Slow Blow Fuses
14.
15.

Block coding provides a method of coding by classes where the number of digits is limited as it provides for more classes with fewer digits than any other type of class coding. Expansion is provided by leaving spare numbers in both the blocks and in the assignment of items within blocks. Subdivisions within blocks is possible. For example:

1–20 BATTERIES

1–6 Flashlight

1. Penlight
2. C Cell
3. D Cell
4. 6 Volt Lantern
5.
6.

7–9 AUTOMOTIVE

7. 6 Volt
8. 12 Volt
9.

GROUP CODES

Codes of this nature depend on breakdown of major and minor classifications as represented by succeeding digits of the code.

1000 Equipment
  1100 Office Equipment
    1110 Furniture
      1111 Desks
      1112 Chairs
      1113 Coatracks
      1114 Bookcases

1120 Machines

    1121 Typewriters
    1122 Adding Machines
    1123 Ditto
    1124 Mimeograph

In this example all digits but the last can be sorted on to create groupings. It is desirable to start numbering with one rather than zero for identification of further group breakdowns. This results in the first item being 1111 rather than 1001. This is a waste of 110 numbers but does provide a more systematic numbering sequence. If the loss of 110 numbers cannot be spared, the same code can be implemented as follows.

1000 Equipment, Office-Furniture

    1001 Desks
    1002 Chairs
    1003 Coatracks
    1004 Bookcases

1010 Equipment, Office-Machines

    1011 Typewriters
    1012 Adding Machines
    1013 Ditto
    1014 Mimeograph

The preceding numbering will not affect the code's efficiency. However, it does make the separation of items into groups less straightforward. Another problem that may be encountered is groups of items greater in number than nine. When this situation occurs two or more sets of numbers can be consolidated to form one group.

20 and 30 Paper

    21 Typing, Letterhead
    22 Typing, Plain White
    23 Typing, Copy Sheet
    24 Typing, Yellow
    25 Typing, Orange
    26 Typing, Green
    27 Typing, Blue
    28 Typing, Onionskin
    29 Legal Size Pads
    30 Desk Pads
    31 Memo Pads
    32 Telephone Message Pads

33 Mimeograph Stock
34 Ditto Stock
35 Hectograph Stock
36
37
38
39

Due to ease of construction these codes are often used where sequence codes or block codes might be more properly used. This type of code is required only when automatic recognition of groups is a necessity. Also, it has the advantage of aiding memorization.

SIGNIFICANT DIGIT CODES

Significant digit codes are arranged so a dimension, measurement, size, or quantity is expressed in the coded number.

12000 Electric Light Bulbs

12025 25 Watt Bulbs
12040 40 Watt Bulbs
12060 60 Watt Bulbs
12075 75 Watt Bulbs
12100 100 Watt Bulbs
12200 200 Watt Bulbs

Significant digit codes have the advantage of reducing the amount of decoding necessary when using a code. The inclusion of a size, quantity, or dimension also aids the memory of people using the code. Expansion of such a code is accomplished by slipping the new item into its correct position in the group.

Significant digit codes are useful in converting old codes to new when old codes are well known. For example:

4000 Pumps

4017 #17 Pump
4024 #24 Pump
4077 #77 Pump
4812 #812 Pump
4997 #13997 Pump

FINAL DIGIT CODES

A final digit code is not a complete code but a modifier to an existing code. The function of the code is to bring out information that is not directly related to the main code. One of the uses of the final digit code is the assignment of business telephone extension numbers on the basis of importance. An extension ending in 0 such as 210 might designate a section head while an extension ending in 00 such as 300 designates a department head.

If more capacity than available with one digit is needed, the next to last digit can be used also. For example:

10 Class 1
20 Class 2
30 Class 3

Under some circumstances the final digit code may be useful. However, assigning numbers on the basis of a final digit reduces the code's capacity. To be a true final digit code the use of extra numbers, letters, or fractions is not allowed. This would be equivalent to an increase of the code's size. The true final digit code adds one or more classifications to the main code without increasing the number of digits of the code.

DECIMAL CODES

Decimal coding was originally devised for indexing library books. Today it is implemented in both business and government as a means of categorizing all forms of data.

000	General	530	Physics
100	Philosophy	531	Mechanics
200	Religion	531.1	Machines
300	Sociology	531.11	Lever and Balance
400	Philology	531.12	Wheel and Axle
500	Natural Science	531.13	Cord and Catenary
510	Mathematics	531.14	Pulley, Simple
520	Astronomy	531.141	Pulley, Compound

The coding to the left of the decimal point is the same as in group coding. The decimal point comes into play to divide and subdivide in a group. The advantage of this system is the ease with which further divisions can be made. The addition of further divisions makes the code that much longer. One of the uses for this coding system is by municipal governments for the numbering of lots and subdivisions of lots. Identification of a lot or sublot is made by noting the parcel number from which the lot came.

PREFIX CODES

Prefix codes are used where it is important to associate data with the frequency with which the data is used.

423821-86	Bumper
284376-21	Carburetor
142938-17	Condenser
343563-19	Fender
235819-58	Generator
167458-92	Points
351763-64	Radiator
473258-41	Roof
120618-38	Spark Plugs

With this example, an auto parts dealer can determine the stock of replacement parts needed. Parts beginning with a one are frequently used. Parts that begin with a three are infrequently used. Few should be carried in stock.

In the following example prefix codes are used to determine classes of material that can be ordered by various sized branch sales offices in an organization. The largest branches are allowed to order material with a code of one, two, or three, whereas the smallest branches are allowed to order only material coded one.

12109	Adding Machine	25108	Ditto Machine
33496	Accounting Machine	23532	Mimeograph
21438	Dictograph	39162	Offset

NUMERICAL-ALPHABETIC CODES

The purpose of numerical-alphabetic codes is to assign numbers to names in alphabetical order. There are many types of numerical-alphabetic codes. The need for different types is due to the degree of alphabetical order that must be retained, the size of the list, and degree of change the list is anticipated to undergo.

Partial Sequence Short List

01	A	
01	01	Aaron
01	02	Acorn
01	03	Adjax
01	04	Adrian
02	B	
02	01	Barney
02	02	Benett
02	03	Billings

In the partial sequence short list the first two digits represent the initial letter of the last name, whereas the second two digits represent the individual name. As originally listed, the groups are in alphabetical order. Additions, which are assigned to the next open number, destroy the complete alphabetical listing. With this system "Mc" is regarded as a separate letter. In the design of such a system the original lists of names should not be so long that certain letter groups would be so large as to prohibit scanning the list for reference to a single name.

Partial Sequence Long Lists

Here the code breaks down the alphabetical groups beyond the initial letter. An example would be:

1- 9	A		40-49	Ai
10-19	Ab		50-59	Ak
20-29	Ae		60-69	Al
30-39	Ag		70-79	An

The original list is in alphabetical order. Additions are placed at the end of the correct group, thereby destroying the complete alphabetical order. Construction of the code starts by ascertaining the total number of names plus an allowance for expansion. This number is divided by the amount of names desired in one division. The number of names in any division should be 10, 20, or 30 but not larger. The list of names is then apportioned by the number selected as the group limit to establish the alphabetical breakdown. If no list is available, a telephone book may be used as as base for estimating name frequency. Alphabetical frequency varies from one geographic location to the next.

Complete Sequence, All Lists

In the following example, alphabetical order on the entire name is required:

00	Saber
01	
02	
03	Sachs
04	
05	
06	Sador
07	
08	
09	Sazen

The first step in constructing such a code is to arrive at an expansion factor by dividing the sum of the number of initial names plus an allowance for additional names by the number of initial names. If this figure is a fraction, the next lower whole number should be used. The second step is to prepare register sheets or a numbered book with the numbers written in order. The first name in alphabetical order is written opposite the first number, the second name is written opposite the first free number following a number of skipped spaces equal to the expansion factor, and so on until the list is complete. As it becomes necessary to add new names to the list, enter them midway between the two existing names that bracket the name to be added. In this manner the list is always in correct alphabetical order. Discontinued names should be removed from the list so the numbers are available for reassignment.

Complete Sequence, No List

This is a form of coding that allows for an alphabetical listing of names when the complete list of names is not available at the time the list must be started. A sampling of the frequency of names is made by referencing a local directory. The alphabet is broken up into groups so each group will eventually contain about thirty names. Pages are prepared with number from one through 99 on each page. The segment of the alphabet and the corresponding sequence number that the sheet is to represent are placed at the head of each page. As the names occur they are placed in the middle of the applicable sheet. Thus, the first name of a sheet is placed on line 50, the second name on line 25 or 75, as the case indicates. Further additions are placed in the free line midway between the names that bracket the name to be added. A typical master code sheet headings table might be:

Sheet Number	Letter
23	Ba
24	Bar
25	Bc
26	Bf
27	Bh
28	Bin
29	Bir

FUNCTION TABLE LOOKUP

Function table lookup codes are used in computer applications. The memory address of the table entry is computed from the corresponding item key. For example, assume a company has 100 products. Each product has a different price. The prices are stored in the computer in the following order:

Stock Number	Memory Cell	Price
1	1001	$ 3.49
2	1002	27.62
3	1003	14.39
4	1004	6.52
. . .	. . .	. . .
. . .	. . .	. . .
. . .	. . .	. . .
100	1100	12.16

To arrive at the price for a product, 1000 is added to the stock number to determine the location of the price. For example, to look up the price for the product with stock number 2, add 1000 plus 2 to get 1002. The figure at this memory address is $27.62, the price of the product. Function table lookup is the most efficient way to look up information in a table.

SELF-CHECKING NUMBERS

It is possible to include in any coding system numbers that check the accuracy of the main code. There are many self-checking number systems, among which are numeric check digit and geometric check digit.

In the numeric check digit system alternate digits of the basic number are doubled and added together. Alternate digits are chosen starting with the least significant digit and moving left. The digits not doubled are added to the total. This total is subtracted from the next highest number ending in zero. The final digit from this subtraction is the check digit and is suffixed to the main code.

Assume a main code of 02456. Alternate digits are doubled and added.

$$
\begin{array}{ccc}
0 & 0 & 6 \\
\times 2 & \times 2 & \times 2 \\
\hline
0 + & 8 + 1 & + 2 = 11
\end{array}
$$

This total is added to the digits not doubled: $11 + 2 + 5 = 18$. This number is subtracted from the next highest number ending in zero.

$$
\begin{array}{r}
20 \\
-18 \\
\hline
2
\end{array}
$$

The check digit of two is suffixed to the main code to form the complete code, 02456 2.

The computer goes through the same procedure that was performed manually. If the computer computed check digit agrees with the manually computed check digit, the program continues normally. If there is disagreement between the two check digits, the computer indicates an error. There are, however, some errors that are not detected by this system. For example, 1213 and 2123 yield the same check digit—eight. Yet, there will be fewer errors with this system than there would be with no check digit.

A more powerful check digit is the geometric check digit. In this system each digit of the main code is multiplied by increasing powers of two, the results of the multiplications are added, and the sum is divided by 11. The remainder of the division forms the check digits. For example, with the main code of 02456 each digit is multiplied by increasing powers of two.

$$\begin{array}{ccccc} 0 & 2 & 4 & 5 & 6 \\ \times 32 & \times 16 & \times 8 & \times 4 & \times 2 \\ \hline 0 + & 32 + & 32 + & 20 + & 12 = 96 \end{array}$$

The sum of the products is divided by 11 to get the check digit.

$$\frac{96}{11} = 8 \text{ plus a remainder of } 8$$

The check digit is the remainder of the division or eight. The check digit of 08 is suffixed to the main code of 02456 to form the complete number 0245608. Fewer than one error in 1000 escapes detection when this form of check digit is used, but two columns are added to the field. The 80-column keypunch has an attachment that automatically generates a check digit.

While the use of check digits detects errors it also adds additional digits to the code. This is a disadvantage. Transposition of numbers accounts for over 70 percent of all numeric misfiles. As the number of digits in a code increases, the number of transposition errors increases geometrically. Thus, the errors double each time another digit is added to the code. Six digits are the maximum that can be handled without confusion. Six digits may be more workable than seven digits including a check digit.

One way to prevent transcribing errors is to break the digits into smaller groups. For example, instead of 123456, 123 456 is more workable. The division in social security numbers eliminates errors that would otherwise be caused by a nine-digit code. Breaking up the code number aids memorization: 054-28-3067 is easier to remember than 054283067.

Assume the following list of numbers is keypunched and then introduced into the computer:

734
285
411
936

If each row of numbers is added and then this total is subtracted from the next highest number ending in zero, there would be one check digit for that row. In a similar manner, add the numbers in each column and subtract from the next highest number ending in zero to provide a check digit for each column. The results are:

734 6   first row: $7 + 3 + 4 = 14; 20 - 14 = 6$
285 5
411 4
936 2

854 3   left column: $7 + 2 + 4 + 9 = 22; 30 - 22 = 8$

The number created by the additional row and the additional column (three) added together with either the digits of the check row or check column produces a multiple of ten ($6 + 5 + 4 + 2 + 3 = 20$, $8 + 5 + 4 + 3 = 20$). This provides a check on the additions and subtractions done to arrive at the check digits for the columns and rows.

Once this matrix-type self-correcting number system is set up, if an error is made in copying one number, the intersection of the discrepancy of row check number and column check number points to the incorrect digit. Assume an error is made keypunching the 285 and it is keypunched as 295. The computer would note that the column and row check digit of the nine in 295 do not tally with the included check digits.

Data Keypunched	Computer Calculation
734 6	734 6
295 5	295 4
411 4	411 4
936 2	936 2
854 3	844 4

In the row with the number in error the check digit as figured by the computer is 4 while the keypunched check digit is 5. In the column of the number in error the given check digit is 5 while the computed check digit is 4. Intersection of these discrepancies points to the 9 of 295. The only digit which corrects this matrix is 8 or 285, which is the correct number. Self-correcting numbers necessitate many extra digits; they should be used only when absolute and automatic control is indicated.

ALPHABETIC CODES

Alphabetic codes use letters as a code. They may be mnemonic. It is possible for *1* to denote a single person and *2* a married person. It is more descriptive to use *S* for single and *M* for married. It is easier for a clerk to recall the *S* or *M* designation than to remember that *1* is for single and *2* for married. Airlines use mnemonics to describe destinations. These codes are of value to ticket agents, porters, baggage handlers, and others that work with or use air travel.

LON	London, England
NYC	New York, New York
PIT	Pittsburgh, Pennsylvania
JAX	Jacksonville, Florida

Mnemonics aid memorization and promote the incidental use of the code by people. In the use of alphabetic codes avoid the use of either *U* or *V*. In handwriting they become confused.

The use of letters is an advantage in that one letter can denote any of 26 things while a number can represent only 10. However, numbers more adequately denote range. Six through 9 is more descriptive than *C* through *F*. Moreover, alphabetics may be more expensive to transcribe and process than numbers. Alphabetic keypunching is slower than numeric and the alphabetic keypunch is more expensive than the numeric.

ALPHANUMERIC CODE

Alphanumeric code uses both letters and numbers and may include special symbols such as dollar sign and asterisk. Alphanumeric code has the advantage that even more classifications can be denoted in a position than can be expressed in alphabetic code. If this advantage is exploited, many of the resulting codes are not meaningful apart from a coding directory. However, such codes can save space by use in areas in which information does not change frequently, such as disability status in a personnel records file. Another advantage is that combinations of letters and numbers yield more easily remembered codes than do numbers alone. If an alphanumeric code is used, avoid the use of *I, O, S,* and *Z.* They look too much like 1, 0, 5, and 2.

Codes of this type have letters and numbers so arranged that they aid the memory of the person using them.

W 5 × 7 C B

This code describes a wooden picture frame five inches in width and seven inches high with cove shaped molding and brown in color. Eventually a point is reached where conflicts and discrepencies result. Depending on the type of operations and equipment to be used the processing of the alphabetic portions of the mnemonic coding may be more time consuming than would be the case with numeric codes.

CONSONANT CODES

Through the use of this type of code words can be abbreviated and become more manageable. The code is created through the elimination of vowels in the clear word.

Harkin	HRKN
Barton	BRTN
Robertson	RBRTSN

If it were not for this type of spelling of street addresses, the size of telephone books for large cities would become enormous. Consonant spelling of names is important in machine work to allow smaller fields, space saving on output forms, and faster sorting times. The disadvantage of this system is the greater chance of error or misinterpretation when words are abbreviated rather than being in the clear.

PHONETIC INDEX CODES

These codes depend on reducing names to phonetic spelling and encoding all but the first letter to numeric equivalents. Prior to encoding in the phonetic index type code a numerical alphabetical relationship is worked out. To create the table, the vowels A, E, I, O, U and the consonants W, H, Y are ignored. An example table is shown below.

1. PV	6. DT
2. BF	7. L
3. KQXZ	8. MN
4. CGJ	9. S
5. R	

Using the table shown above the following names are encoded as:

Name	Phonetic Spelling	Encoded
Harkin	HRKN	H538
Barton	BRTN	B568
Robertson	RBRTSN	R25698

This type of coding has the value of reducing searching time for misspelled names. For example, Johnson, Johnsen, and Jonsen all have the phonetic spelling of JNSN and the coding J898. If it were necessary to search for a misspelled name of one of the three, all of them would be located. The correct one could be selected.

INFORMATION IN THE CLEAR

For information in the clear language and spelling must be standardized to allow efficient computer handling. If abbreviation is adopted, rules for abbreviation must be adopted so one man's abbreviation is the same as the next man's.

MANUAL CONTROLS

Manual Review

Data can be manually checked for validity. For example, freight rates are assigned by agents at railroad stations. These assignments can be manually checked for accuracy at a collection point. Such review need not be exhaustive. A sampling procedure may be adequate.

Count Controls

For example, an individual or department can be made accountable for a group of prenumbered documents.

TRANSCRIPTION OF INFORMATION

To avoid the inaccuracies that arise in manual communication and transcription, information should be converted to machine language as close to the information source as economically possible. A consideration in setting up the point of machine language transcription is that equipment in outlying areas costs more for maintenance and supplies.

CARD DESIGN

There are two elements to card design.

1. The fields should be arranged so the keypunch operator can punch

the card by reading the source document from top to bottom and from left to right.

2. The card design should take advantage of the features of the equipment used.

There are instances where these goals conflict. To gain maximum utility from the card it is sometimes necessary to compromise between the two.

If designing the source document so it is easy to fill out and designing the card so keypunch utilization is optimized means the keypunch operator must skip all over the document to punch the card, a transmittal form can be used. This form is designed so the operator can read it from top to bottom and left to right as she keypunches. It is completed by an editor who copies the information from the source document. Use of a transmittal form means the introduction of one more clerical step during which error can occur.

To take advantage of keypunching equipment the system designer must be familiar with the equipment operation. In particular, with respect to the 80-column keypunch and verifier, the system designer should be familiar with the program card used on this equipment. The program card is roughly equivalent to the tab bar on a typewriter but is more flexible. It should be exploited to the fullest to obtain keypunching economy.

The following are some rules for optimizing equipment utilization:

1. The card is a unit record. It is a documentation of a single transaction.

2. Design each field to be large enough to accommodate the maximum number of digits.

3. Group keys and arrange them from left to right and from major to minor. If they are arranged in this manner, editing is avoided on the computer.

4. Use overcapacity punching sparingly. Overcapacity punching increases computer editing.

5. Use some control to key the card to the source document from which it came. In this way the card can be traced back to the document from which it was punched. Such tracing may be necessary in the case of later detection of erroneous data.

6. Minimize right justification. The keypunch operator is more likely to make an error in this operation than in any other.

7. Identification data punched into multiple use cards should be punched in both card types in the same columns. This makes future identification easier.

8. On 80-column cards, group columns not being used at the end of the card. This arrangement allows an early eject operation which

speeds up keypunching. Duplicated information can be automatically copied from one card to the next. Group duplicated and skipped columns together to allow the keypunch operator maximum time to select and orient the next item of source material. Fields are generally arranged on 80-column cards from left to right as duplicated fields, manually punched fields, and blank columns.

On 90-column cards place information of a fixed nature (dates, sequence number, code number) to the left of the card. In arranging the card in this manner it is possible to make use of margin controls on the keypunch so constant information can be set in once and then automatically be included on succeeding cards. Putting variable information to the right of the card reduces the number of times the keypunch operator has to align the carriage of the machine.

9. On 90-column equipment the intermediate marginal stops can be utilized to index the carriage to the proper position for semivariable information and thereby save time for the keypunch operator. An example of semivariable data is an invoice number for a group of cards for one invoice. This data can be punched once for the group and then, by utilizing the intermediate marginal stop, there is no need to key it again until the number changes. When the number does change the old number can be erased and the new number inserted.

10. On 90-column equipment the left-hand margin of the upper and lower half should be in line vertically to provide a common home point for the marginal stop and intermediate stops. This eliminates a lot of spacing and skipping.

11. On 90-column equipment restrict data to the upper half of the card to save the operator the added time of flipping the upper and lower punching-control lever. If it is necessary to have some portion of the lower half used, have the lower portion punching extend to the right beyond the punched upper half. If this is done, when the card is tripped all data is erased.

In some cases adherence to one of the preceding principles causes violation of another. Make the best possible compromise between conflicting principles.

Once the card layout has been decided the next step is the physical design of the card and the headings to be applied. For this step consider the following:

1. Cards of similar design can often be combined in a multiple use card. The multiple use card has more than one heading per field. It reduces the amount of card types required by an installation.
2. Headings should be clear and descriptive.

3. Limits of fields should be delineated clearly by printing on the card.
4. If data which has been punched is to be interpreted, space must be allotted so the printing is legible.

Cards often make excellent source documents. Some advantages of using cards as a source document are:

1. The source document and the card are the same. This eliminates the need for handling a separate source document to obtain the required information.
2. The source document, once punched, is machinable in sorters, which adds an additional degree of flexibility for filing and reference.

If the card is to be used as a source document, the following considerations must be taken into account:

1. With 90-column equipment any place on the card may be used for handwriting as the whole card is visible to the keypunch operator. With 80-column equipment consider the blind spot in determining where information is to be entered on the card. If the columns to be punched from this information are placed to the far left or right of the 80-column card, the respondent can record the information on the card almost anywhere.
2. Take care that information written on the card is not obliterated by punching.
3. Protect the card from mutilation in recording and in transit.

Minimize variability of formats between different card types. Two types of excess in format variability are (1) too many card types and (2) too many exceptions. Too much format variability results in (1) a slowdown of keypunching production and (2) the creation of a keypunching control problem. On 80-column equipment the operator must frequently turn off program card control to punch an exception. After the exception is punched the operator may turn on program card control. Information to be duplicated is duplicated from the exception card rather than from the preceding standard card and is in error. This is the type of error most likely to get past verification without being detected. The verifier operator is apt to make the same mistake the keypunch operator did. After punching an exception card the proper procedure for both keypunching and verifying is to punch one normal card prior to returning to program card control.

In some cases the data comprising an item requires more space than is available on one card. In such cases the data must be punched into more than one card. Such a sequence of cards is referred to as a header card together with one or more trailer cards. With headers and trailers, each header card and associated trailer cards should have punched into them an association code to allow trailers to be properly associated with their headers. For example, in the case of file addition items to a payroll application, where each addition requires more than one card, employee number can be used as an association code and should be punched in the same columns of all cards, headers and trailers.

Trailers for one header should have a sequence code to identify the sequence of the trailers. For example, a header could have a zero punched in a certain column, the first trailer could have a one punched in the same column, the second trailer could have a two, and so on.

If the number of trailers that may follow a header is variable, the number of trailers for each header must be identified in some fashion to protect against the loss of trailers. One way to achieve this goal is to have the number of trailers punched into the header. This approach has the disadvantage that the number of trailers for a header must be determined before the trailers are punched. A technique that avoids this disadvantage is to use a sequence code of zero for the header, one for the first trailer, two for the second, and so on, and punch something, say a one, in a given column of the last trailer. The corresponding header and other associated trailers could have a zero punched in this column. The combination of this "last-card" column and the sequential nature of the sequence code provides sufficient information to detect the loss of a trailer.

Controls on card operations are as follows:

1. Do not allow keypunch operators to make up program cards for 80-column keypunching equipment. The operators should be required to use standard program cards that have been designed as part of the system.

2. Beware of the X skip key on the 80-column keypunching equipment. This key creates an X punch that will be converted by the computer and cause erroneous results. Require operators to use the skip key.

3. Where possible minimize the use of card equipment. The computer is the more accurate piece of equipment. Put the data on the computer as soon after it has been originated as possible to provide greater accuracy.

If input cards are being prepared at the computer site and are to be converted to magnetic tape prior to being fed into the computer, convert them as soon after punching as possible. If cards are to be transported over a geographical distance to a computer center, the following precautions should be adopted:

1. Tabulate a transmittal list.
2. Create control totals.
3. Duplicate the deck if there is some danger that the card deck will become lost during transmittal.
4. Print everything punched in the cards on the transmittal list.
5. Use an alphabetic tabulator to create the transmittal list if the punching includes alphabetics.
6. Use the tabulator at the time the transmittal list is created to:
   a. Check item counts and control totals.
   b. Create other batch totals.
   c. Make consistency checks.
   d. Check for the presence of a code such as a card type code.
   e. Test for overpunches.

PAPER TAPE DESIGN

Paper tape may be oiled or nonoiled. Oiled paper is longer lasting. In addition to paper tape there is plastic tape and edge punched cards which are available as containers of information produced by punched paper tape equipment. For some office machines, MYLAR tape and edge punched cards are used to hold master information for the automatic reproduction of the predictable parts of the printed output and associated output tape. For a message that is to be repeated over and over again, a master loop, paper or MYLAR, is used. There are various codes, four-, five-, six-, seven-, and eight-channel. These codes include *function codes* which cause accounting machines with paper tape reader attachments to perform editing functions. For example, on five level tape there are LTRS and FIGS function codes to provide shift and unshift facilities on the typewriter. Another use of function codes such as LTRS, FIGS or blanks is to take up space on paper tape that is to function as input to a printing device with a reader attached. The purpose of such space is to provide for the mechanical time lag that occurs during printer operations such as carriage return and paper feed.

Presuming an accounting machine, for example, a typewriter, with a paper tape reader and punch attached, this array of equipment can be used as follows.

1. Information can be read off a tape by the reader and punched in a blank tape fed through the punch.
2. Information can be read and printed on paper inserted in the typewriter.
3. Information can be read, punched in a blank tape, and printed on paper.

4. Information keyed on the typewriter can be printed.

5. Information keyed on the keyboard can be punched and printed.

These operations can be performed in a selective fashion. The selection can be controlled by function codes punched in the input tape fed into the reader or by the manual manipulation of switches on the typewriter or by both. In addition there are manual controls to allow the following.

1. A series of punches that would normally print a line to be passed through the reader without the occurrence of printing

2. A series of punches that would normally print a message to be passed through the reader without printing

3. A strip of tape to be read that would normally cause printing and have the typewriter respond only to the editing symbols punched in the strip

More than one tape can be fed through the reader at one time. This allows information from one tape to be superimposed on a delete area of another tape. More than one reader and more than one punch can be attached. Punched paper tape can be converted to 80- or 90-column cards, magnetic tape, edge punched cards, or can be read by a computer. Paper tape equipment may be a paper punch and reader; multiple punch or multiple reader combinations; paper tape reading and punching plus typewriter combinations; or paper punching and reading, typewriter, and calculator combined. Attachments for simultaneous paper punching can be put onto adding machines, cash registers, accounting machines, and other key-driven machines.

With five-channel equipment it is possible to transmit the information on the paper tape via wire to a distant geographical location. In such communications systems combinations of function codes are used to operate *stunt boxes,* which are used to provide such operations as switching, selective calling, and classification of messages. For example, if three branch offices are receiving from a headquarters, headquarters can transmit continuously, but by operating stunt boxes, each branch receives only the information pertinent to it.

When paper tape is fed into the computer consider the following:

1. Editing out function codes.

2. Information on paper tape is character organized. Therefore, field size does not have to be fixed. If field size is not fixed, markers are used to separate fields. If such is the case, field markers must be stripped and the fields may have to be word organized. Even if fixed field size is used, the data may not be word organized. In such a case the computer must justify fields within words and space or zero fill.

3. Reorganizing the fields for optimum computer item layout.

4. Stripping typing characters such as the decimal point, dollar sign, and comma.

5. Performing the reverse operations when coming out of the computer to make the information suitable for paper tape equipment. This includes:

   a. Editing in function codes and typing characters.
   b. Editing out fill.
   c. Reorganizing fields for paper tape usage.

Consider an application of an accounting machine using paper tape input. Procedures must be formulated for use of this equipment. Write these procedures down for reference purposes. For example, for a typewriter operated from paper tape consider the following in developing procedures:

1. The margins must be set at least as wide as the typewriter producing the tape to prevent character pileup at the end of lines.
2. Tab stops must be set for horizontal format.
3. Paper must be placed properly in the typewriter for vertical format.
4. If the typewriter uses a spacing disk to control vertical format, the proper disk must be inserted and synchronized with the form feed.
5. If tape is being taken up on a reel and is then to be used again, a special centerfeed reel must be used or the tape must be rewound.

FORMS FOR CHARACTER READING DEVICES

Input documents bridge the gap between the measurement and recording of some phenomenon, such as hours of work or units of material issue, and the computer. In some engineering, production recording, process control, and other applications, the devices sensing the data may be able to deliver signals directly to an on-line computer. In most business applications, this is not the case. Instead the data is recorded in documents and converted subsequently after some delay and handling to a medium directly sensible by the computer or its peripheral support equipment.

In fact, a major purpose of recording the information in documentary form rather than transmitting it directly upon sensing and acquisition is a need to deliver some or all of the data to human beings for processing and especially for interpretation to prepare it for the computer or for processing quite independent of ultimate computer manipulation. In such documents, it is not sufficient to use instrument-generated marks only intelligible to the appropriate reading instrument and not simultaneously intelligible to humans. Most input forms are in the category of documents showing information in unencoded English text or possibly some obviously abbreviated variant thereof and in standard numerical representations having obvious quantitative significance.

Such forms cater to the ease of comprehension by the humans who will perform the precomputer operations and make more or fewer gestures in the direction of lowering costs in the subsequent steps of encoding and data conversion. Two types of devices have been introduced for machine sensing and interpretation of alphanumeric characters in order to achieve economies in encoding and conversion. One of these devices senses information optically and the other magnetically.

Neither of these devices has reached the stage of logical sophistication in development in which the information to be sensed can be casually inscribed in individualistic calligraphy or type font. Even so, they tend to be expensive and should not be used if data can be recorded in more conventional encoded machine language and medium at the source.

The devices which read documents directly impose three classes of limitations on forms design. Each has a pure mechanical aspect: The facilities for forms handling. These limit some or all of the physical characteristics of the forms: their horizontal and vertical extent, the thickness and nature of stock, tear strength, freedom from mutilation, number of pages or parts per form, and so forth. Secondly, the scanning systems of these character reading devices are such that their fields of observation, optical or magnetic, are zoned to limited portions of the forms and input data must be confined to these zones. This imposes additional dimensional tolerance limits for the form itself and for the positioning the data on it. Thirdly, the limitations in logic of the character recognition systems may restrict the opacity of the form, type of ink, ink-absorbing qualities of the form stock, character size and shape, tolerance for dirt or tears, or other deterioration of signal-to-noise ratio.

In spite of this imposing array of problems, forms and data entry procedures have been custom tailored for numerous successful operations of optical and magnetic ink character recognition devices. These have found wide application in banking for checks and deposit slips; in inventory systems for material charge out and other documents; in the trucking industry for waybills; and elsewhere.

In the usual application, fixed information is preprinted and variable information, if any, is entered with special imprinting devices. In some cases, the data on the document is split into two streams: fixed data read and converted directly by character recognition devices, and variable data which is keyboarded and entered into the computer by more conventional means. More generally, there is a mixture of variable data entered by special imprinting devices at the source and fixed data, both of which are read and converted directly by the devices; and these data are accompanied by handwritten or other supplementary variable data which must be keyboarded. An example is a gasoline station credit card system in which the station identification and charge slip serial number may be preprinted, the customer identification and date may be entered from a credit card matrix in a special imprinting device, and item and quantity detail of sale as well as the price may be handwritten.

COMMUNICATIONS

Consider the following questions for information communication in a data processing system.

1. What is the most economical method of communication consistent with the time schedule? If the tolerable delay is large, shipping documents in bulk may be the most economical method of transporting information.
2. Can the communications system handle the data transmission peaks?
3. What is the possibility for error in the communications system?

From an economic viewpoint the larger the field of information to be communicated, the more characters per second have to be sent to transfer the information at a given rate of speed. The more characters per second, the more the communication costs. Keep fields to be communicated at a minimum size.

With extension of the family of terminal equipment for communication services, there is less need than formerly for conversion to and from a communicable medium. Terminal equipments include specialized key sets such as in airlines reservations, card readers and punches, standard typewriters and page printers, perforated tape punches and readers, magnetic tape readers and recorders. Transmission path facilities have also expanded and a greater variety of services are available in terms of bits per second. Also, error detection and correction facilities can be included in terminal equipment.

10

OUTPUT FORM
CONSIDERATIONS

A data processing system produces two types of output: Historical records to be stored for possible future reference, and active reports used by management as a basis for decision. There is no point in reviewing historical records in detail once they have been produced, as there is an excellent chance they may never be used. Active reports, however, should be reviewed for acceptability by the recipients of the reports. Control should be exercised by the computer center to ensure that these reports are prepared according to the proper procedure and time schedule. These procedures should be written.

The system designer's primary responsibility in output form design is form layout. Then if he can specify the following a form supplier can guide him as to the quality of paper needed, carbon requirements, volume, and lead time:

1. What equipment handles the form
2. Who the recipients of the form are
3. The number of copies required
4. The volume and frequency of the report
5. Storage and filing requirements for the form
6. Any unusual requirements the form must satisfy, such as for checks, bills, subsequent punching, or mailing

PREPRINTED OR BLANK FORMS

Blank forms are available in a variety of sizes, colors, plain or semi-lined, and single or multipart combinations. Standardized stock is less expensive than preprinted forms and does not entail the problems of supply and storage inherent with preprinted stock. The decision to use plain or preprinted stock is based on the following considerations.

The requirements of the recipient

For example, the government requires certain preprintd forms such as W2 forms. Another example of special requirements is an invoice or statement going to a customer. For presentability such a document should be preprinted.

The form requirement

If the form is too complicated, it may have to be preprinted. For example, on an invoice it is impractical to print terms of sale, company name or trademark, and similar information with a printer. Other requirements can complicate a form:

1. A great number of columns across the page requires preprinted column headings to delineate the fields of information.
2. The amount of information in the captions may be too great to allow printing of the captions on the printer.

There are ways to modify standard blank stock so the expense of preprinted forms can be avoided. Consider these alternatives:

1. Have paper prepared where columns are prelined yet have no captions printed. This type of paper can then be used for a variety of reports.
2. Print only the body of the report on blank paper stock. Supply a template with the report that contains the captions used for the columns of the report. If it is desired to bind the report, bind the pages to flip to the left and have the template on the right so the template can be used on any page. If columns have more than one heading, or if headings are different for totals, there can be two templates or one dual heading template.

OPTIMIZING PRINTER USE

Some ways of increasing printer utilization are as follows:

1. Minimize tape passes on the printer by creating similar documents simultaneously on the printer. Examples of documents that lend themselves to this type of operation are shipping instructions and invoices and check registers and check transmittal sheets. One way to effect this simultaneity is by printing the two forms side by side. An alternative is multiple part forms with strip carbons which have the ability to produce only required sections of the original on copies. Another means of doing

selective printing on copies is to have blocked-out areas on the copy. Printing is done in the blocked-out area but is illegible.

2. Printing time can be minimized by printing forms two or three up, that is, side by side. For example, printing two up doubles printer speed measured in document pages per minute without requiring higher line speed.

3. Design output forms to require the least number of lines to be printed per document. Keep these lines adjacent and capitalize on printer ability to fastfeed from one document to the next.

4. Setup time on the printer can be minimized by the following methods:

a. Standardize the left-hand margin of all forms. This allows the printer-operator to leave the left-hand tractor in the same position for all runs. Paper alignment is thereby simplified.

b. Use standardized form widths to minimize adjustment of the printer-feeding device. For a large volume of reports that are to be bound, 11 by 14 inches is always an applicable size, as these reports are invariably stored by stacking.

FORM DESIGN CONSIDERATIONS

The following are some questions to ask about output forms.

1. Is the sequence of the form logical and easy to follow?
2. Are the filing data and margins consistent with the filing equipment or binders to be used?
3. Are the captions easily understood?
4. Will titles, numbers or colors facilitate routing, dispatching or handling?
5. Have the space requirements of each field been verified?
6. Is there any part that needs emphasizing?

Other things to take into consideration are as follows.

1. Where there is a line, a carbon edge, or a perforated edge on a form at least one character space should be left free.
2. Forms should be marked for horizontal and vertical placement in the printer.
3. If a part of the copy is to be blocked out, use a pattern rather than a solid area.
4. Do not use stapled multipart forms. The staples tear the carbon.

REPRODUCTION OF PRINTED DOCUMENTS

The need for from one to several hundred copies of computer output varies with the nature of the application. Inventory records, of use to many departments as well as a central control section, often need to be duplicated. A midwestern wholesale grocery chain with 1000 retail outlets hopes, by using telephone communication links, to maintain a daily inventory for each store and each item. Copies of the printed output of the inventory run will be sent to each store to double check its inventory, to each divisional warehouse to chart delivery dates and reorders, to the central warehouse to plan for divisional shipments, to a central purchasing department to purchase materials for stock replenishment, to a production department to plan production of the needed items, to a central inventory section, and to district sales managers to provide them with information on leading items and to aid them in planning sales.

In some circumstances it can be more economical to reproduce output documents using the printer than using offset presses. In other cases, even though it may not be less expensive to use the printer, the time savings effected using the printer may prove to be advantageous.

Assume a printer that can produce six copies in one run. For more than six copies there is a choice of:

1. Rewinding the tape and rerunning it, thereby getting six copies each pass, until the desired number of copies is reproduced
2. Printing a reproducible master on the first pass from which additional copies are printed on offset printing equipment

REWINDING AND REPRINTING

Determine the relevant costs for an on-line printer in a concurrent processing computer configuration. Assume a printer that rents at $1650 a month. If a month consists of 176 hours (10,560 minutes), the rent per minute on the printer is 1650 divided by 10,560, or 0.1562 dollars per minute.

Assume that a tape handler to read the tape to be printed rents at $500 a month. The rent per minute on the tape handler is then

$$\frac{500}{10,560}$$

or 0.0473.

Assume that the pay rate of the printer operator is four dollars an hour. The operator cost per minute is then four divided by 60, or 0.0667.

Assume a printer that prints 700 lines a minute. In one hour the printer prints 700 times 60, or 42,000 lines. In one 8-hour day the printer prints 42,000 times 8, or 336,000 lines.

Assume that the printer prints 32 computer words on one line. Then the printer prints 336,000 times 32, or 10,752,000 words a day.

Assume that the printer is driven by a tape blocked at 500 words per block. Then the printer prints 10,752,000 divided by 500, or 21,504 blocks a day. (A similar calculation can be made for character addressable devices.)

Assume that tape can be read at 0.0223 seconds per block. The tape synchronizer is then tied up 21,504 times 0.0233, or 480 seconds. Four hundred and eighty seconds is 8 minutes. There are 480 minutes in an 8-hour day. Thus, the printer uses eight divided by 480, or 0.0167 of the synchronizer's time.

Assume that the synchronizer rents for $3250 a month. The rent per minute on the synchronizer is then

$$\frac{3250}{10,560}$$

or 0.3078. The printer's share of this per minute cost is 0.0167 times 0.3078, or 0.0051.

Assume that the printer consumes 24 minutes of the computer's time, three times as much as is consumed on the synchronizer. Thus, the printer uses

$$\frac{24}{480}$$

or 0.05 of the computer's time.

Assume that the computer rents for $9400 a month. The rent per minute is then

$$\frac{9400}{10,560}$$

or 0.8902. The printer's share of this cost is 0.05 times 0.8902, or 0.0445.

The sum of these developed costs, 0.1562 + 0.0473 + 0.0667 + 0.0051 + 0.0445, or 0.3198, is the cost per minute to operate the printer.

Assume that 30 lines per page are printed. At 700 lines per minute 23.3334 pages per minute are printed. Dividing the cost per minute, 0.3198, by pages per minute, 23.3334, gives a cost of 0.013 dollars per page.

A representative paper cost for 1000 sets of 6 ply blank paper 17 inches wide and 11 inches long is $74. The cost per set is then 0.074 dollar. Adding printer cost per page, 0.013, to paper cost per page, 0.074, yields a cost of 0.087 a page. A page consists of six copies. Thus, the cost per copy is 0.087 divided by six, or 0.015 dollar. If x copies of a report are to be produced, the cost per copy for each page, C, is expressed in the following formula.

(1) $$C = 0.015x$$

PRINTING BY PRODUCING A MASTER
AND OFFSET PRINTING THE COPIES

Printer cost (previously illustrated)	0.013
Plastiplate master 18 × 11 in. at $10 per 100	0.100
Depreciation on offset equipment: a $3000 machine with a 7-year life depreciates $1.714 per day based on 250-day years. Assuming that 30 jobs are run per day, regardless of the number of copies reproduced, the per job depreciation is	0.057
In New York City a pressman receives approximately $60 for a 40-hour week. Assuming 30 jobs per day, labor cost per job is	0.400
Total fixed costs per job	0.570

Paper costs are $1.50 per 500 sheets or $0.003 per sheet. The cost per copy for each page can be expressed as follows.

(2) $$C = 0.57 + 0.003x$$

CONCLUSIONS

The graphs of formulas (1) and (2) are shown in Figure 10-1. Solving equations (1) and (2) simultaneously indicates that the breakeven point between the two methods is at 48 copies.

$$0.015x = 0.57 + 0.003x$$
$$x = 47.5$$

Under this set of assumptions, when 48 or fewer copies are to be made, it is more economical to rewind the tape and reprint it. For over 48 copies it is less expensive to print and run a master. Cost is not the only consideration involved in such a decision. A fairly high number of copies can be produced faster on the printer than by supplementing the printer with reproducing equipment. Also, the pages of a printer run can be made on continuous fanfold forms which do not require collating and can be simply and inexpensively bound. Even multipart forms can be simply decollated with a *waterfall decollator*. By contrast, the pages of reproduced copy must be sorted, collated, and physically secured.

On the other hand, use of the printer to produce copies removes the

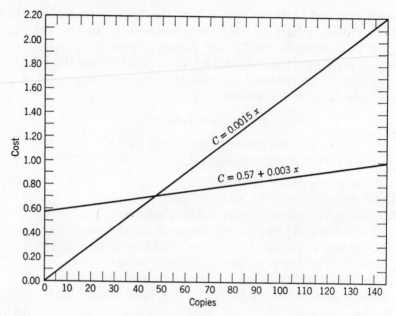

Fig. 10-1 Comparative Costs for Reproducing Copies

possibility of using the printer to produce other reports. Also, the quality of copy must be considered. The last copy of a multipart form is inferior in quality to the original. It may be necessary to reduce the number of parts below six to make copy acceptable in a particular application. Any reduction of the number of copies per printer pass will increase the printer copying cost developed here and favor using off-line reproduction equipment. In some applications, carbon copies will not be acceptable in any degree. This makes it even more difficult to justify repeats of the printer run as an alternative to reproduction.

PART THREE

The Approach

11

DESIGN AND

INSTALLATION STEPS

A capsule description of the seven steps involved in the design and installation of a computer data processing system is presented in this chapter. It is an outline for the remaining chapters of this book.

Survey

Survey is the determination of whether a proposed computer data processing system is feasible; that is, whether it will give improved operation at lower cost or satisfy other objectives. Initially, someone gets the idea that there may be benefits to be reaped by computerizing some data processing operation or that the computer can be used to solve certain problems for the first time. A survey of the area is made to determine the feasibility of such a step. If computerization is feasible, objectives are defined, and responsibility for the construction of the new data processing system is detailed.

System Investigation

System investigation consists of two phases: defining area objectives and reviewing existing procedures. In defining area objectives, the scope of the area to be covered is analyzed, the overall objectives are determined, and the functions required to meet these objectives are evaluated. Also, an appraisal is made of how this area relates to other data processing operations and to the company as a whole.

In reviewing existing procedures, a study is made of the operation with emphasis on exceptional as well as routine characteristics. All documents are reviewed as to origin, distribution, material, and format. All outputs are studied to determine whether they contribute to an operating objective. Another part of this study determines operating restrictions which must be adhered to in the new system.

System Design

The system design step begins with a study of the documentation prepared during system investigation. This study is to determine the relationships between all parts of the system. Next, a layout is prepared depicting the major relationships in the proposed system and giving consideration to the reference records that must be created. Following this, an analysis of the reports to be generated is made with emphasis on the fulfillment of legal and management control requirements. The source and reference data required to produce the desired reports are then defined. A process chart is constructed to show the processing needed. The last function of the system design step is to prepare run descriptions which describe the operations to be performed on the computer.

Programming

During programming the run descriptions are parceled out to programmers. The programmer's first step is to analyze the run description and prepare a flow chart picturing in detail how his run is to be executed on the computer. The flow chart is used for coding the run in computer language. After the coding has been completed, the run is tested for accuracy by processing specific transaction material on the computer (this is the debugging process). On completion of the testing, a run book and computer center procedures are prepared.

Filemaking

Filemaking involves construction of the records used for reference to obtain information or to accumulate data. For example, in a payroll system, a file is maintained on tape of all employees' records. Arrangements must be made to enable the clerical organization to gather the necessary data and establish the file. The data is then converted to tape and an audit of the file is made. Finally, subsequent to establishing the file and prior to going into production, the file is brought up to date.

Preparation of Clerical Procedures

The installation of a new computer system involves changes in clerical routines and thereby requires documentation of these manual procedures. After documentation has been completed, training must be provided for all personnel involved in the new system. After the training phase has been accomplished, the new system is tried with test data before it is installed on a production basis.

Program Testing

The last step is the testing and installation of the computer system. This step involves testing the system prior to installation and making the necessary changes to produce the required data. The system is then turned over for operation.

12

SURVEY

This chapter introduces the steps which lead to the decision to computerize a data processing operation and explains the initiation of the effort to effect this computerization. It provides background as to what may have transpired before the system designer begins to participate in the computerization effort.

Most commonly, the interest in computerizing a data processing area and the survey to determine the feasibility of such computerization is generated and sustained by a planning group. Consequently, this chapter in no way pretends to tell how to conduct a survey.

Initially, someone has the idea that the application of computer data processing to a company operation might solve a problem, affect economies, provide new management techniques, or deliver other desirable benefits. This person could be in the line operation or in a staff planning department. The idea could have been suggested to him by a number of means. Perhaps it was the realization that a data processing problem exists in his operation. Perhaps it was the announcement of the availability of a new type of equipment. Perhaps some distinctly different approach to managing the company or some of its functions obsoletes existing procedures and demands a new information system.

This idea, in the form of a suggestion, is channeled to the company's planning group where, if the idea has appeal, a preliminary phase of the survey is entered. During this phase several steps are taken. The needs of the project are defined in greater detail. What has to be done? How far reaching would the computer system be? Would the computerization result in centralization or some other reorganization? What equipment demands would be made? Many other questions arise as the implications of computerization are examined in detail.

When the project needs are more clearly outlined, the feasibility of the project is investigated. What potential does the computer system offer? Is it an easily measured potential, such as so many hundreds of

226

thousands of dollars in data processing costs saved each year, or an intangible savings, such as better management control, or more accurate and up-to-date reporting? Is the potential worth considering? Can the project be sold to management on the basis of the potential indicated?

In conjunction with the definition of project needs and the determination of potential, a rough block diagram of the data processing system may be drawn up to aid in this definition and determination. It is often the case that the system designer who will be given responsibility for the system design of this computerization is brought in to work with the planning group on this block charting, need definition, and potential determination.

If this phase substantiates the feasibility of the project, a second stage is entered during which a finer delineation of the methods to be used in the computer data processing system is made, the interdepartmental relationships implied by the system are investigated, and the areas of greatest potential are pinpointed and more fully outlined. The project is then ready for presentation to management.

Management is given a definition of potential, a block diagram of the proposed system is explained, and the methods to be used in the system are discussed. The purpose of the presentation is to ask management for a project team to carry out the computerization. If they are sold on the suggested data processing system, they define the objectives to be met by the computerization and detail the responsibilities for the construction of the new system. Design of the computer data processing system begins.

13

SYSTEM INVESTIGATION

INTRODUCTION

Ideally, when the system designer enters a data processing area scheduled for computerization, the only information he needs is a complete description of the output required from the data processing system in terms of content and timing. The system designer can then set about constructing the optimum computer data processing system within the restraints imposed by equipment limitations, company policy, availability of required input, and so on.

In practice, the situation is seldom this clearly defined. Instead, the system designer finds himself operating in a situation that manifests considerable sponginess. There is no formal definition of the total output requirements of the system. There is no line official who is familiar enough with the spectrum of output to create such a definition. The purpose of some of the output presently produced is not clear. The recipients of other output are not satisfied with the information they are getting but are not sure what information they would like to receive.

Assuming that the system designer gets the output defined, he then generally discovers that the character of the restraints within which he is to build his system are not the most desirable. Policy that governs a particular course of action is riddled with exceptions and is so fuzzy as to be subject to several interpretations, all of which have been used at one time or another in the history of the operation. Other policy, still in operation, is designed to take advantage of a market situation, working capital or tax position that has since passed into oblivion. Too much information is available for some processes. Not enough is available for others.

In the light of the situation in which the system designer finds himself, it is impossible to start his system design from a formal definition of what is required. Instead, he must begin by trying to develop some overall feeling for the data processing area to be computerized. The method generally grasped to develop this feeling is to begin with a study of the system that is presently in operation in the data processing area. In the great number of cases, such a system is available for investigation.

Although most data processing areas in which computerization is going on have already-functioning systems operating within them, the chance that the procedure presently in force is documented is less likely. If a procedure manual does exist, it is a good place to start the investigation of the data processing system, since it will provide some clue as to the structure and purpose of the system and will act as a guide to the system designer's study by pointing out to him some of the lines of thought that should be followed up in his review. However, a procedure manual should never be relied on completely as a definition of the current system. A procedure manual is characteristically drawn up at the time a procedure is instituted, and then, even if efforts are made to keep the manual up-to-date, the rate at which the manual changes hardly ever keeps pace with the rate at which the procedure changes. It is often the differences between the system as it operates and the system as it is described in the procedure manual that are the most crucial characteristics of the system. After all, the system changed for a reason.

INFORMATION TO BE GATHERED ABOUT THE DATA PROCESSING AREA

In investigating the data processing area, the system designer must gather information on the following subjects.

1. The objectives of the system
2. The existing procedures
3. The organization doing the job
4. The policies governing the area
5. The working papers used
   a. Reports
   b. Forms
   c. Records
6. The effectiveness of the procedure

During system investigation, the system designer is only incidentally interested in the computer data processing system. The design of this system is his goal. He can never forget it completely. However, during system investigation his primary interest is the present system, what makes it up and how it works.

It is difficult to analyze the information required by the system designer into categories. As soon as the attempt is made, it becomes obvious that the categories chosen are interrelated to the point where it is hard to discuss one category without becoming involved in others. For example, existing procedures cannot be discussed independently of organization. Procedures are a function of the organization set up to effect them. It is through knowledge of organization that knowledge of procedures is gained. Similarly, procedures cannot be discussed independently of the forms used in those procedures. The content and format of the forms are a documentation of the procedures. Consequently, the division of the following discussion into areas is a division of emphasis rather than of mutual exclusion.

OBJECTIVES

Information regarding objectives in a data processing area must be clear, detailed, and complete. For example, it is not enough to observe that the objective of sales statistical procedures is to provide the information required for planning, implementing, and controlling a company's marketing operations. Instead the objective might be stated as follows. The sales statistical procedures objective is to produce the internal sales data needed for effective planning and control of the following types.

1. Sales planning:
   a. establishing quotas by territory and industry
   b. developing the advertising budget and planning the allocation of funds for local advertising
   c. evaluating the character and size of the product line
   d. developing additional outlets and new channels of distribution
   e. determining the need for and location of additional warehouses
2. Control over sales by
   a. distribution channel
   b. geographical area
   c. type of customer industry
   d. product group
   e. salesman

There are numerous ways to determine objectives. One method is to ask management officials what they are trying to accomplish, what decisions they are faced with, how they measure performance, and what information they must have to control operations. Having the consumer specify what he wants has some merit but is only partially satisfactory. The consumer may have a good notion of the value of information he receives but is likely to have little idea of the plausibility of supplying information through the solution of technical data processing problems, not to mention the cost of gathering and processing the data required to produce the information. Since the net advantage of knowing something depends on both the cost of learning it and the benefit from using it, determination of what information is useful involves cooperation by data originators, processors, and users. Lacking any other way for determining system objectives, the usual approach is to start with the existing information structure and modify it to meet known deficiencies and foreseeable new requirements.

EXISTING PROCEDURES

The procedures in existence can be mechanized or clerical. Besides the steps constituting the procedure, the system designer is also interested in quantitative data. (What are the volumes of transactions? How long does it take to prepare a particular source document?) He needs frequency distribution information of all transactions, the number of this type and that; the frequency of need for the procedure, and the frequency with which the alternative procedure is used. A description of all exception as well as normal processing must be known. The scheduling of input and output (when source documents will be available for processing, when reports must be prepared) is required. Work-flow information (how smooth it is, and where it peaks) and any legal or other requirements that are imposed on the system from without are other considerations.

Mechanized Procedures

Process charts for the existing mechanized procedures probably exist. Consequently, to understand the mechanized aspects of a procedure little more needs to be done than acquire these charts and study them to ascertain the procedures involved. The system designer needs to check with key people within the organization to determine whether the charts are up-to-date, and if not, how they can be brought up-to-date. For example, if a data processing operation is being done on punched card equipment, one of the byproducts of the development of this system is a process chart drawn up at the time the system was created. This chart shows all equipment operations and their sequence, and identifies all cards entering each operation and all cards produced by each operation. If this chart is up-to-date, it will, with samples of each type of card used in the system, provide documentation of the existing system.

Clerical Procedures

It is possible that a clerical procedure is as completely documented as a mechanical one. There is no bar to producing a process chart of a clerical operation. Many clerical procedures are documented in this way. Moreover, many companies have clerical procedures detailed in the form of procedure bulletins and job descriptions. The more of this documentation there is, the easier the job of investigating clerical procedures becomes.

However, in many cases, documentation of clerical procedures is rudimentary, if it exists at all. In these cases, the procedure being followed and the job descriptions of the people working in the procedure exist only in the minds of the men who are involved with the procedure, either from an operating or supervisory viewpoint. In such cases, the procedure must be documented. Aspects of the procedure that are pertinent to this documentation are the types of equipment, the forms, and the work aids used by the clerical force.

Knowledge of the equipment used is of importance because in many instances characteristics of the procedure being followed are included to take advantage of some feature of the equipment or to compensate for some lack on the part of the equipment. The system designer wants to be aware of these characteristics. It may be advantageous to alter them when adapting the procedure to computer processing.

The forms used in the clerical procedure, particularly the work forms used by the clerk in developing his work, are important in documenting the procedure. Each form, to some extent, embodies within it the procedure involved in filling it out. Details of the information to be gathered about forms are covered in the section on working papers.

The manual work aids, the tables, the charts, the encoding and decoding directories, and the price lists that are used in the clerical procedure are also important. Some method for supplying this information to the computer system must be provided.

Finally, clerical procedures are generally segmented. One of the aspects of a clerical operation that the system designer wants to know is how this operation fits into the overall procedure in the data processing area.

Quantitative Data

With respect to any procedural step, it is useful to know:

1. *The quantity of work being performed.* That is, how many units of work go through this step in a meaningful period of time? For example, how many invoices does the billing department handle each week?

2. *The time required.* That is, how long does it take to perform this step on one unit? For example, how long does it take to extend an invoice?

There are many uses for this information. It may pinpoint bottlenecks. Also, volume and timing figure are indispensable to evaluating alternative approaches to a procedural problem. A document count is a useful measure of volume. If forms are prenumbered serially, such counts are easy to obtain.

Frequency Distribution Information

The system designer is interested in the types of transactions and the distribution of the volume among types. For example, in freight accounting the system designer is interested in the spectrum of possible loads from, say, coal to mules. He is also interested in the distribution of volume over the loads. How much coal is shipped in a month? How many mules?

This information is important because it has an influence on the method fixed on for handling a procedure. For example, to return to the previous illustration, if the carrier were located in a coal mining area, a lot of coal would be transported each month, but few consignments of mules would be handled. In such a case the freight accounting system could be biased so a coal shipment is handled expeditiously at the cost of a relatively inefficient method for processing shipments of mules.

In accounts payable useful information is the percentage of customers who pay from monthly statements and the percentage who pay from invoices covering individual shipments. In order-processing the following is useful information:

1. The number of items in the product line
2. The average, maximum, and minimum number of items per order
3. The volume of backorders and partial shipments
4. The volume of order changes (a reduction or increase in quantity; a substitution, deletion, or addition of items)
5. Those items involved in most backorders

Exception Processing

Related to frequency distribution information is the concept of exception processing. In describing a procedure it is easy to describe the normal case and forget to mention the exceptional case. Consequently, the implication is that the normal procedure is the only procedure. Then, when the new system is designed on the basis of this information, it is discovered that the system does not handle exceptional cases. The completely mechanical handling of procedure by a computer data processing system makes it imperative that the system designer be informed of all aspects of procedure from the most normal to the most exceptional. One of the important aspects of normal versus exception processing information is the percentage of occurrence of each type of processing.

Input-Output Scheduling

It is crucial to know when source documents are available for processing and when reports must be ready for distribution. These times set limits within which a system must operate. Pay cannot be computed before time cards are available. Paychecks that are not available on payday create a negative effect on morale.

In some instances, the system designer can work back from a due date for a report, determine from the amount of processing required how long before the due date the source data must be ready, and set up a cutoff point for source data on this basis. If current input organization procedures do not meet this cutoff date, the system designer may be able to rearrange these procedures to meet the date.

Work Flow

The system designer is interested in the flow of work through a data processing area and the degree of stability of that flow. He is interested in the size and frequency of peaks and valleys in the work load, their effect on procedure cost and time, and their causes. Irregularities in work volume are indicated by symptoms such as backlogs of work, delays in work, overtime, and idletime. Is there little to do at certain times and at other times does the volume swamp the staff?

The cause of such irregularities may be internal to the data processing area or they may be external. They may also be controllable or uncontrollable. If the causes are internal and controllable, eliminate the irregularities. If the causes are external or uncontrollable, be aware of these variations so the system can be built to minimize the shock of the variations.

If uniform quantities of work are available at the start of a procedure, irregularities appearing later are internal to the procedure and are controllable. Some questions that are appropriate in such a situation are as follows:

1. Is a department or position accumulating in-process work and dumping it in batches into the next department or position?

2. Is special, irregular, or nonstandard work permitted to interrupt the normal routine?

3. Do the number of workers assigned to various operations accurately reflect differences in time required to perform the operations, or is one group of personnel overloaded and another underloaded?

4. Is the schedule arranged to keep work from reaching critical stages toward the end of the working day?

5. What delays are incurred in getting approving signatures on forms before they can be released for action?

Legal and Other Requirements

Many procedures are prescribed by governmental or other restrictions. For example, the Internal Revenue Service has requirements for tax reports. The W2 form is a case in point; even the form is prescribed. State and local governments have tax regulations that must be met. A labor agreement may bind the company to certain procedures. Industry associations may place requirements on data processing operations. For example, the members of the Association of American Railroads have agreed on forms and procedures to be used in interroad transactions. Be aware of these constraints on procedure, since the system designed must conform to them.

THE ORGANIZATION

Concern with the organization implementing the current procedure is confined to its impact on the procedure to be studied. Organization has an effect on procedure. For example, complex procedure may be more the result of faulty organization than of complexity in the operation. Know enough about the organizational structure to separate procedure, per se, from procedure resulting from organization. Moreover, it is hard to understand the significance of records and reports without a comprehension of what responsibilities are involved in the organization.

Knowledge of organization is important for another reason. Such knowledge guides the determination of how much interviewing is needed to gain insight into the nature of the procedure, who should be interviewed, and in what sequence the interviews should be conducted. For example, in the case of a mechanical procedure already documented in process chart form, the proper personnel within the organization must be contacted to determine whether the process chart is up to date, and if not, what information is necessary to accomplish this updating. Knowledge of organization guides the system designer to the proper people to gain this information.

Information desired regarding organization is as follows:

1. The structure of the organization: the position titles and the lines of authority among them
2. The names of the people manning the organization
3. The functions of each unit in the organization

To the extent that they exist, organization charts reflect the first two types of information. Job descriptions reflect the third type. However, use of these documents is predicated on the basis of two requirements:

1. The documents must be up-to-date. If not, investigation is required to bring them up-to-date.
2. The documents reflect the situation as it is. Often it is the difference between the formal organizational plan and job descriptions and the actual organization and unit functions that represent the more significant aspects of organization structure.

One of the more important aspects of organization information is the relationship between departments on matters of common interest in the area under study. For example, the following questions regard division of functions that might be raised in a study of the order processing, invoicing, and shipping procedure of a manufacturing company.

1. Are separate organization units responsible for order processing and invoicing? If so, what is the line of demarcation between their functions?

2. What is the relationship between field sales offices and the headquarters credit department on establishing lines of credit and approving orders?

3. To what extent do field sales offices deal with the manufacturing departments?

4. To what extent do sales headquarters, order, production control, or manufacturing departments have contact with customers regarding orders or shipments?

5. What are the relationships among the order, production control, and factory departments on establishing shipping dates, on determining the manufacturing sequence of orders, or on specifying the plant from which the order will be shipped?

6. What are the relationships between the order department and the sales force on determining the priority of shipments?

7. Is there a clear and logical distinction of duties among the sales, order, and production departments regarding the control and replenishment of finished goods inventories?

8. If the company manufactures several products at several plants, are the functions of the order department divided among the personnel on a product basis, a plant basis, or a clerical activity basis?

POLICY

Policies are criteria for performance which originate on a level higher than that on which the study is being made. For example, policy may be set up by management dictates; it may be tradition; it may be habit. A policy is an artificial, although in many cases justifiable, restraint placed on a system from "above." Policies may exist with respect to every area of a business. They may be formal, written, and publicized. They often are informal, undocumented, and undeclared doctrines adhered to as rigidly or flexibly as formal policies.

Labor relations policies may prescribe that no employee be dismissed for routine reasons within five years of normal retirement age or at any age without a month's severance pay. Inventory policy may dictate shortage costs to be considered in optimizing inventory level. Policies for stockholder relations may cover dividend maintenance and growth or the time and form of stockholder correspondence and meetings. Policies may be indeed profound in that they may define what are acceptable objectives for the business and its functions.

Be aware of policy restraints, since one of two courses of action must be taken with respect to them. If it is worthwhile from the point of view of the system being devised, it may be worthwhile to take steps to get the policy changed. If not, the system must conform with policy.

Examples of policy are as follows. In a billing procedure there are pricing and discount policies. In an order processing procedure there are sales and credit policies. In payroll there are compensation policies. In any data processing system there is a records retention and disposal policy. Questions to which answers are needed are as follows.

1. Are policies reduced to writing?
2. Are policies uniformly understood by those who execute them?
3. If policies are not uniformly followed, what is the nature and frequency of the exceptions?
4. Are there any important recurring matters on which policies have not been established?

WORKING PAPERS

The working papers of a department consist of the reports it turns out, the records it keeps, and the forms it uses in accomplishing its objectives. A necessary tool is a collection of all reports, records, and forms annotated as to content, periodicity, routing, etc. In some instances such a collection is kept as a part of procedures documentation. To the extent that this documentation exists, system investigation in this area is complete. To the extent to which this documentation is lacking, effort must be expanded to compile the information. The following are data required with respect to reports, records, and forms.

Reports

Any information a department supplies or is held responsible for supplying is a report. Thus, reports include not only summaries and other management reports, but documents such as paychecks, invoices and bills.

Moreover, reports are not exhausted by the normal reports that are turned out at periodic intervals. All special reports that have been turned out in the past and which may be asked for in the future fall into this category. If information is rendered in response to a telephone call, this, too, constitutes a report and must be included for consideration.

Besides the report forms, the following information must be supplied for each report.

1. Information reported: What data does this report contain? To the extent that this information is not clearly indicated in the captions of the form, a description of the information required should be entered in the columns and sections of the report. Often captions on reports are abbreviated and are meaningful to the originators and users of the report but are unintelligible to the uninitiated.

2. Period covered by the report: Does the report reflect a month's experience? A year's? Other?

3. Frequency of preparation: How often is the report prepared?

4. Age of information reported: How much lag time is there between the cutoff date for source information and the appearance of the report based on that information?

5. Source of each part of the information: Where does it come from? Records? Source documents? Which ones?

6. Method of preparing the report

7. Method of compiling data

8. Checking procedures

9. Responsibility for preparation: by organization unit and position title

10. Man hours required: How long does it take to prepare the report?

11. Number of copies: How many are prepared?

12. Routing of each copy: Where and to whom do they go?

13. Purpose of report: What does it accomplish? Show?

14. Use made of each copy by recipients: This is information that will not be available in any procedure binder but will have to be determined.

15. Effectiveness of report: Does it meet the requirements?

Forms

Most of the points in the above checklist are applicable to forms. In addition, the following constitute useful information.

1. Volume of use: How many copies are used during the processing cycle?

2. Information entered at time of origination

3. Volume and significance of errors: How often do they happen? What is their nature? What is their impact on procedure?

4. Information added subsequent to origination

5. Approving signatures required

6. Use made of each piece of information in the form

7. Information transcribed to other forms, records or reports: Which

information is it? To what other document is it transcribed?

8. Disposition of each copy

Records '

The following information concerning records is to be gathered.

1. Information recorded in each column or space
2. Source of each entry
3. Volume of postings
4. Frequency of posting
5. Responsibility for maintenance
6. Man hours required
7. Methods of verifying posted data
8. Method and frequency of summarizing posted data
9. Equipment in which record is filed
10. Filing arrangement including type and frequency of visual indexing
11. Purpose of record: What is the nature and frequency of reference to it and of inquiries for the information it contains? What reports are prepared from it? Are copies made? What are they used for?
12. The time the record remains on file before it is destroyed.
13. Legal or company requirements governing retention of the record

To the extent that files or forms, correspondence and other documents are referred to and analyzed, they become a type of record, and together with this checklist of information on them, should be included in the forms binder.

QUALITY

Information on the quality of the work being performed includes the degree of error the procedure can tolerate, where mistakes are least important and where they are crucial, and the steps being taken to control the quality of the output of the data processing area. This information is an indication of which validation and checking procedures need to be incorporated into the system. Information on the volume and types of errors detected and the volume and types of corrections necessary at various checking points is also of interest. Another useful point of information on quality concerns any difficulties experienced because of undetected errors. The new system may be able to eliminate them. Consideration of the possibilities of defalcations and frauds and the expected damage causable thereby should be included. Audit trails and reviews, separation of responsibilities, crosschecks and other devices should be considered for coping with these control problems.

INFORMATION-GATHERING METHODS

There are two methods of gathering information about a data processing area. One is to review such documents as organization charts, procedure flow charts, work distribution charts, work layout charts, supervisor's control guides, procedure instruction manuals, job descriptions, and pertinent correspondence. The other is to interview the line official and the people within his organization who are placed in spots crucial to the data processing operation.

To the extent the information required is documented and to the extent to which this documentation is up to date, it is easy to acquire complete details concerning the operations in the data processing area. To the degree that data processing operations are not documented, the people who have the procedures "in their heads" must be freed for interview. This interviewing will interrupt the normal operating procedures of the line official's staff. The interruption is unfortunate but unavoidable, and some solution that will keep it to a minimum must be found. The system designer must inform the line official of his plans for interviewing far enough ahead to allow the line official to adjust both his own and the system designer's schedules for minimum interference with normal operating procedures. The system designer cannot appear on short notice and announce that he must talk to "so and so" today regardless of how this may affect the line operation. It is the system designer's responsibility to supply the line official with the schedule.

INFORMAL INFORMATION

Up to this point, the subjects in this chapter, the information sought and the methods for obtaining it, have been formal. There is, however, an informal area of information which is of equal importance to the formal knowledge gained about a data processing system, and which can be supplied only by the line official and the people he depends on in his organization. These people have an intimate, long-term acquaintance with the area undergoing computerization. Given the benefit of this experience, the system designer can supply the line official with a data processing computing system which is more effective, more tailored to the line official's needs, and more oriented to the solution of the problems peculiar to this data processing area than would have been possible otherwise. Examples of this type of information are as follows.

The line official is probably aware of a host of small problems occurring on a day-to-day basis within the data processing operation. One of these problems may be requests for information that the line operation has not been able to satisfy. Most likely, these problems have never been documented or solved. The line official should make the system designer aware of these problems. It is possible that several are due to the equipment in use, and if recognized, can be avoided in the computer data processing system. Others may be amenable to solution because of the advanced equipment design of which the system designer is aware. The system designer may be able to provide for the solution of these problems when he redesigns the system.

The line official, in informal discussions with the system designer, has the opportunity to tell not only the imperfections in the present system, but also the hopes for the future. The line official should detail how he would like to see the system improved. All his ideas on future needs and improvement should be discussed.

As an example of how a slight but significant addition to a data processing procedure can make the difference between an average system and an outstanding one, consider the following case. One user reports an annual savings of $250,000 realized from the production of a year-to-date engineering labor distribution report for budgetary control. Although preparation of this report requires the input of a negligible amount of additional information in the regular labor accounting distribution application, it produces savings greater than the total savings anticipated from conversion of payroll and labor accounting.

The line official should point out to the system designer the fundamental problem areas which exist in the data processing operation. Perhaps, with the introduction of the computer, these problems can be solved. Or perhaps they can be solved concurrently with the system redesign for the switch to a computer data processing system. For example, at present a company may be plagued with too many pay dates. The payday of one group of employees may be weekly; of another group, semimonthly. The payday of one group rarely coincides with the payday of the other. With the switch to an electronic payroll system, it may be possible to introduce a universal pay system, or at least, weekly and biweekly paydays for the two groups. There is nothing about a computer system which is essential to this change. The weekly and semimonthly payrolls could have been carried over to the computer system unchanged. But the company has already committed itself to farreaching change when it decided to use a computer for data processing. Consequently, it is easier for operating departments to secure approval for other changes from their management at this time than it normally is.

The line official should describe the ideal solution of his data processing problems to the system designer even if he does not think it is achievable. It may be more realizable than he thinks. And even if the system designer cannot develop a system reflecting this ideal, the ideal will still give direction to his thoughts.

DOCUMENTATION AND REVIEW

During information gathering there must be documentation of the information gathered to insure that the system designer is receiving accurate and complete knowledge of the line operation. If the document exists and is up-to-date, documentation consists of acquiring a copy. If documents do not exist, information must be gathered through interviews. In such instances, the system designer should document what he has been told. This documentation should be reviewed by the line official, to be certain the system designer is being correctly and comprehensively informed.

One aspect of this review is vocabulary. Every data processing area—sales accounting, inventory, production control—has a nomenclature all its own. There are words in the terminology of the area that have precise meanings shades away from the general meaning of the word. The system designer must learn the jargon and in using it, understand the words to mean the same as the line organization does, or communication is faulty.

There are documents that either should be in existence before system investigation begins, or should be developed during the course of this investigation. One of these is the annotated binder of reports, forms, and records referred to earlier in this chapter. Another necessary document is an output analysis chart, which cross references each field of information produced by the procedure with all the reports and records being produced. An example of such a chart is shown in Figure 8-1. A third document that it is necessary to produce is a list of the controls against error and defalcation incorporated into the data processing system. This list is used as a guide during the development of the computer system.

A document that may be developed during system investigation is a process chart of the present system. If such a chart exists, it is used as part of the documentation. If the chart does not exist, the question of whether it should be developed depends on the objective in the data processing area. For example, in payroll, where there are many external restraints, such as union agreements and tax structure, impinging on the system, a process chart of the present system should be developed to give documentation to the substantial part created by these restraints which must be retained in any new system. On the other hand, in sales analysis, where very few restraints operate, it may be decided to install a new reporting system using the computer and to phase the old reporting system out as the new one takes hold. Under such circumstances a process chart of the old system is not entirely useful and is not completely developed. In those instances in which these remarks are applicable, the system designer has an obligation to develop the associated documents.

One way the system designer documents his understanding of a procedure is by means of a block chart. Figure 8-2 is an example of a block chart. The system designer may make a block chart the basis of his review with the line official. Outside the area of these basic documents, ground rules for communications must be developed by the line official and the system designer. From the line official's point of view, documentation and his review of it are his guarantee that the system designer has understood what he was told during the last interview. The extent of this documentation must be determined by the line official as system investigation progresses. Throughout this period the line official works closely with the system designer and has an opportunity to appraise him. The line official, on the basis of this evaluation, decides how much documentation is necessary.

However, despite the line official's judgment, one phase that must be documented is the decisions agreed to between the line official and system designer. Whenever there are alternative procedures by which an end may be reached, and the line official and system designer agree on the choice of one procedure, this choice must be documented. The alternatives available and the reasons why one was chosen over the others should also be documented. In the discussion of the alternatives, the advantages and disadvantages of each are clearly outlined in the mind of each man involved. However, after the decision has been made, people's memory of the reasons for a decision begin to fade. Documentation of a decision, with alternatives and reasons, as soon as the decision is made, avoids repetitive discussion to refresh memories on points once clear to all.

SUMMARY

The purpose of system investigation is to gather information on the data processing area. This information is concerned with: the objectives of the data processing system; the output the system produces; the input provided; the processing required to produce the output from the input; the organization performing the processing; the policies the system operates under; the quality of the output produced; the suggestions made for improvement to the system; the concept of the ideal system; and the problem areas that exist in the system. The information collected in these areas forms the base from which the system designer begins his design of the computer data processing system.

The importance of system investigation cannot be overemphasized. Installing a computer data processing system is always difficult. In one instance in which installation went more smoothly than usual, the system designer was asked why. It developed that a man who had worked in the line operation undergoing computerization for many years had been assigned full-time to the system designer's staff. This man was always accessible to the system designer for consultation. According to the system designer, the use of this "sounding board" against which to test his understanding of the system was the most important element in the installation's success.

14

SYSTEM DESIGN

INTRODUCTION

During system design, the system designer's job is to develop the blueprint of the data processing system to be implemented by the computer.

GENERAL APPROACH

When designing a data processing system, have in mind certain objectives which relate to improving operations and decreasing cost. Some of these objectives are as follows:

1. Attempt to achieve standardization among like units. For example, if a company has two plants, make the payroll system of both as much alike as possible. One of the system designer's watchwords is "standardize."

2. Eliminate unnecessary functions—company operations that no longer serve any purpose. Integrate others which are currently separated.

3. Eliminate unnecessary reports, records, and forms.

4. Eliminate superfluous data—items on reports that make no contribution.

5. Establish necessary controls and eliminate excessive ones. For example, if statistical data are kept on punched cards, question the advisability of verifying the keypunching of the data.

6. Eliminate unnecessary refinement of quality requirements. For example, if information on month and year is adequate, there is no need to supply day also. A supervisor of a government agency eliminated four man months of punched card work per year by eliminating a superfluous day entry on a form.

Another example of an unnecessary refinement of quality requirements took the form of a transportation display in one of the larger cities of the country. This bulletin read "75,544,868+ passengers rode the city rapid transit service in the first 5 years." Carrying out this figure to the units digit was excessive refinement. A figure of 75,000,000 or perhaps 75,-500,000 would convey the same information. As a matter of fact, such a figure would have conveyed more information. The plus after the figure indicates that the suppliers of the figure are not sure of its accuracy, and the figure presented leaves the reader uncertain as to the degree of inaccuracy: Is it in the units digit, the tens digit, or where? A figure rounded to the nearest thousands or ten thousands conveys degree of accuracy as well as magnitude.

7. Eliminate duplication of function. For example, a situation in which not only purchasing buys an article, but stores also buys it, and the user of the article within the company buys it, too, is a duplication of function. Duplication is not necessarily a bad thing; in some cases it may be more economical than not duplicating. Be willing to accept such a situation. To say that the attempt to eliminate duplication of function should be made is not to say that duplicate functions should be eliminated wherever they appear. It means, rather, that the system designer has an attitude which makes him sensitive to duplication of function, since he has been able to affect economies in such areas in the past.

8. Eliminate duplication of purpose. One of the most widely publicized instances of such duplication in recent history was the parallel development of missiles within the armed forces. Reflection on this situation lends emphasis to the principle that duplication of purpose is a fertile area for economizing. Some duplication may be purposeful, such as that deliberately engaged in for competition, cross checking, and so forth.

9. Eliminate duplication of operations, such as the multiple filing of the same reports in the same office.

10. Eliminate duplication of information and forms. If two forms are the same except for format, or if the information on two different forms overlaps, consolidate the forms. "Consolidation" is another of the system designer's watchwords. Slight variations in report content may exist in different departments. Integration of function will tend to encourage consolidation of variants.

11. Smooth out work flow and eliminate peaks and valleys in this flow.

To this end consider such things as

a. Reduction of waiting time: for example, consider switching from a semimonthly payroll to a weekly payroll to provide weekly accounting for labor distribution.
b. Elimination of bottlenecks: with the increased capacity of the computer to automate procedure, a procedure which has created a bottleneck can often be integrated into the overall procedure so the work is smoothed out and the bottleneck disappears.

c. Advancing of the cutoff date for source documents so the data enter the data processing system at an earlier point in time.
d. Setting up the system so that part of the work is performed ahead of schedule. For example, on a weekly payroll in which clockcards are available to the accounting office daily, instead of batching them for processing at the end of the week, set up the system so each day's cards are processed as far into the system as possible.

In preparing his system design, the system designer asks certain questions.

1. Can the procedure be improved so its basic objective is more fully achieved?
2. Can the procedure be simplified or the work volume reduced by modifying such external factors as policies, organization structure, or the practices or performances of other departments?
3. Is each operation necessary?
4. Does it duplicate or overlap another operation? Can it be integrated with others?
5. Can the work be performed in a simpler, faster, or more economical way?

POLICY

The following avenues in the policy area should be explored. Can work volume be reduced by making adjustments in policy? For example, can pricing or discount policies be made more uniform without loss of income but with simplification of invoicing procedures? An instance is a concern with a complicated rate structure built up over a number of years to stimulate trade in special areas of the market where rates peculiar to those areas were offered. With the passage of time and the increase in data processing costs, it may now appear desirable to simplify the rate structure to realize a simplification in procedure. The problem to be resolved is whether customer dissatisfaction will result from the simplification of rate structure, and if it does, whether it would be more than outweighed by the data processing savings possible. This type of problem is very real when conversion to computer data processing is being considered, since the use of extensive tables is one of the more expensive computer applications. On the other hand, mechanization of the application of such tables is a source of major clerical economies in computer applications.

Another example is the routine for handling customer complaints, where a reduction in the amount of tracing to be done before settlement is made may often be instituted safely. A related example occurs in the accounts payable area, where the policy for handling overshipments, overcharges, and damage claims comes under question. In many companies a large percentage of these discrepancies and claims represent dollar amounts smaller than the cost required to straighten them out.

A third example concerns the debiting of purchased items of low unit value at the time of acquisition rather than charging them to inventory accounts and debiting them individually on withdrawal from stores. One company found that 35 percent of its stores' requisitions covered items which represented less than 5 percent of the values of inventories. For many of these items, the cost of maintaining inventory records, pricing, withdrawals, and charging them to jobs was greater than the value of the item.

A second question in the area of policy is: Can the administration of policies be made more uniform? Reduction of the number of exceptions in a data processing system reduces system cost.

PROCEDURE

When external factors, such as policies, have been explored, analyze the procedure. Eliminate those parts of the procedure that are unnecessary or unprofitable. Some questions to ask about procedure are:

1. Are all steps in the procedure necessary? If they are, are they being performed in their most logical order?

2. Are all checks necessary, particularly the double checks? Should every unit be checked or should a sampling procedure be established as part of a statistical quality control procedure?

3. Where else is work similar to this being done? Does duplication of work exist? If so, where do these steps belong?

4. Are all forms necessary? If they are, are they the best that can be derived? Can two or more be combined into one?

5. Is a document being routed through too many individuals?

6. Are there parts of the procedure now performed in one section that functionally belong in another section?

7. What is the output of the system being used for? Is it the best for its purposes?

The basic question to ask when concentrating on procedure is: How does this operation or document relate to the objectives of the procedure as a whole? Subsections of this question are

1. Does the operation or document make a contribution to the quality or progress of the work?

2. Is the value of the contribution greater than the cost? In many cases the cost of producing some document amounts to more than the value of the document in use.
3. What would happen if the step were curtailed or eliminated?

During system design the system designer's philosophy with regard to any procedure is to think of at least one other way to accomplish the procedure's purpose and to compare the alternatives. In many cases, the alternative chosen is the original procedure. It is the system designer's attitude this chapter is trying to document, not the result of his actions.

Exception Reporting

In many operations, such as savings bank accunting, bill payment, billing, and so on, amounts and quantities must be exact. However, in operating control areas, such as production, cost, inventory, and sales, exact and detailed information is not crucial. Nevertheless, more than likely such data are accumulated over a period of time, and for instance, at the end of the month, a report is prepared. The purpose of such a report is to indicate trends to management so bad trends can be identified and corrected before they become serious. Frequently, because of the data's age, such reports, instead of indicating trends at their inception, depict trends that have reached a degree of maturity. Thus, rather than giving management a tool with which to work, the report is a source of exasperation, for it reveals what might have been done. Technically, this is known as a historical report. Familiarly, they are often referred to as "hysterical."

The advent of the computer as a data processor has made it less necessary to resort to such reporting procedures. The increased ability of the computer to automate procedure allows an investigation of trends to be built into the processes designed to handle the standard operations on data. For example, one payroll produces, as a byproduct of normal payroll procedures, an average labor rate that is used by management as an indication of labor cost movements.

Estimates of performance in production, cost, inventory, sales, and so on, can be constructed from past experiences. Then, performance can be measured against these estimates as an aspect of normal processing. In each instance where the performance deviates from the estimates, an appropriate notation can be placed on an exceptions report. For example, a sales analysis for the sales manager of a large company was prepared monthly. The report contained a complete record of the previous month's sales broken down by product, district, and salesman. The report contained over 5000 entries and was designed to aid the sales manager in determining the answers to the following questions.

1. Are sales up to schedule?
2. Are sales being made in the districts and markets as planned?
3. Are the salesmen realizing their potential?

To get the answers to these questions it was necessary for the sales manager to waste time digging through a 5000-entry report. Or, what was more probable, the sales manager's examination of the report was superficial. Consequently, the report never answered the questions posed. In either case there was waste: in the former case, waste of the sales manager's time; in the latter, waste of data processing time. With the computer as a data processor, and with an approach to this problem as previously described, the sales analysis system can be set up so the entries that do not deviate significantly from expectations are eliminated from the report. This approach leaves only those items requiring the sales manager's attention in the report.

This approach to management reporting is known as *management by exception* or *reporting by exception*—one of the most effective ways for eliminating unnecessary operations in a data processing system. Utilizing management by exception, an organization isolates the problem areas earlier, spends less time pinpointing problems, and has more time to spend solving them. This approach allows management to spend more of its time in significant activity and less of its time on unimportant jobs.

To take advantage of management by exception, certain requirements must be met. First, criteria must be formulated to determine what constitutes a normal or acceptable occurrence and what constitutes an exception. Second, a method of evaluating exceptions must be established so all exceptions that are insignificant are screened out, leaving only important exceptions to be reported. For example, for one interested in the status of the stock in an inventory from period to period, there is no point in including items on which there has been no activity during the last period. Further refinement of this system might also make it possible to eliminate from the stock status report those inventory items on which the amount of activity for the past period was insignificant. On the other hand, a special report of slow-moving items might select out for reporting only those items for which there was little or no activity.

Elimination of Duplication of Operation

An example of the way the application of computer data processing makes it possible to eliminate a duplication of operation is as follows. One of the jobs of a railroad company is the construction and maintenance of track. Before computer data processing in one railroad company, the foreman of each maintenance-of-ways crew working on track kept a running record of the labor, material, and other expenses his crew incurred. The purpose of these reports was to serve as the basis for producing summaries in the form of unit cost statements. This recording of cost information was a duplication of operation. The information required for the unit cost statements was already recorded in other documents, such as time cards and material requisitions. With the advent of computer data processing, the payroll, stores, and other applications were designed so this cost information was captured. The unit cost statements are prepared automatically by the computer on the basis of the captured information, and it is no longer necessary for the foreman to keep a running record of his costs.

Elimination of Duplication of Forms

The immediate way to uncover duplication of forms is to bring all the forms used in a department together at one time. This is one of the reasons for creating the collection of reports, forms, and records discussed in the previous chapter. A manager of a large department of a public utility decided to try this approach to forms analysis. He anticipated that about 200 forms would be gathered. In actuality, 792 different forms were discovered, and many duplications were noticed just in collecting the forms.

Another example of form duplication took place in the receiving system of an industrial plant. The old receiving system had grown up over the years to meet varying requirements—to aid in the control of quality and quantity of shipments, to facilitate storage and availability of material to production, to enable the accounts payable department to pay, and to help the cost department carry out its function. The old system included three forms for each shipment, involving seven copies, and a summary. Because the information had to be written four times, there were many errors in transcription and long delays before the summary could be made. The new system uses an eight-part form completed on receipt of a shipment, and consequently, eliminates the three forms previously required. As a consequence, the delay and error that made the old system disadvantageous are eliminated also. This outcome is one instance of the general rule that elimination of waste effects an improvement in both the speed at which a document is produced and the quality of the result. The two watchwords of the system designer, standardization and consolidation, are at work here. Consolidation of reports that have slightly different purposes into one report generally results in a standardization of report format.

The Most Useful Output Possible

Construct a data processing system that produces the most useful output possible. For example, in one organization, the payroll system requires that a timecard be prepared for each employee each day. This card represents a day's work and contains the employee's identification number, the number of the department in which he works, the location at which he is working, the classes of work in which he was employed that day, and the breakdown of hours between these classes. Before the use of a computer, these cards had to be prepared daily as part of the input organization procedure of the data processing system.

The computer now prefabricates these cards as part of its normal operation, and each card has the identification, department, and location numbers already punched in it. In addition, as part of its normal record-keeping, the computer keeps a history of the classes of work for each employee. On the basis of this history the computer predicts the employee's class of work on the day represented by the card produced for him. This prediction is printed on the card. The computer also keeps a record of its predictions. These prefabricated cards are then shipped to the field. If the employee works as predicted, the card is returned directly to the computer center. No keypunching is necessary. On the basis of the card and the prediction, which it has recorded, the computer computes the man's pay. Only if an employee does not work as predicted is any keypunching necessary, and then, only information concerning his work experience has to be keypunched. All identifying information has been prepunched in the card by the computer. The company's experience has been that 25 percent of their employees work as predicted. Thus no keypunching is required in these cases. Another 40 percent of the employees work substantially as predicted. Only a minimum of keypunching is necessary for them. Through design of output to make it as useful as possible, the designer of this computer system has, by anticipating future operations in the system, reduced the amount of work required to organize input for the system.

One question to ask in evaluating the usefulness of output is, "Will this report help someone do his job better?" The higher the echelon to which a report is directed the more condensed the report should be. One possibility to consider is the production of the report in a different order from that which is presently being used, with the purpose of making the report more meaningful, or reducing the volume of the report, or both. Also, measure the value derived from the output against the cost of producing that output. Producing output is profitable only if its use yields more than its production costs.

Determination of the Real Use of Output

It is crucial to determine the real use of the reports developed in a system as opposed to their apparent or intended purpose. Information on report distribution is necessary to this determination.

For example, in the headquarters sales organization of a consumer goods company, a survey was made of sales statistical procedures, records, and reports. Among the records was a file containing a card for each of the company's customers to which postings were made from copies of branch office sales orders, factory shipping notices, and invoices. Maintenance of the record required three clerks. On being questioned about the use of this record, one of the company's sales executives stated, "This is the score sheet that tells us how we stand with each of our accounts. It enables us to call to the attention of each branch sales manager those accounts in his territory that need special attention."

Further investigation revealed that complete sales information by individual account was also available in a monthly punched card listing and that the product managers relied on this and other tabulated reports for sales control purposes. Pursuing the inquiry further, the system designer then talked with the three clerks who maintained the hand-posted customer card record. From them he learned that most of the inquiries they received were from a group of headquarters order expediters who usually wanted to know the factory order number assigned to the most recent order received from a specific customer.

A conversation with one of these expediters produced the following facts.

1. Branch offices assigned their own serial numbers to orders which they forwarded to headquarters for processing.
2. In converting this form to an order on one of the company's factories, the headquarters sales department assigned a new number known as the "factory shipping order number."
3. In following up the factory in response to a branch office inquiry regarding the status of an order, the customer card record was the only means of relating the original branch order number to its corresponding factory shipping order number.

After determining the use being made of the record, the system designer proposed that factory shipping order numbers be discontinued and that the numbers assigned by branch offices serve as the reference throughout the order filling process. Adoption of this change made possible elimination of the customer card record.

Questions to put to the recipient of a report to determine its validity are as follows:

1. How many other persons use it?
2. How essential is it to the work of your unit?
3. How often do you use your copy of this report?
4. How much of this information on this report do you not use?
5. Is the data on this report necessary for:

   a. making decisions to take action?
   b. keeping you informed on current conditions?
   c. checking accuracy of other matters?
   d. establishing control over operations?

6. What would be the effect on your work if you:

   a. did not receive the report at all?
   b. received it less frequently?
   c. received less information than at present?
   d. received more information than at present?

7. The cost of preparing this report has been estimated at x dollars. Do you consider that your use of the data justifies this expense?
8. What other reports, records, or forms are prepared from data on this report?
9. Can the data on this report be had from any other source?
10. Is this report easy to read and use?
11. How long do you keep your copy of this report?
12. How and where do you file it?
13. How often do you refer to it after its original use?

The late Ben S. Graham, former director of the Systems and Procedures Division of the Standard Register Company, one of whose main products is paper and forms, had the following to say about the purpose of output: "From many experiences with a variety of companies, the indication is that between ten and 30 percent of the records created do not serve any valid purposes."

WEAKNESSES OF THE SYSTEM DESIGNER

There are common failings of system designers which should be guarded against. System designers may display a tendency to jump to conclusions about existing procedures without full comprehension of them. This fault forces the new system into a mold that is not always best for it.

Related to this first weakness may be a tendency for the system designer to fail to discuss his conception of the operating system with the line official or others in a position to know the facts. The result is that he is unable to determine whether he has an accurate picture of the situation. Under such circumstances it is possible for the system designer to acquire and cultivate misconceptions concerning the system.

A third facet of the system designer's lack of appreciation for the system at hand is that he may come to feel he knows what the line official needs more than the line official does. If this is so, a system designer can be slightly overbearing.

Another area in which he may falter is in keeping the line official informed of his plans. This failure can create complications in the operation of the line organization and the furtherance of the system designer's work. Making people available for interview on short notice may cramp the line organization's efforts, and the system designer may be stymied, if the people with whom he has planned to work are unavailable.

A final failure is that, after the system investigation is complete, the system designer may work out the design of the system he intends to propose without reviewing its development step by step with the line official. It is the line official and the organization which he heads that must "live" with the new system. Consequently, the line official must review the proposal for the new system to be sure it meets his needs. A complete computer system design proposal is a bulky package. If the package is completed before any of it is submitted to the line official for review, an adequate review is an impossibility. Consequently, the line official must review the system concurrently with the designer's development of it. In this piecemeal fashion the line official can evaluate the material as it is presented to him in sections, and as a result, his review is complete.

The concurrent review has advantages as far as the system designer is concerned, too. It affords an everpresent sounding board off of which he can play his system design ideas. He is protected against going astray in his thinking. If he incorporated some misconception into his system early in his design and did not submit his design for review until it was complete, the effects of this misconception might propagate themselves throughout the system. As a result, when the line official did unearth the misconception, the system designer would have a major redesign job on his hands. Concurrent review avoids such catastrophes.

GENERAL DESCRIPTION OF
A COMPUTER DATA PROCESSING SYSTEM

A computer data processing system can be thought of as a *production line* with data moving from stage to stage through the line. The raw material for this production operation is source documents: forms such as time rolls, material application reports, orders, and requisitions, that are generated by the company's physical operations. These documents are usually sent to and gathered in divisional, regional, or central offices.

In this gathering, controls are instituted to protect against the loss, duplication, and corruption of information. They may involve checkoff lists to see that all documents belonging to a particular office have been received, the numbering of documents with a Bates stamp, or the generation of a total of various quantities included in the document on an adding machine. Information on these documents may then be encoded. For example, a three-character alphanumeric code may be substituted for a major patron's name and plant designation.

Punched cards are then keypunched and verified with the coded information corresponding to the data in the document. They may pass through some precomputer processing on tabulating equipment. For example, the cards may be listed and the totals accumulated for comparison with document counts and totals produced earlier by manual means from the source documents.

As a final step in the preparation of input for the computer system, it is necessary to transport the punched cards to the computer center. This may be a physical movement of data or transmission via commerical or private communication services. At the computer center the punched card information is converted to magnetic tape. The data is then processed. Payrolls are produced, revenue accounting is performed, and major customer activity is analyzed.

When the processing is completed, magnetic tape output files produced during the processing are converted to either punched cards or printed copy. Prepunched clockcards, dividend checks, and proxies are examples of this output. The output is then handled in some way. Forms are decollated, burst, bound, and signed where needed. Next it is examined for reasonableness. For example, certain totals such as salary amounts or quantities requisitioned may not be allowed to exceed predetermined amounts.

At all points in the system—precomputer processing, computer processing, output checking—unacceptable information is rejected. For example, control totals may not check out, data fed into the system may not bear any recognizable identification, and reasonableness checks may not pass. Error correcting procedures must be established to handle these rejects. Finally, the output is distributed (perhaps labelled and mailed) to the user, the paycheck to the employee, and the sales analysis to the sales manager.

The procedure is summarized in the following chart.

Company operation
Source document
Control
Encoding
Keypunching $\qquad$ Input Organization
Verifying
Precomputer processing
Transmission
Conversion to magnetic tape
Computer processing $\qquad$ Computer Operation
Conversion from magnetic tape
Handling
Review $\qquad$ Output Organization
Distribution
User

DOCUMENTATION

The proposed computer system design is reflected in a variety of documents. One that assumes central importance in this documentation is the process chart. A process chart is a set of symbols designed to represent various operations that are connected by arrows to indicate the sequence of operations. In general, the operations can be of any type, manual, punched card, and so on. However, when "the" process chart is referred to in computer system design, the operations symbolized are computer operations, and the process chart is the master plan of the computer data processing system. Figure 14-1 is an example of a process chart.

Although the only operations shown on a computer process chart are computer operations, the previous section of this chapter indicates that there is more to a computer data processing system than computer operations. Therefore, there is certain information that cannot be derived from a process chart.

To some extent the process chart can be used to determine whether the system timing commitments have been fulfilled. For example, it can be determined from the process chart whether weekly reports are produced weekly; monthly reports, monthly; and so on.

In some instances estimates of how long each run takes are included on process charts. If so, it can be determined from the process chart how long after source documents are available to the system in computer intelligible form the output is available for distribution. Whether or not these estimates are included in the process chart, they have to be made.

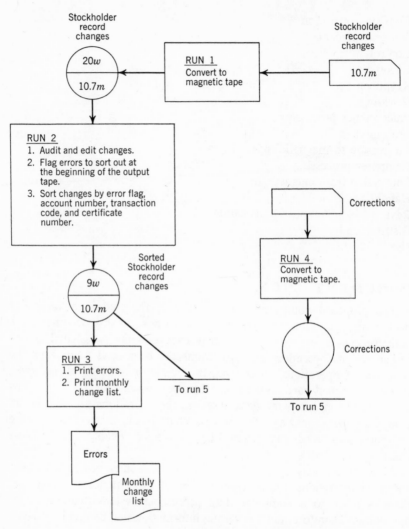

Fig. 14-1 Example of a Process Chart: Stockholder Record System. Page 1: The Monthly System

A running time estimate is not the only factor determining whether a system meets its deadlines. Estimated running time for a system may produce the output on time, but if the schedule for other applications makes little computer time available when the system is to run, there may be a scheduling problem—for this system, at any rate. For example, a system must turn out a report eight hours after the last source document is in. The system may be designed to produce the report from the source

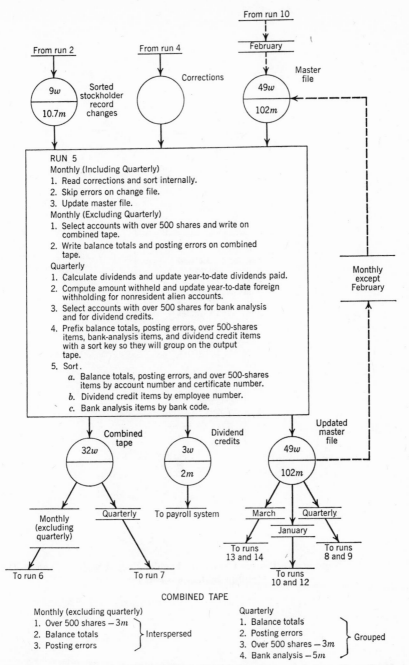

Fig. 14-1 Example of a Process Chart: Stockholder Record System. Page 2: The Monthly System (cont'd.)

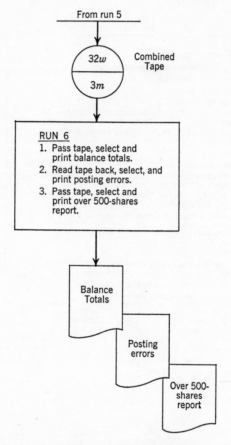

Fig. 14-1 Example of a Process Chart: Stockholder Record System. Page 3: The Monthly System (cont'd.)

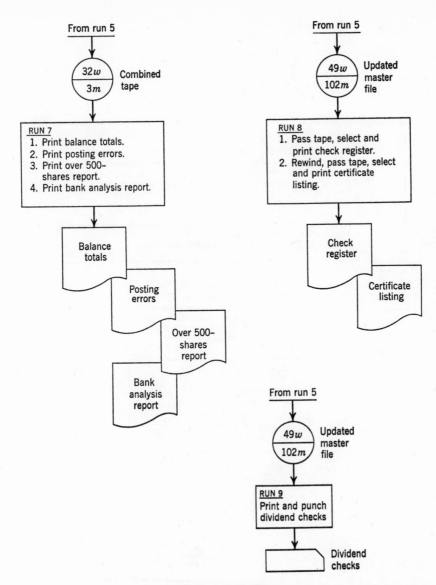

Fig. 14-1 Example of a Process Chart: Stockholder Record System. Page 4: The Quarterly System

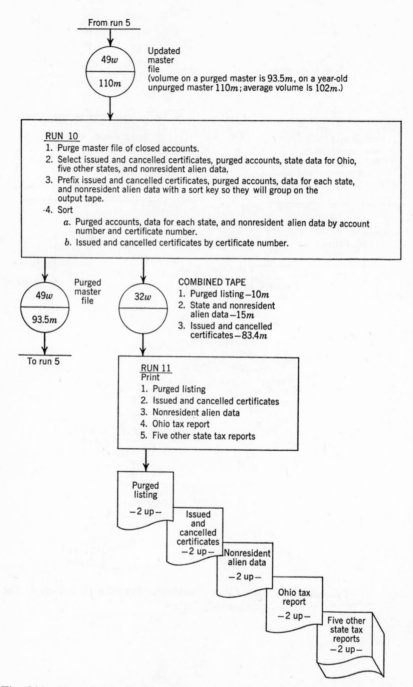

From run 5

49w
110m

Updated
master
file
(volume on a purged master is 93.5m, on a year-old
unpurged master 110m; average volume is 102m.)

RUN 10
1. Purge master file of closed accounts.
2. Select issued and cancelled certificates, purged accounts, state data for Ohio,
   five other states, and nonresident alien data.
3. Prefix issued and cancelled certificates, purged accounts, data for each state,
   and nonresident alien data with a sort key so they will group on the
   output tape.
·4. Sort
   a. Purged accounts, data for each state, and nonresident alien data by account
   number and certificate number.
   b. Issued and cancelled certificates by certificate number.

Purged
master
file

49w
93.5m

To run 5

32w

COMBINED TAPE
1. Purged listing—10m
2. State and nonresident
   alien data—15m
3. Issued and cancelled
   certificates—83.4m

RUN 11
Print

1. Purged listing
2. Issued and cancelled certificates
3. Nonresident alien data
4. Ohio tax report
5. Five other state tax reports

Purged
listing

—2 up—

Issued
and
cancelled
certificates
—2 up—

Nonresident
alien data

—2 up—

Ohio tax
report

—2 up—

Five other
state tax
reports
—2 up—

Fig. 14-1   Example of a Process Chart: Stockholder Record System. Page 5: The
January Annual System

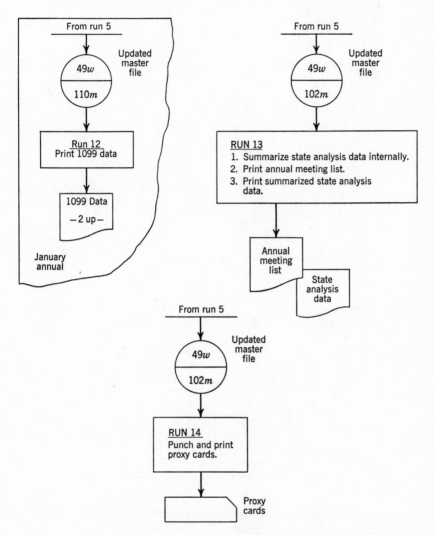

Fig. 14-1 Example of a Process Chart: Stockholder Record System. Page 6: The January Annual System (cont'd.); The March Annual System

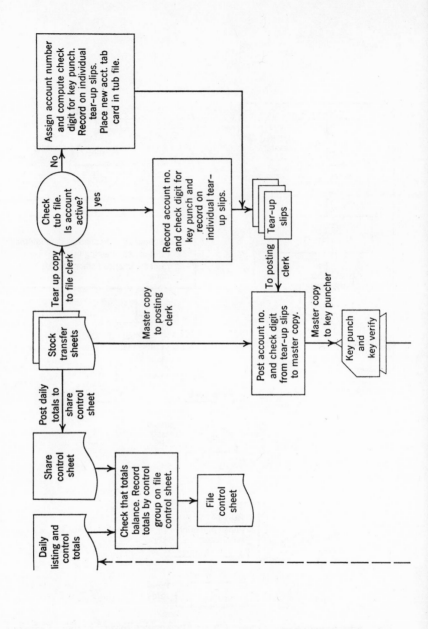

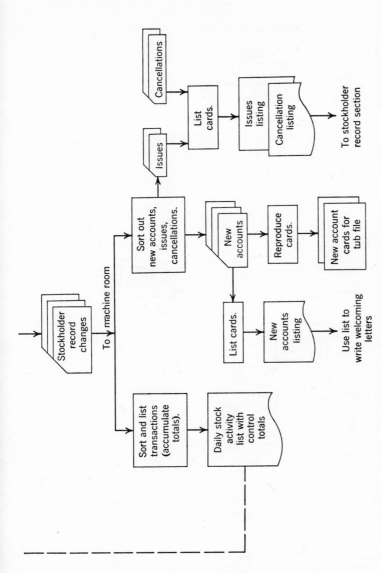

Fig. 14-2 Example of a Procedure Chart: Stockholder Record System. Page 1: Daily Transaction Preparation

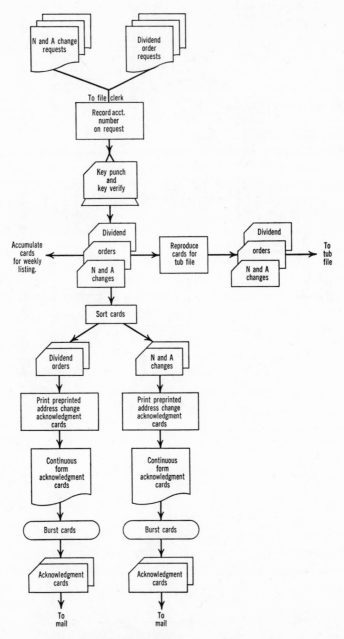

Fig. 14-2 Example of a Procedure Chart: Stockholder Record System: Page 2: Daily Transaction Preparation

documents in four hours of computer time, but if only two hours are scheduled between the time at which the documents are available and that at which the report is due, the system is in difficulty. Consequently, one other timing document is the computer schedule set up with the computer center for the proposed system. This schedule shows the date and time each run in the system is placed on the computer.

From the process chart it can also be determined how far errors introduced into the system with source data can penetrate it. For example, the process chart in Figure 14-1 indicates that, by the time run four is completed, the source documents, in this case, stockholder record changes, are "purified."

It can be determined from the process chart what output the system produces. Another indication supplied by the process chart is the nature of the source documents the computer system requires.

But despite the information a process chart contains, there are also facts it does not reveal. Not only is it restricted to computer operations in the data processing system, it is also a general document that shows the flow of operations without specifying details.

The process chart reveals nothing about the manual and punched card procedures that may both precede and follow the computer operations. To document this aspect of the total data processing system design, procedure charts that indicate these processes must be produced. For example, Figure 14-2 depicts the procedure charts that incorporate the manual and punched card procedures preceding the introduction of the stockholder record change file into the computer data processing system in the form of a card deck, as is shown in run one of the process chart in Figure 14-1.

Neither does the process chart show the content and format of the items of information on the magnetic tape files depicted on it. This information is supplied in the form of item designs. An example of item design is shown in Figure 14-3. This figure depicts the item layout for stockholder record changes that appear on the stockholder record change file shown in the process chart in Figure 14-1. Item designs show the complement of fields contained in an item and the number of digits or characters allocated to each field.

A third factor which the process chart does not show is the layout of the source documents of the system. This information is supplied on a separate document. For example, Figure 14-4 depicts the form layouts for the transfer sheet tearup slips and stockholder record change punched cards referred to in the procedure chart shown in Figure 14-2.

The process chart does not give any indication of output forms design. This information is also supplied as a separate set of documents.

For example, shown in Figure 14-5 is the forms layout for the dividend check register produced by run eight of the computer system in Figure 14-1.

A fifth factor undisclosed by the process chart is the controls incorporated into the data processing system. For example, run two of the process chart in Figure 14-1 indicates that each stockholder record change card being read into the system is subject to an audit and that

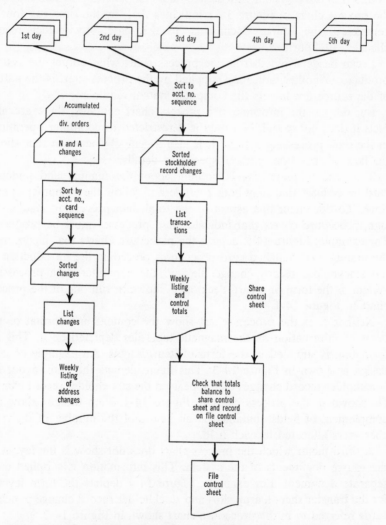

Fig. 14-2 Example of a Procedure Chart: Stockholder Record System: Page 3: Weekly Transaction Processing

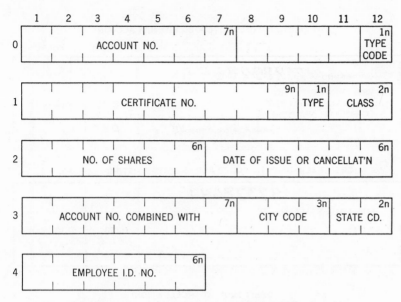

Fig. 14-3 Example of Item Design: Stockholder Record Changes

all such cards containing errors are tossed out of the system for correction. However, the process chart does not specify which tests for validity the cards are run against during this audit. Consequently, one of the records developed as part of the documentation of a system design is a list of all controls envisioned for incorporation into the new system.

This situation is not peculiar to validation runs. No run is described in detail on a process chart. To acquire this detail a set of *run descriptions* must be prepared, each of which describes what processing is to take place during the computer run with which it is associated. These descriptions indicate which discriminations are to be made between different data types, which tables of values are to be stored internally in the computer's memory from the instruction tape, and so on.

Finally, the process chart does not show the impact of the computer data processing system on the line organization. What clerical procedures and work groups now in existence are no longer required? What clerical procedures and work groups not presently in existence must be established? What changes in organization are required? Can these changes be negotiated with the union? Procedure manuals, job writeups, a list of organizational changes, and a labor negotiation package must be produced to supply answers to these and related questions.

In summary, the proposed computer data processing system is documented with at least the following documents.

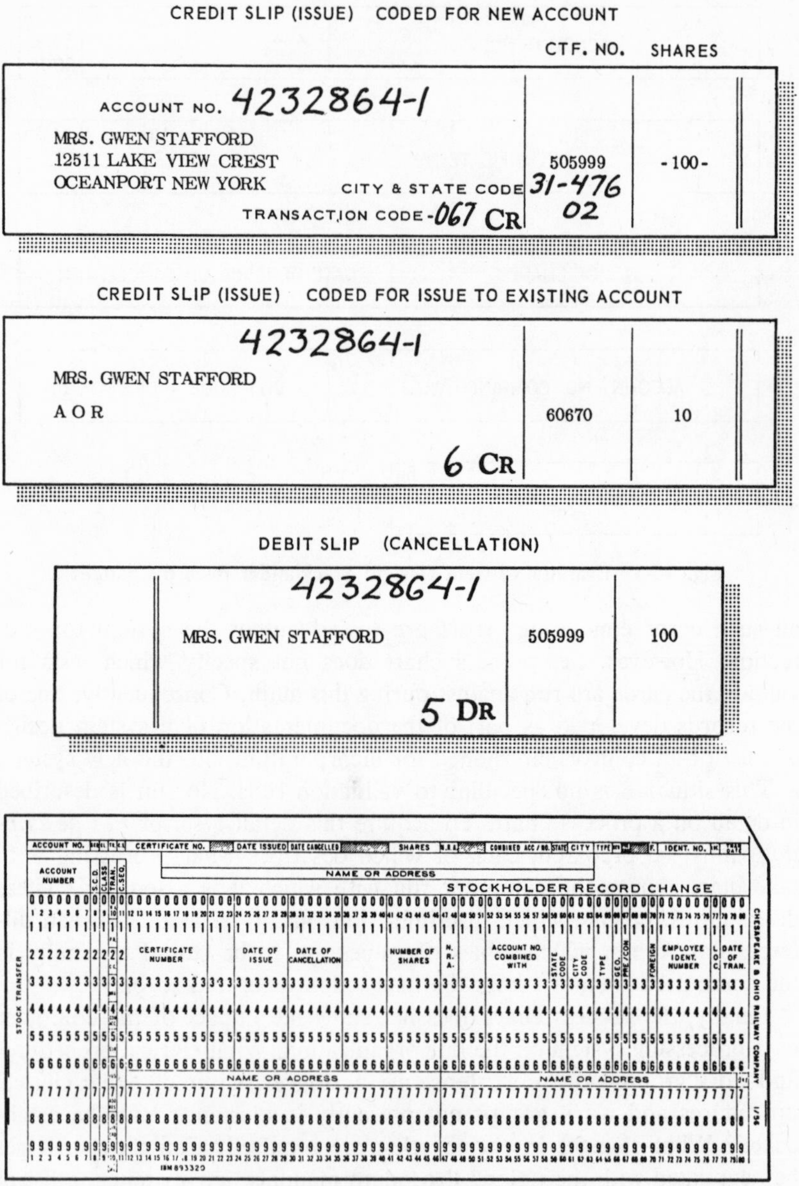
CREDIT SLIP (ISSUE) CODED FOR NEW ACCOUNT
CTF. NO.
SHARES
ACCOUNT NO. 4232864-1
MRS. GWEN STAFFORD
12511 LAKE VIEW CREST
OCEANPORT NEW YORK
505999
-100-
CITY & STATE CODE 31-476
TRANSACTION CODE -067 CR
02
CREDIT SLIP (ISSUE) CODED FOR ISSUE TO EXISTING ACCOUNT
4232864-1
MRS. GWEN STAFFORD
A O R
60670
10
6 CR
DEBIT SLIP (CANCELLATION)
4232864-1
MRS. GWEN STAFFORD
505999
100
5 DR
ACCOUNT NO.
CERTIFICATE NO.
DATE ISSUED
DATE CANCELLED
SHARES
COMBINED ACC / NO.
STATE
CITY
TYPE
IDENT. NO.
NAME OR ADDRESS
STOCKHOLDER RECORD CHANGE
ACCOUNT NUMBER
S.C.D.
CLASS
TRAN.
C.SEQ.
CERTIFICATE NUMBER
DATE OF ISSUE
DATE OF CANCELLATION
NUMBER OF SHARES
N. R. A.
ACCOUNT NO. COMBINED WITH
STATE CODE
CITY CODE
TYPE
GEO.
PRE/CON
FOREIGN
EMPLOYEE IDENT. NUMBER
L O C.
DATE OF TRAN.
STOCK TRANSFER
CHESAPEAKE & OHIO RAILWAY COMPANY
NAME OR ADDRESS
NAME OR ADDRESS
IBM 893329

Fig. 14-4 Example of Source Document Layout: Transfer Sheet Tearup Slips and Stockholder Record Change Card

DIVIDEND CHECK REGISTER

ARP. NO. 112				DIVD. NO. 186		MAR 20 1958		PAGE NO. 12061

CHECK NO.	NET AMT.	%	AMT. WITH-HELD	GROSS AMT.	NO. SHRS	NAME AND ADDRESS		ACCT. NO.
92769	8.50	15	1.50	10.00	10	FREDERICK HERBERT SANDERS 557 QUEEN STREET CHATHAM ONTARIO CANADA	425738	8051852
92770	8.50	15	1.50	10.00	10	ARTHUR FRANKLIN TURNER 130 CHURCHILL CRESCENT ST. THOMAS, ONTARIO CANADA	425955	8051882
92771	10.00			10.00	10	NELLIE MAE WALKER 6 119 GENERAL MOTORS BLDG. DETROIT MICHIGAN	425545	8051915
	26009.20		22.80	26092.00	26092	TOTAL SHAREHOLDERS	1715	

Fig. 14-5 Example of Output Layout: Dividend Check Register

1. Computer Process Chart
2. Procedure Charts for Punched Card Operations
3. Item Designs
4. Source Document Layouts
5. Output Document Layouts
6. Run Descriptions
7. List of Controls
8. Timing Estimates
9. Computer Schedule
10. Procedure Manuals
11. Job Descriptions
12. List of Organizational Changes
13. Labor Negotiation Package (If Appropriate)

15

PROGRAMMING

Programming consits of taking the plans developed for the computer data processing system during system design and implementing them in the form of programs to be run on the computer. The nature of the computer runs must be communicated to the programmer. The system designer is accountable for seeing that the program the programmer writes conforms with the run specifications.

The point at which programming begins is significant. Until now the system designer has been investing months of time and effort in system investigation and design. Nevertheless, any change, any fact previously neglected, generally does not cause delay or jeopardize work already done. Usually all that is required to rectify the matter is to add a note in some record, change a notation on a process chart, or delete a line on an item layout. However, once the programming begins, the picture changes.

The situation is analogous to the building of a house. As long as the house is on the drawing board, a change is inexpensive. It requires little more than a rub with the architect's eraser and a few new lines with a pencil. But when the building is started each change is an "extra" whose cost is directly related to the state of completion of the house. Each program instruction written for the system is another brick laid and mortared in the construction of the overall job. A change or addition that would have been innocent during system design may be costly in terms of revisions to programs already written. Each step taken during construction more firmly imbeds the steps previously taken in the erection of the structure and increases the difficulty of change. Moreover, changes have ramifications beyond the alteration of already written programs. With the step into programming, documentation proliferates. There is now a team of programmers, each of whom possesses documentation of the system to the extent to which it is applicable to the run or runs he has been assigned to program. Each change involves an administrative problem in keeping this documentation up-to-date.

It is easy to make changes to a data processing system before it is programmed, but it is difficult afterward. Make certain the proposed system is correct and complete before releasing it for programming.

There are additional reasons for this precaution in organizations which make heavy or unquestioning use of COBOL and other so-called problem-oriented automatic programming systems. The system design up to and through run description becomes the last critical opportunity to preserve the design efficiency which stems from deliberate hardware orientation in design. Remember that basic aspects of the computer itself demand operands in the application to be distinctly hardware oriented in mode, radix, size, and so on; otherwise, the computer process is burdened with time-consuming conversions and compensations. Also remember that the limitations of the instruction repertoire of a computer demand preferential use of a restricted subset of possible logical organizations of a run; otherwise, the computer process is burdened with time-consuming construction of logical equivalents to another order code and with failure to exploit the availability of operations perhaps peculiar to that computer.

It is up to the system designer to restrict to the utmost the amount of damage a programmer can do to the system efficiency. For example, he should decide, and reflect this decision in his process chart, whether the application will be organized for random access processing or sequential batch processing. If it is a random access application, he should decide whether the application contains a single file—with only high-activity items, all of which will fit on magnetic disks or drums—or whether these will be two files—high-activity items on discs or drums with nonmatching low-activity items passed on for batching and longer cycle sequential processing, and so on. As the use of automatic programming techniques grows, it is increasingly important that system design envision the hardware characteristics which determine whether a source program fed into a particular compiler will produce even a reasonably efficient object program. In short, good system design is the last bulwark of good programming in the world of automatic programming

16

FILEMAKING

The preparation of the programs for the runs of the computer data processing system is not the only implementation of the system design. Another is the creation of the master files of the system.

The majority of the permanent records, accumulations, and other information maintained in a computer data processing system is stored on magnetic tape, punched cards, drums, disks, and so forth. Examples of such information are the employee data of a payroll application, the inventory information of a stock control system, and the vendor information of an accounts payable system. Before the introduction of the computing system this information is usually kept in a variety of punched card files, index card files, visible files, ledger cards, and binders of various types.

Another distinction between computer master files and these files in other data processing systems is the greater degree of consolidation of information in the former. For example, the employee information contained in a magnetic tape file might be stored in four or five card files in a punched card application. Another example of information consolidation is in the insurance field. For ordinary life insurance an insurance company may have four departments to handle premium billing and accounting, policyholder dividends, policy loans, and valuation. In a noncomputer data processing system each of these departments would maintain its own records. In a computer system these records are consolidated into one policyholder file.

The collection of this master information from a number of sources varying in type as well as in location and the organization and coordination of this data into a single stream of information which must then be converted to magnetic tape is quite an undertaking. The item design of the master file was fixed during system design. This item design specifies what information the master file is to contain and the format in which the data is to appear. What must be done to collect, organize, and convert

274

the master file to the form specified by the item design is to set up a procedure for this purpose.

File conversion boils down to a system design problem. It is an exercise for the system designer. He knows what output he wants. He knows the sources for his information. He must design a system that produces the output from the input. But the system designer cannot create and implement this procedure independent of the line official. He must be certain that his filemaking system does not access the current records in a way which would disrupt current procedures. He must be apprised of the quantity and quality of the clerical work force that will be available to him for the implementation of the procedures. For the answer to these and other questions the system designer must turn to the line official. With cooperation similar to that involved in their work during system investigation and design, the system designer and line official can work out a procedure for creating the master file.

Since the end product of this filemaking example is a magnetic tape file, file conversion involves one or more computer runs to accept the file information, generally in punched card form, and record it on magnetic tape in the format specified by the master file item design. One part of these conversion runs is the audit of the information being converted. This audit consists of a validity check of all information submitted for incorporation in the master file. Its purpose is to catch errors introduced into the master file because of mistakes made during the filemaking process. However, the audit delivers an added benefit. When master records are converted to magnetic tape the audit unearths inconsistencies and other mistakes in the existing records which were undetected for years.

Once the conversion of the master file to magnetic tape is complete some procedure must be instituted to keep the master file up to date. Because the master file has been converted does not mean that the company operation associated with that file, whether it is payroll or accounts receivable, is going to cease to operate. The company operation will continue. Moreover, it is unlikely that the computer procedures associated with the master file become debugged and go operational at the same instant that the master file conversion is completed. The current data processing procedure, whether it is punched card, manual, or other, must continue to keep the reports and records up to date with respect to the company operation. The master file no sooner gets converted to tape than it is threatened with the danger of going out of date. To prevent this situation a procedure for keeping the master file up to date must be prepared. Some special runs can be programmed for the purpose of keeping the master file up to date during the interim period between the master file conversion and the cutover to the computer data processing system.

There is one alternative to an independent filemaking operation that is feasible under certain circumstances. For example, in a sales statistics application the master file may consist of an accumulation of information on sales experience as it occurs. In such a situation it is possible for the computer application to start out with no master file and have the computer data processing system build the master file over a period of time on the basis of the transactions that occur.

In some cases the master file may be created by the method described here, even though an existing master file must be in evidence when the computer data processing system is inaugurated. The way this approach is implemented is to introduce, immediately before the cutover to the computer system, bogus transactions that cause the system to create a master file which duplicates the records required to be carried into the new system from the old.

Some provision for conversion of master information to magnetic tape or other internal medium is a necessary step in computerization. It is up to the system designer to propose and implement the conversion procedure.

17

CLERICAL PROCEDURES

When people talk about computers and clerical procedures the remarks made are generally that computer data processing allows the elimination of certain clerical procedures and effects a reduction in the clerical work force. Such remarks are true. The contribution to data processing that is unique to the computer is the automation of procedure. As a result, personnel previously required to implement procedure are no longer needed.

However, the pre-eminence of such remarks distracts emphasis from an aspect of the relationship between computer data processing and clerical procedures that is crucial: The introduction of a computer data processing system creates clerical work in the area of originating data for the computer system, of investigating and correcting errors thrown out by the computer, and of handling and distributing the reports and records turned out by the computer system. These areas of clerical procedures have their counterparts in the previous data processing system. Here attention is drawn not so much to a creation of procedure where there previously was none as to a substitution of new procedures for old. Nevertheless, although the computerization of a data processing operation reduces the amount of clerical procedure associated with the operation, it far from eliminates this procedure and may change the nature of the remaining procedure. Because of these changes in the clerical procedures of a data processing operation which is being computerized, adequate preparations must be made for the smooth transition into these new procedures. Two areas in which preparation is necessary are documentation and training. A third area, which comes into being if the clerical work force is unionized, is labor negotiation.

If the clerks are unionized, the introduction of a computer data processing system is going to create a change in working conditions. It is a responsibility of the system designer to develop a labor package that can be taken by the company to the bargaining table as a basis for negotiation.

In the area of documentation there are two types of documents that must be prepared. One is the work aid, which is any document a clerk uses in the pursuance of his work. For example, the encoding directory to which a clerk refers to decide what code should be assigned to a sales account or city is a work aid. The system designer is responsible for the content and form of all work aids used in a clerical procedure whose design he has originated.

The other type of documentation necessary in the development of a clerical procedure is the job descriptions and procedure manuals which specify what this procedure is. This type of documentation is important for a number of reasons. The development of a procedure manual forces decisions on policy and procedural details that otherwise might never be considered until the situation arose in the performance of the procedure. It also facilitates the training of personnel. The time required for training decreases substantially when training is done with documentation rather than without it. The effectiveness of the training also increases with the use of documentation.

A procedure manual promotes uniformity of performance. More people will perform a procedure the same way and with the same accuracy if they have a model of that procedure available for reference. A procedure manual also establishes a basis for control. It states what the proper procedure is and allows the question of whether a particular method is acceptable to be resolved once and for all. A procedure manual preserves experience. The details of a procedure can never be lost with the loss of a man if the procedure is documented. Finally, the procedure manual, as an objective document, facilitates the examination and revision of procedures and acts as an aid in job evaluation.

For these reasons it is important that acceptable procedure manuals are made up. Also, a workable set of mechanics for keeping the procedure manuals up-to-date should be set up when the procedure is instituted and the inevitable changes in procedure begin to occur. In addition to adequate documentation, proper orientation and training are essential ingredients in a successful clerical operation. New forms must be filled out, new procedures followed, and clerks must be adequately trained for jobs. The provision of adequate training is the responsibility of the line official. However, the system designer should be available to assist in this training.

Setting up the associated clerical procedures is one more aspect of the computerization of a data processing system and is as important to the success of the computer system as is the conversion of the master files to magnetic tape or the programming of the runs of the system. Aspects of the clerical procedure that are important during this establishment are the documentation of the procedure, orientation and training of the personnel slated to implement the procedure, and if appropriate, negotiation of the agreement for the procedure with the clerical labor union.

18
TESTING THE SYSTEM

INTRODUCTION

The last step in the computerization of a data processing system, and a step that phases into the cutover to the computer data processing system, is the testing of the system to see whether it performs as it should. This testing takes place in three phases—run debugging, system testing, and parallel running.

RUN DEBUGGING

The development of the programs for a system is carried on by programmers working under the supervision of the system designer. Each of the programmers is assigned to program several runs in the system, but the runs assigned to a programmer bear no necessary relationship, one to another, as far as the system is concerned. Runs should be assigned to programmers on the basis of the following criteria:

1. Assign similar runs to the same programmer so what he learns in technique while programming one run can be carried over to other runs. For example, if there are three summary runs in a system, they might all be assigned to the same programmer.
2. For the same reason assign runs to a programmer that are similar to any he has programmed before on other systems.
3. Match the complexity of the run to the competence of the programmer.

As a result the programming of the system is a run-by-run affair. A programmer is assigned a run, he is told what input is to be fed into the run, he is told what output he is expected to develop from his run, he is given some idea of the procedures to be accomplished in his run, and he then is allowed to program the run.

One of the responsibilities of the programmer is to debug the run to which he has been assigned. That is, after he has written the coding that constitutes the program for his run he must have the program run on the computer to ascertain whether it performs as expected. The programmer makes up some test data that he believes conforms to the description of the input given to him. The system designer may cooperate in the construction of this data. The programmer runs his program against this test data in debugging. These debugging sessions reveal inadequacies in the program being debugged—inadequacies created by misunderstandings and inadvertent slips on the programmer's part. The programmer corrects and improves his program on the basis of the results of the debugging session and once more submits the program for test running. When by repetitions of this debugging and correcting cycle the programmer becomes satisfied with his program's performance, it is turned over to the system designer as a debugged run.

SYSTEM TEST

When programming is complete the system designer has a set of programmed runs, each of which is attested to by the programmer assigned to it as being correct in terms of the manner in which he understands the run's requirements. It must now be determined whether these runs fit together as a functioning system. Perhaps because of faulty communication when the programmer was told what a run is supposed to do, the programmed run does not meet the system designer's requirements. Perhaps the individually programmed runs are inconsistent one with another and consequently, as a whole, do not make up a functioning system. It must be ascertained that the individually tested runs do not have these faults and do, as a result, constitute an acceptable data processing system. This aim is accomplished by the system test.

In the system test the sequence of runs making up the system is run as it would be in the functioning system. In this way inconsistencies between runs and inadequacies of the computer system are pinpointed in much the same way as the errors in each run were isolated during run debugging. Test data is used to perform the system test except that now the test data is the same for the whole system, instead of being made especially for each run. This test data may be invented, or use may be made of data from some previous cycle of the data processing system the computer system is designed to replace. In the latter case the data may be altered to make it conform to the purpose at hand.

Preparation of test data for a system test is the responsibility of the system designer. In preparing system test data make it as exhaustive as possible. That is, have it incorporate as many of the situations which could arise in operations as possible to test the system from every angle. System test is a cyclical procedure in which errors are isolated on the computer, programs are modified to correct these errors, and the corrected system is rerun to pinpoint any remaining errors. Some guiding principles in system test are included here.

If the system is large—ten or more tailored runs—schedule the system test in parts. The first time the system is run it will probably not run through to completion anyhow. Scheduling for a complete system run just ties up more time in the computer room schedule than is needed for the initial phases of the system test. Later when the major errors have been weeded out of the parts into which the system has been broken for testing purposes, the system can be run as a whole. Check out the file establishment and file maintenance runs first so they can be used for their purposes while the rest of the system is being tested out.

Begin the test with a low volume of data, just enough to test major controls and the integration between runs. When the errors have been eliminated from these areas more extensive data can be used to test the finer details of the system. Start at the beginning of the system and work through it so the gross errors are eliminated first. When the system more or less hangs together the finer errors can be weeded out.

A computer system usually generates several intermediary tapes, output of one run that constitutes input to a subsequent run. Print these tapes. Such printouts constitute an aid in error location. They can be checked for conformance with expectations just as are final outputs. In checking output, pay particular attention to the first and last items of a file. They are the most likely to be in error. Normal procedure may be performing well when initial and windup procedures still contain errors.

Programmers should be on hand for system test. They may be able to spot the reason for some errors more readily than the system designer. Be sure to check out the system for recycled data such as corrections to errors as well as normally introduced data. For a system to be operating correctly all parts of it must perform equally well.

A record of all changes to the documentation of the system brought about through the discovery and correction of errors must be kept until the documentation is revised. Otherwise there is a gap between the documentation of how the system works and how it actually works. All such changes must be communicated to the programmers involved so, if a change has a repercussion on a programmer's program, he is aware of it and can change his program accordingly. The more such a procedure is adhered to, the less frequently will the correction of one error lead to the creation of another error.

PARALLEL RUNNING

After the successful completion of system test the computer data processing system is installed. However, the previous system is not disestablished. Instead the two systems are run in parallel as a further test. The old system is the one depended on to produce the results. The purpose of running the two in parallel is to see whether the new system comes up with the same results as the old. In parallel running the line official and his organization become involved in the testing of the computer data processing system. Most line officials agree that parallel running is a necessary step in safeguarding the accuracy of the procedures for which the line is responsible. On the other hand, parallel running places strains on his organization. Since two data processing systems are running, the line official must take adequate steps to avoid being swamped by the demands of both.

For instance, a temporary increase in personnel is inevitable. The line official, with adequate warning from the system designer, must anticipate this need, arrange for the additional personnel, and provide for their training. Second, the line official's organization is not only keeping two systems going, but is also participating in a check of the performance of one against the other. The purpose of parallel running is to see if the computer system comes up with the same answers as the previous system. The only way to achieve this purpose is to check the output of the two systems against each other. Because a considerable amount of data must be handled by a data processing system to make computerization feasible, magnitude of this cross-checking job is great. The only way to avoid being overwhelmed by the job is to be adequately prepared for it.

It is part of the system designer's job to develop for parallel running the most economical procedures possible for testing the adequacy of the computer system's results. Without such procedures the weight of the paper work involved would be overpowering. The following techniques may be utilized:

1. All printed material that must be reviewed and compared with other material should be produced in an edited, easy-to-read form.
2. All output produced in a mechanical form should be checked by mechanical means. For example, if both the computer system and the previous system produce a deck of punched cards for the same purpose, a punched card system for testing the consistency of the two decks should be devised.
3. Advice should be given for the applicability of sampling techniques

to the testing of output. In many cases, particularly where numeric data are involved, a check of a sample of output proves as effective as 100 percent review. However, even where sampling is applicable cases that constitute exceptions should be inspected on a 100 percent basis.

4. In many cases the reports turned out by a data processing system contain subtotals of the information detailed in the report. In a good proportion of these instances the requirements of the parallel check are satisfied if the subtotals are checked out and the detail information is investigated only where it bears on a subtotal that has failed to measure up. Advice should be given when such an approach is permissible.

The system designer should provide adequate procedures for conducting the testing procedure involved in parallel running. However, the decision as to when the output of the computer system is acceptable and cutover, that is, discontinuation of the previous system, can occur is the line official's.

The parallel running phase provides the ideal occasion for a "dry run" of procedures for the clerical work force that will service the computer system. During parallel running as much of the computer system as possible should be put into operation to see if it hangs together. Parallel running is the first opportunity for the error detection, correction, and reinsertion procedures to be tested in their entirety. All error printouts from the computer system should be routed to correction points as called for by the system setup; the errors should be investigated and corrected, and the corrections should be sent back for reinsertion into the computer system. These procedures should be followed to determinine whether they are adequate for their purpose, whether control is being maintained over this avenue of transactions, and whether the procedure fits within the established time schedule. Parallel running is the time to revise timing estimates originally made for the system to a more realistic level.

One problem is in the area of source documents. The source documents designed for use with the computer system are different from those used in the present system. There is no point in originating two sets of source documents even during parallel running. Before parallel running begins the introduction of the new source documents forms and their associated procedures should have started. This allows time for training in the use of the new forms and in the following of the new procedures. Although these new forms will eventually be used exclusively with the computer system, for the present time and on up through parallel running they must serve the present system as well. Consequently, to the extent that the new documents differ from the old, the personnel in the line organization must be trained in the use of the new documents for the present system.

SUMMARY

The testing of the system is done in three phases: run debugging, system test, and parallel running. The line organization takes part during the third phase. At this time two data processing systems are operated. The performance of the two is compared, and it is part of the system designer's job to develop workable procedures for this comparison. When the line official determines that the results of the parallel running are satisfactory, the previous system is disestablished and the computer system takes over.

19

ADMINISTRATION

It is a responsibility of the system designer to make commitments to his management as to the results he can produce and the completion dates for these results. He must plan ahead so the work of the line organization, the system team, the programmers, equipment and forms suppliers, and consultants is integrated. A timetable for computer implementation must be drawn up. This timetable must outline the work to be done from the time of the approval of the system design to the cutover to the computer system.

A second job in this planning for system implementation is to fix the responsibility for the jobs specified in the timetable. This manual has been written in terms of "the" system designer for facility in exposition. In actuality a system staff is working together. No single person can do all the work; the work is delegated. If people are going to operate effectively and keep to the schedule set up in the timetable, responsibilities and authority must be spelled out.

The jobs that must be included in this timetable have been described in the last four chapters. They include preparing the programs; orienting personnel to the coming changes in procedure; making preparatory changeovers, such as creating the master files and introducing the new source document forms; ordering new forms; preparing work aids and procedure instructions; seeing about labor negotiations for filemaking, parallel running, and the computer system; revising related procedures; training personnel; scheduling computer time; and testing the system.

As implementation is entered, planning involves the attempt to keep on schedule, the revision of the schedule when necessary, and the making of emergency decisions and in-process changes when the need arises. In many cases the implementation of a computer data processing system is segmented and rolled up piecemeal by means of a gradual cutback in the operating of the previous system. For example, in installing a computer payroll system the gross-to-net pay computation operation might be cutover first and then the time-to-gross pay computation systems might be cutover department by department.

When a system is in production forms-control, reordering and such are handled by the computer center. However, for the first running of the system in testing it is up to the system designer to order the forms in time to have them on hand when he desires their use.

GLOSSARY

Absolute address Actual designed location in storage of a particular unit of data; address that the control unit can interpret directly

Absolute coding Coding written in basic numeric language acceptable to the machine without further modification. In particular, written with absolute addresses.

Access time (1) the time interval between the instant at which information is: (*a*) called for from storage and the instant at which delivery is completed—the read time; or (*b*) ready for storage and the instant at which storage is completed —the write time; (2) the latency plus the word time.

Accounting controls Various procedural and arithmetic steps established within a system for checking internal consistency and accuracy of accounting results, for inhibition of fraud and defalcation, for detection of inadvertent error, for adherence to company authority and standards, etc. (*See also* **Control.**)

Accumulator A register in arithmetic unit which stores operands and in which arithmetic results are formed.

Accuracy "Correctness," or freedom from error. Accuracy contrasts with precision: e.g., a four-place table, correctly computed, is accurate; a six-place table containing an error is more precise but not accurate.

Activity Any information which results in use or modification of the information in a master file.

Activity ratio The fraction of the records in a master file which have activity in a given period.

Addition record A record which, when processed, results in the location of a new record in the master file.

Address A label such as an integer or other set of characters, identifying a register, location, or device in which information is stored.

> **Absolute address (Specific address, Actual address)** The label(s) assigned by the machine designer to a particular storage location.
>
> **Indirect address** An address requiring modification by a counter or by other information.
> (*See also* **Relative, Symbolic.**)

Address computation Computer operations which result in the creation or modification of the address part of instructions.

Address modification Refers to the automatic change of the address part of an instruction by means of a subroutine or computer operations.

Allocate To assign storage locations to the main routines and subroutines, thereby fixing the absolute values of any symbolic addresses. In some cases allocation may require segmentation. Also, to assign facilities of both memory and other units to a routine.

Alphanumeric Characters which may be either letters of the alphabet, numerals, or special symbols.

Arithmetic unit That portion of the hardware of an automatic computer in which arithmetic and logical operations are performed.

Assemble (**Assembler, Assembly program**) To integrate subroutines (supplied, selected, or generated) into the main routine, by adapting or specializing to the task at hand, by means of present parameters, by adapting, or changing relative and symbolic addresses to absolute form, or incorporating, or placing in storage. (*See* **Routine**).

Asynchronous Computer in which initiation of the next operation is dependent on a signal that the previous operation is completed, rather than on a fixed time cycle (synchronous).

Audit (**Input Audit**) Operations designed to check the authenticity and validity of data being introduced into a data processing system.

Automatic Checking (**Computers**) Provision, constructed in hardware, for automatically verifying the information transmitted, manipulated, or stored by any device or unit of the computer. Automatic checking is "complete" when every process in the machine is automatically checked; otherwise it is partial. The term "extent of automatic checking" means either (1) the relative proportion of machine processes which are checked, or (2) the relative proportion of machine hardware devoted to checking.

Automatic programming Any technique whereby the computer itself is used to transform programming from a form that is easy for a human being to produce into a form that is efficient for the computer to carry out. Examples of automatic programming are compiling routines, interpretive routines, etc.

Available Time (**Machine**) Time during which a computer has the power turned on, is not under maintenance, and is known or believed to be operating correctly.

Band A group of recording tracks on a magnetic drum or disc.

Base (**Radix**) A number base; a quantity used implicitly to define some system of representing numbers by positional notation.

Batch A number of records or documents grouped together for the purpose of processing as a single unit.

Batch process Applies to process where units of material are accumulated into a batch for sequential processing; in contrast to on-line processing where each unit of material is processed without delay at the time of presentation to the head of the processing sequence.

Binary Involving the integer 2, as in a binary number system (base 2), a binary choice (between two alternatives), or a binary operation (combining two quantities).

Binary (Coded decimal) *See* **Decimal.**

Binary notation The writing of numbers in the scale of two. The first dozen numbers zero to eleven are written 0, 1, 10, 11, 100, 101, 110, 111, 1000, 1001, 1010, 1011. The positions of the digits designate powers of two; thus 1010 means 1 times two cubed or eight; 0 times two squared or four; 1 times two to the first power or two; and 0 times two to the zero power or one. This is equal to one eight plus no fours plus one two plus no ones, which is ten.

Bintry number A single digit or group of characters or symbols representing the total, aggregate or amount of units utilizing the base two; usually using only "0" and "1" digits to express quantity.

Binary search To find an element in an ordered table by successively halving a search interval and looking at the remaining half where that element is known to exist.

Biquinary A form of notation utilizing a mixed base, odd digit positions using a base of 5 and even digit positions using a base of 2. (*See also* **Notation.**)

Bit A binary digit; a quantum of information; a single pulse in a group of pulses.

Black box A generic term for any integral unit or device, especially electronic devices. (*See also* **Kludge.**)

Block A group of characters or words considered or transported as a unit, particularly with reference to input or output. The term is used sometimes in connection with magnetic tape as a synonym for record, or for grouped records on tape. (*See also* **Item** and **Message.**)

Block diagram A graphic representation of a sequence of operations of data processing machines using symbols to represent functional steps and elements involved and not physical structural details. The scope of a block diagram is an entire application system, all the equipment units and supplies used therein, and the sequencing of gross operations which are detailed further in flow charts.

Blocking Combining two or more items or groups of items into one block of information, especially on magnetic tape to decrease the number of starts and stops and the number of gaps on tape.

Branch, Branching A conditional jump; a computer operation in which a selection is made between two or more possible courses of action depending upon some related fact or condition.

Breadboard A roughly constructed, experimental model of a circuit, device, or process.

Buffer An isolating circuit used to avoid any reaction of a driven circuit upon the corresponding driving circuit; e.g. a circuit having an output and a multiplicity of inputs so designed that the output is energized whenever one or more inputs are energized. Thus, a buffer performs the circuit function or isolation which is equivalent to the logical "OR."

Buffer storage Facilities linked to: (1) An input device in which information is assembled from external or secondary storage and stored ready for transfer to internal storage; (2) An output device into which information is transmitted from internal storage and held for transfer to secondary or external storage. Computation continues while transfers between buffer storage and secondary or external storage or vice versa take place. (3) Any device which stores information temporarily during data transfers.

Built-in check A device that is included in data processing equipment by the manufacturer as a means of verifying the accuracy of various operations performed by the machines.

Burst To separate sheets of a continuous form.

Bust Programmer or operator malperformance.

Call, call number Identification for a closed routine.

> **Calling sequence** Instructions used for linking a closed routine with a main routine, basic linkage plus list of parameters.

Capacity The upper and lower limits of the numbers which may be processed in a computer register—in the accumulator. Quantities which exceed the capacity usually interrupt the operation of the computer in some fashion.

Card Heavy, stiff paper of uniform size and shape, adapted for being punched in an intelligible array of holes. The punched holes are sensed electrically by wire brushes, mechanically by metal feelers, or optically by photoelectric pickup cells or tubes. One standard card is $7\frac{3}{8}$ inches long by 5 and $\frac{1}{4}$ inches wide and contains 80 columns in each of which any one of 12 positions may be punched.

Carriage, automatic A typewriting paper guiding or holding device which is automatically controlled by information and program so as to feed forms or continuous paper to a set of impression keys and to provide the necessary space, skip, eject, tabulate, or performing operations.

Carry (1) The digit to be added to the next higher column when the sum of the digits in one column equals or exceeds the number base; (2) the process of forwarding the carry digit.

Cell A storage location for one unit of data such as a character or word.

Change record A record which results in the modification of some of the information in the corresponding master file record.

Channel A path along which information, particularly a series of digits or characters or units of information may flow or be stored.

Character (1) One of a set of elementary symbols such as those corresponding to the keys on a typewriter. The symbols may include the decimal digits 0 through 9, the letters A through Z, punctuation marks, operation symbols, and any other single symbols which a computer may read, store, or write. (2) A pulse-code representation of such a symbol.

Character reader An input device which reads printed characters directly from a document.

Character recognition Reading, identifying, and encoding a printed character by magnetic, optical, or other means.

Check A means of verification.

> **Built-in (Automatic) check** Any provision constructed in hardware for verifying the accuracy of information transmitted, manipulated, or stored by any unit or device in a computer.

Duplication check A check which requires that the results of two independent performances (either concurrently on duplicate equipment or at a later time on the same equipment) of the same operation be identical.

Twin check A continuous duplication check achieved by duplication of hardware.

Forbidden combination (Illegal Combination) Tests for the occurrence of a nonpermissible code expression.

Mathematical check A check making use of mathematical identities or other properties, frequently with some degree of discrepancy being acceptable—checking multiplication by verifying that $A \cdot B = B \cdot A$, checking a tabulated function by differencing, etc.

Redundant check A check which uses extra digits, short of complete duplication, to help detect malfunctions or mistakes.

Summation check A redundant check in which groups of digits are summed, usually without regard for overflow, and that sum checked against a previously computed sum to verify accuracy.

Parity check A summation check in which the binary digits, in a character or word, are added (modulo 2) and the sum checked against a single, previously computed parity digit—a check which tests whether the number of ones is odd or even.

Check digit(s) One or more digits carried in a word or symbol, often called a self-checking number, which are computed from the remaining digits. The check digit(s) is recomputed at certain points during processing and compared with the original check digit(s) as a check on the remaining digits of the number.

Clear The replacing of information in a storage unit with zeros or blanks; the passing of a data medium through a station, such as the clearing of punched cards through the reading station or the clearing of the output card stackers.

Clock A time-keeping, pulse-counting, frequency-measuring or synchronizing device within a computer system.

Master clock The source of pulses required for computer operation, consisting of a time-pulse generator (master oscillator) and associated control apparatus.

Programmable clock A clock whose time values are transmitted into a clock register, which may be accessed as dictated by clock instructions in the program.

Real-Time Clock A clock which measures elapsed time in the same scale as external events it will be used to describe.

Code (noun) A system of symbols and of the rules for their use in representing information.

Computer code (Machine code) The code representing the operations built into the hardware of the computer.

Instruction code The symbols, names, and definitions of all the instructions which are directly intelligible to a given computer or a given executive routine.

Operation code That part of an instruction which designates the operation to be performed.

Macro code A form of pseudo code in which each symbol represents a complete subroutine or block on a diagram.

Pseudo code An arbitrary code, independent of the hardware of a computer, which must be translated into computer code if it is to direct the computer.
Pulse code Sets of pulses to which particular meanings have been assigned; the binary representations of characters.

Universal code A form of macro code using standard notation applicable to any computer.

Code (verb) To prepare problems in computer code or in pseudo code for a specific computer.

Coder A person who translates a sequence of instructions for an automatic computer to solve a problem into the precise codes acceptable to the machine.

Coding The list, in computer code or in pseudo code, of the successive computer operations required to solve a given problem.

Absolute, relative, or Symbolic coding Coding in which one uses absolute, relative, or symbolic addresses, respectively.

Automatic coding Any technique in which a computer is used to help bridge the gap between some "easiest" form, intellectually and manually, of describing the steps to be followed in solving a given problem and some "most efficient" final coding of the same problem for a given computer. Two basic forms, defined under **Routine**, are compilation and interpretation.

Collate To merge or combine two or more similarly ordered sets of items to produce another ordered set composed of information from the original sets. Both the number of items and the size of the individual items in the resulting set may differ from those of either of the original sets and of their sums.

Collation sequence The sequence into which the allowable characters of a computer are ranked.

Collator A machine which has two card feeds, four card pockets, and three stations at which a card may be compared or sequenced with regard to other cards so as to select a pocket in which it is to be placed; the machine is suitable for matching detail cards with master cards, merging cards in proper sequence, etc.

Column (card) One of a number of columns in a punched card into which information may be entered in the form of punches controlled in row-position.

Column (digit column) One of the character or digit positions in a positional notation representation of a unit of information. Columns are usually numbered from right to left, zero being the rightmost column if there is no point, or the column immediately to the left of the point if there is one.

Command A pulse, signal, or set of signals initiating one step in the performance of a computer operation. (*See also* **Instruction**.)

Common language A machine-sensible information representation which is common to a related group of data processing machines.

Compare To examine the representation of a quantity for the purpose of discovering its relationship to zero, or of two quantities for the purpose of discovering identity or relative magnitude or order relation.

Comparison The act of comparing and, usually, acting on the result of the comparison.

Compile; Compiler; Compiling routine; Compilation *See* **Routine.**

Compiler A program-making routine, which produces a specific program for a particular problem by determining the intended meaning of an element of information expressed in pseudo code, selecting or generating the required subroutine, transforming the subroutine into specific coding for the specific problem, assigning specific storage registers, etc., and entering it as an element of the problem program, maintaining a record of the subroutines used and their position in the problem program, and continuing to the next element of information in pseudo code. (*See also* **Routine.**)

Complement A quantity which is derived from a given quantity, expressed to the base n, by one of the following rules and which is frequently used to represent the negative of the given quantity. (a) Complement on n: subtract each digit of the given quantity from $n - 1$, add unity to the least significant digit, and perform all resultant carrys. For example, the twos complement of binary 11010 is 00110: the tens complement of decimal 456 is 544. (b) Complement on $n - 1$: subtract each digit of the given quantity from $n - 1$. For example, the ones complement of binary 11010 is 00101; the nines complement of decimal 456 is 543.

Computer Any device capable of accepting information, applying prescribed processes to the information, and supplying the results of these processes; sometimes, more specifically, a device for performing sequences of arithmetic and logical operations; sometimes, still more specifically, a stored-program digital computer capable of performing sequences of internally-stored instructions, as opposed to calculators on which the sequence is impressed manually (desk calculator) or from tape or cards (card-programmed calculator).

Computer limited A section of program in which there is a significant excess of central computer time required, as contrasted to input-output time. (*See* **Input limited, Output limited, Tape limited.**)

Concurrent processing Processing of more than one independent task simultaneously by a single computing system involving interlaced time-sharing of at least one section of hardware, generally the control unit and memory address register or the multiplexing unit for selecting individual control units and memory address registers for each task. The operation of a computer which has some or all of the program for more than one run stored simultaneously in its memory and which executes these programs concurrently by time-shared control. (*See also* **Multiprogramming.**)

Conditional Subject to the result of a comparison made during computation; subject to human intervention.

Contents The information stored in any storage medium. The symbol ( ) is used to indicate "the contents of"; e.g., (m) indicates the contents of the storage location whose address is $m;$ (A) indicates the contents of register $A;$ (T_2) indicates the contents of the tape on input-output unit two.

Control (1) Usually, those parts of a digital computer which effect the carrying out of instructions in proper sequence, the interpretation of each instruction, and the application of the proper signals to the arithmetic unit and other parts in accordance with this interpretation. These include controls over accuracy of performance. (2) Frequently, one or more of the components in any mechanism responsible for interpreting and carrying out manually initiated directions. Sometimes called manual control. (3) In some applications of mathematics, a mathematical check. (*See also* **Control total, Accounting controls.**)

Control console Main operating position of a computer system, a position for human communication with the computer system.

Control key A set of characters within a record, having a logical order of significance and used to identify the record and to determine its place in a file or in an ordered sequence of records.

Control panel A removable wiring panel on punched card (accounting) machines and other data processing equipment on which external wiring may be performed to complete connections between the equipment's internal circuits; a fixed panel on any unit of equipment for visual display of machine status and setting of external controls of status.

Control register A counter built into the control unit and used for sequencing instructions to be executed. It normally contains the address of the next instruction to be performed.

Control sequence Normal order of selection of instructions for execution. In some computers one of the addresses in each instruction specifies the control sequence. In most computers, the sequence is consecutive except where a jump occurs.

Control total A sum formed by adding together some field from each record in an arbitrary grouping of records; usually has some significance as a number; used for checking machine and program data reliability. (*See also* **Hash total.**)

Control unit That portion of the hardware of an automatic digital computer which directs the sequence of operations, interprets the coded instructions, and initiates the proper commands to the computer circuits to execute the instructions. Specialized control units, such as tape control units, direct operations of a specialized unit of a computer system subject to higher level direction from the main system control unit to the specialized control unit.

Conventions Standard procedures in programs and systems design.

Conversion (1) Changing the form of representation of information, such as from the language of one type of magnetic tape to that of another. (2) The process of changing the information and (sometimes) methods of a data processing operation to a different method. For instance, we speak of conversion from tabulating equipment to computer processing.

Convert To change numerical information from one number base to another (e.g., decimal to binary) and/or from some form of fixed point to some form of floating-point representation, or vice versa; to change any data from one coded representation or medium to another representation or medium. Also, to convince a previously unbelieving executive of a company that electronic data processing is useful. Also, to make the transition from manual, electromechanical, and other earlier systems to electronic data processing.

Converter A unit which changes the language of information from one form to another to make it available or acceptable to another machine; e.g., a unit which takes information punched on cards to information recorded on magnetic tape, possibly including editing facilities.

Copy To reproduce information in a new location, replacing whatever was previously stored there and usually leaving the information unchanged at the original location.

Core storage A form of high-speed storage in which binary information is represented by the direction of magnetization of the ferromagnetic material serving as a core to a transformer.

Counter A device, register, or storage location for storing integers, permitting these integers to be increased or decreased by unity or by an arbitrary integer, and capable of being reset to zero or to an arbitrary integer.

Crossfoot To add several horizontal fields of information from cards or across a document.

Cycle (noun) (1) A set of operations repeated as a unit; (2) a nonarithmetic shift in which the digits dropped off at one end of a word are returned at the other end in circular fashion; cycle right and cycle left.

>**Major cycle** The maximum access time of a recirculating serial storage element; the time for one rotation—of a magnetic drum or of pulses in an acoustic delay line. A whole number of minor cycles.
>**Minor cycle** The word time of a serial computer.

Cycle (verb) To repeat a set of operations a prescribed number of times including, when required, supplying necessary address changes by arithmetic processes or by means of a hardware device such as a B-box or cycle counter.

>**Cycle count** To increase or decrease the cycle index by unit or by an arbitrary integer.

>**Cycle criterion** The total number of times the cycle is to be repeated; the register which stores that number.

>**Cycle index** The number of times a cycle has been executed; or the difference, or the negative of the difference, between that number and the number of repetitions desired.

>**Cycle reset** To return a cycle index to its initial value.

Data (plural) Any facts or information, particularly as taken in, operated on, or put out by a computer or other machine handling information.

Data processing Handling information in a sequence of reasonable operations, a generic term for all operations carried out on data.

Data processor A machine for handling information in a sequence of reasonable operations.

Data select A special selection operation in which one set of items is extracted and printed or punched from several sets presented on tape. (*See also* **Select**.)

Dating routine   A routine which computes and/or stores, where needed, a date such as current day's date, expiration date of a tape, etc.

Dead time   Any definite delay between two related actions. It is measured, obviously, in units of time.

Debug   To isolate and remove all malfunctions from a computer or all mistakes from a routine.

Debugging   The process of determining the correctness of a computer routine, locating any errors in it, and correcting them. Also the detection and correction of malfunctions in the computer itself.

Decimal, coded, binary   Decimal notation in which the individual decimal digits are represented by some binary code; e.g., in the 8-4-2-1 coded decimal notation, the number twelve is represented as 0001 0010 for 1 and 2, respectively. Whereas in pure binary notation, it is represented as 1100. Other coded decimal notations are known as: 5-4-2-1, excess three, 2-4-2-1, etc.

Decision   The computer operation of determining if a certain relationship exists regarding words in memory or registers, and taking alternative courses of action; effected by conditional jumps.

Deck   A set or pack of cards.

Decode   To ascertain the intended meaning of the individual characters or groups of characters in the pseudo-coded program.

Decoder   A device capable of ascertaining the significance or meaning of a group of signals and initiating a computer event based thereon; often, a character translator as in matrix decoder.

Decollate   To separate the parts in a multipart form and remove the carbons if any are present, to disperse cards or other data. (*See also* **Disperse**.)

Delete   To remove a record from a master file.

Deletion record   A record which results in some corresponding record(s) being deleted from a master file.

Diagnostic routine   A computer program for performing equipment debugging or preventive maintenance; a routine for performing some program debugging functions.

Diagram   *See* **Block diagram, Flow chart.**

Digit   One of the n symbols of integral value ranging from 0 to $n - 1$ inclusive in a scale of numbering of base n, especially one of the 10 decimal digits, 0, 1, 2, 3, 4, 5, 6, 7, 8, 9.

>   **Check digit**   One or more redunant digits, in a character or word, which depend upon the remaining digits in such a fashion that, if a digit changes, the malfunctions can be detected.

>   **Coded decimal digit**   One of ten arbitrarily selected patterns of ones and zeros used to represent the decimal digits.

Digit, binary   A whole number in the binary scale or notation; this digit may be only 0 (zero) or 1 (one). It may be equivalent to an "on" or "off" condition, a "yes" or a "no," etc.

Digit, decimal, coded *See* **Digit.**

Digital The quality of utilizing numbers in a given scale of notation to represent all the quantities that occur in a problem or a calculation.

Digits, check *See* **Digit.**

Disk storage A storage device which uses optical or magnetic recording on flat disks.

Disperse To distribute items among more sets than originally presented. It is possible for an input item to the process to be distributed to and appear in more than one of the output sets.

Document (noun) Any representation of information which is readable by human beings; usually on paper.

Down time The period during which a computer unit is malfunctioning or inoperative due to machine failures, to mistakes in library programs furnished by the computer manufacturer, or to malfunctioning of supplies such as tapes furnished by the computer manufacturer. It has been extended to include otherwise "good" time to repair damage to a system or process inflicted during down-time. (*See also* **Rerun.**)

Drum, magnetic A rotating cylinder on whose magnetic-material coating information is stored in the form of magnetized dipoles, the orientation or polarity of which is used to store binary information.

Dummy A fictitious fact, record, or other item used to test machine operations or to space between pieces of valid data.

Dump To withdraw all power accidentally or intentionally, to clear data (*see* **Clear**).

    DC dump The condition resulting when DC power is withdrawn from a computer which uses volatile storage—loss of stored information.

    Memory dump Read out data with or without clearing of a portion of any storage, especially the main memory of the central processor (*see* **Memory**).

Edit To rearrange information. Editing may involve the deletion of unwanted data, the selection of pertinent data, the insertion of invariant symbols such as page numbers and typewriter characters, and the application of standard processes such as zero suppression. It includes the arrangement of data into desired format.

EDP Electronic Data Processing.

Electronic Pertaining to the application of that branch of science which deals with the motion, emission, and behavior of currents of free electrons, especially in vacuum, gas, or phototubes and special conductors or semiconductors. Contrasted with electric which pertains to the flow of large currents in wires or conventional conductors.

Erase To clear, especially to remove data from a tape or other storage medium.

Error The amount of loss of precision in a quantity, the difference between an accurate quantity and its calculated approximation. Errors occur in numerical methods; mistakes occur in programs, coding, data transcription; and operating malfunctions occur in computers.

    Inherited error The error in the initial values; especially the error inherited from the previous steps in the step-by-step integration.

Rounding error The error resulting from deleting the less significant digits of a quantity and applying some rule of correction to the part retained.

Truncation error The error resulting from the use of only a finite number of terms of an infinite series, or from the approximation of operations in the infinitesimal calculus by operations in the calculus of finite differences.

Exception reporting An approach to systems design in which reports furnished contain only data which differ from that which was predicted, i.e. exceptions and variances are reported. Other events or results equalling expectations or predictions can be inferred.

Extract To select certain characters (as specified by an extractor) of a word as an operand rather than the entire word, to replace the contents of specific columns of a quantity (as indicated by some other quantity called an extractor or extract pattern) by the contents of the corresponding column at a third quantity; to remove from a set of items of information all those items that meet some arbitrary criterion. (*See also* **Field selection**.)

Feed, card A mechanism which moves cards serially into a machine.

Feedback The process of returning portions of the results of an operation for the purpose of modifying later operations.

Field A set of one or more characters (not necessarily all lying in the same word) which is treated as a whole; a unit of information. (*See also* **Item, key**.)

> **Card field** A set of card columns fixed as to number and position into which the same unit of information is regularly entered.

Field selection or addressing Designation of a field within one or more words of storage as an operand, designation of a set of adjacent characters as an operand. (*See also* **Extract**).

File A sequential set of items (not necessarily all of the same size).

File maintenance The run or group of runs during which a file has all pertinent changes, additions, and deletions applied to it.

Filing system A plan of organizing and identifying records so they can be found quickly when needed. There are two principal filing arrangements, alphabetic and numeric, on which all filing systems are based.

Fixed point A notation or system of arithmetic in which all numerical quantities are expressed by a predetermined number of digits with the arithmetic point implicitly located at some predetermined position; contrasted with floating point.

Fixed word length Refers to computers in which a computer word always contains the same number of characters. Contrasted to variable word length.

Flag A sentinel, tag, label, distinctive symbol, or set of symbols identifying a record.

Float To shift one or more characters to the right or left into position as determined by the structure of the data, such as to float a dollar sign to a rightmost nonspace position, to float asterisks to right and left of a numerical field. (*See also* **Justify**.)

Floating Point A notation in which a number x is represented by a pair of numbers y and z (and two integers, n and m, which are understood parameters, m

being the number base to which y is expressed and n the base of the exponent z, in any given representation) with y and z chosen so that $x = y \cdot n^z$ where z is an integer and where m and n are usually 2 or 10. The quantity y is called the fractional or mantissa; the integer z is called the exponent or characteristic, e.g. a decimal number 241,000,000 might be shown as 2.41, 8, since it is equal to 2.41×10^8. Here the 2.41 is assumed to be the base 10.

Flow chart A graphical representation of a sequence of operations, using symbols to represent the operations such as compute, substitute, compare, jump, copy, read, write, etc. A flow chart is a more detailed representation than a block diagram. The scope of a flow chart is a routine or subroutine, of a block diagram an entire application system.

Force To intervene manually in a routine and cause the computer to execute a jump instruction.

Format The predetermined arrangement of characters, fields, lines, page numbers, punctuation marks, etc. Refers to input, output, and files.

Frame A row of bits running literally across a tape transverse to direction of tape advance.

Function table Two or more sets of information so arranged that an entry in one set selects one or more entries in the remaining sets; a dictionary; a device constructed of hardware, or subroutine, which can either (*a*) decode multiple inputs into a single output or (*b*) encode a single input into multiple outputs.

Garbage Unwanted, meaningless, or dummy information in memory or on tape. Also called "hash."

General purpose computer A computer designed to operate on more than one program of instructions for the purpose of solving many types of data processing problems rather than being designed to fulfill a single function or type of function. (*See also* **Special purpose computer.**)

Generate To produce a needed subroutine from parameters and skeletal coding. (*See also* **Routine.**)

Generator A program for a computer which generates the coding of a problem; a mechanical device which produces an electrical output. (*See also* **Routine.**)

Hang up An unexplained machine stop, program bust.

Hard copy A document produced at the same time that information is transcribed to a form not easily readable by human beings. Also called page copy.

Hardware The mechanical, magnetic, electronic, and electrical devices from which a computer system is fabricated; the assembly of material forming a computer system. Any piece of data processing equipment.

Hash In particular, garbage deliberately recorded on magnetic tape as filler to comply with restrictions on block size, starting and ending conventions, etc. (*See also* **Garbage.**)

Hash total A control total developed from a specific number in each record processed and which has no significance accounting-wise other than as a control or check on processing accuracy.

Head A device which reads, records, or erases information in a storage medium, usually a small electromagnet used to read, write, or erase information on a magnetic drum, disc or tape or the set of perforating or reading fingers and block assembly for punching or reading holes in paper tape. Also, reading assemblies for magnetic ink readers and optical scanning devices.

Header (**card, record, item, etc.**) A record containing common, constant or primary identifying data for a group of records (trailers) which follow.

Hit The occurrence of a match of a transaction item with a file item in file maintenance. (*See also* **Activity.**)

Housekeeping The portion of a program which involves the setting up and checking of contestants and variables to be used in the program. Operations in a routine which check compliance with programming and operating standards. The housekeeping must be done before any productive work is done by the computer.

Ignore A typewriter character indicating that no action whatsoever be taken. (In Teletype or Flexowriter code, all holes punched is an ignore).

Indexed addressing or coding Coding in which the apparent address of the operand must be modified by the contents of a specified index register to obtain the true address of the operand. (*See also* **Index register.**)

Index register A register which contains a quantity which may be used automatically to modify addresses (and for other purposes) under direction of the control section of the computer.

Indirect addressing Coding in which the apparent address of the operand is the location of a further indirect address of the operand or is the location of the operand itself.

Information A set of symbols or an arrangement of signals that designate one out of a number of alternatives; an aggregation of data which may or may not be organized.

Input Data introduced into a data processing machine from an external source, information transferred from secondary or external storage into the internal storage of the computer.

Input block A segment of internal computer storage reserved for receiving data transferred from input devices.

Input equipment or unit (**computers**) The equipment used for taking information into a computer.

Input limited The state of a section of program in which central processing is obliged to await the further delivery of fresh input to the process. Its counterpart for output units is "output limited." (*See also* **Tape limited.**)

Inquiry Request for information from storage. (*See also* **Keyboard inquiry.**)

Inquiry Station Device from which inquiry is made.

Instruction A set of characters which defines an operation together with one or more addresses (or no address) and which, as a unit, causes the computer to operate accordingly on the indicated quantities. The term instruction is preferable to the terms command and order; command is reserved for electronic signals; order is reserved for the order of the characters (implying sequence), the order of the interpolation, etc.

Breakpoint instruction An instruction which, if some specified switch is set, will cause the computer to stop.

Conditional breakpoint instruction A conditional jump instruction which, if some specified switch is set, will cause the computer to stop, after which either the routine may be continued as coded or a jump may be forced.

Zero-address instruction An instruction specifying an operation in which the location of the operands is defined by the computer code, so that no address need be given explicitly.

One-address instruction (single-address instruction) An instruction consisting of an operation and exactly one address. The instruction code of a single-address computer may include both zero- and multiaddress instructions as special cases.

One-plus-one or **three-plus-one-address instruction** A two- or four-address instruction, respectively, in which one of the addresses always specifies the location of the next instruction to be performed.

Multiaddress instruction An instruction consisting of an operation and more than one address.

Two- Three- or **Four-address instruction** An instruction consisting of an operation and two, three, or four addresses, respectively.

Integrated data processing (1) Data processing carried out, organized, and directed according to a systems approach including common use of information pools by separate functional authorities. (2) A collection of data processing techniques built around a common language in which duplication of clerical operations, especially successive transcription of data, is minimized and intercommunication between machines is facilitated.

Interblock gap Space on magnetic tape separating two blocks of data.

Interlace To assign successive storage locations to physically separated storage positions, to intermingle operations.

Interlock To prevent operation of one portion of a computing system while another portion is operating.

Internally stored program A sequence of instructions (program) stored inside the computer in the same storage facilities as the computer data, as opposed to being stored externally on punched paper tape, pin boards, etc.

Interpret (1) The translation of coded characters into standard letters, numbers, and symbols. (2) To print on a punched card or tape all or some of the information punched in it. (3) To subject to an interpreter (device) or interpretative routine (process).

Interpreter (programming) An executive routine which, as the computation progresses, translates a stored program expressed in some pseudocode into machine code and performs the indicated operations, by means of subroutines, as they are translated. An interpreter is essentially a closed subroutine which operates successively on an indefinitely long sequence of program parameters (the pseudo-instructions and operands). It may usually be entered as a closed subroutine and left by a pseudo-code exit instruction.

Interpreter (Hardware) A device for translation from one language and machine to another, especially for printing on punched cards activated by the holes therein.

Interrupt Inhibiting of current control sequence, especially a jump triggered by signals from on-line peripheral equipment or the results of programmed tests.

> **Automatic interrupt** Not controlled by programmer, inherent to operation of devices or built into an Executive Routine, e.g. error interrupt.

> **Cycled interrupt** Passing of control among each of several tasks in a predetermined sequence and sometimes predetermined rate.

> **Perpiheral interrupt** Interrupt caused by a readiness or completion signal from a peripheral unit.

> **Priority interrupt** Interrupt which seizes control of computer system sequencing and assigns it to the device generating the interrupt signal.

> **Programmed interrupt** Interrupt dictated by programmer.

Item A set of one or more fields containing related information; a unit of cor-related information relating to a single person, object, transaction, or event.

Item advance In grouping of records, a technique for operating successively on different records in memory.

Item design Specifications of fields making up an item, order in which the fields are to be recorded, the mode and number of characters to be allocated to each field.

Item size Number of characters and/or words in an item.

Jump An instruction or signal which, conditionally or unconditionally, specifies the location of the next instruction and directs the computer to that instruction. A jump is used to alter the normal sequence control of the computer. Under certain special conditions, a jump may be forced by manual intervention.

Justify To align a set of characters horizontally into a prescribed format. Justification may take place in a word, field, item, line, or other unit of data as defined by context or specifications. (*See also* Right-hand justified, left-hand justified.)

Key A set of characters, forming a field, used to identify an item. Also, the im-peller of a manually activated device.

Keyboard inquiry A technique whereby the interrogation of the contents of a computer's storage may be initiated at a keyboard.

Key driven Said of any device for translating information into machine-sensible form which requires an operator to depress a key for each character.

Kludge In computer humor, the archetypical, farcical, or apocryphal black box and computer system. The Kludge Komputer Corporation and the Kludge device are the butts of much computer humor. Also, term of endearment for computer as household pet, as in "our Kludge."

Label A specialized record used to identify an associated collection of data. Ex-amples: Tape label, label card, label block, etc. Also, to assign an identification to a body of data and create a specialized record associated with it.

Latency In a serial storage system, the access time less the word time—the time spent waiting for the desired location to appear under the drum heads.

Left-hand justified A number (decimal, binary, etc.) which exists in a memory cell, location or register possessing no left-hand zeros; i.e., $\boxed{3}\boxed{9}\boxed{2}\boxed{7}\boxed{6}\boxed{4}\boxed{0}\boxed{0}\boxed{5}\boxed{0}$, is considered to be left-hand justified. A field in which nonzero and nonspace characters are shifted as far to the left as possible. (*See also* **Normalize, justify.**)

Library An ordered set or collection of standard and proven routines and subroutines by which problems and parts of problems may be solved and from which sequences of commonly occurring batches of instructions can be drawn in the formulation of a program; usually stored in relative or symbolic coding. (A library may be subdivided into various volumes, such as floating decimal, double-precision, or complex, according to the type of arithmetic employed by the subroutines).

Line printing Printing an entire line of characters across a page as the paper feeds in one direction past a type bar or cylinder bearing all characters on a single element.

Linkage Portion of a compiler routine which lists specifications for variables contained in a subroutine called from a library, a technique for providing a reentry to the routine from which a closed subroutine was called.

Location A unit storage position in the main internal storage, storing one or many computer characters or words; a storage register. (*See also* **Cell.**)

Log 2 look-up *See* **Binary search.**

Logical operations (computers) The operations of comparing, selecting, making references, matching, sorting, merging, etc., where in essence ones and zeros corresponding to yes's and no's constitute the elements (yes-or-no quantities) being operated on.

Loop The repetition of a group of instructions in a routine. Associated with a loop are loop initialization, loop computing, loop modification, and loop testing. (*See also* **Cycle.**)

  Closed loop Repetition of a group of instructions indefinitely.

Machine Language Information in the physical form which a machine can handle or punched paper tape is machine language to a system equipped with a paper tape reader; printed characters on paper are machine language only if the system is equipped with an optical character reader capable of handling the paper and recognizing the characters.

Machine-sensible Information represented in a form (medium, coding) which can be read by the machine in question.

Macro, Macrocode, Macroinstruction, Macroprogram A source language statement, intelligible to a processor aided by an interpretative routine, capable of resulting in the production of one or many instructions in machine language. The coding produced is an open-ended sequence of machine operations which may consist in part of a linkage to a closed subroutine.

Magnetic core *See* **Core storage.**

Magnetic disc A circular disc, one or both surfaces of which are coated with a magnetic material on which information may be stored as small polarized spots.

Magnetic drum A rapidly rotating cylinder, the surface of which is coated with a magnetic material on which information may be stored as small polarized spots.

Magnetic tape Tape made of paper, metal, or plastic, coated or impregnated with magnetic material, on which polarized spots representing information may be stored.

Main chain That part of the program for a run which processes the unexceptional input items, exclusive of branches for exceptional items.

Main Frame Central processing unit of a computer, the main part of a computer.

Malfunctions A failure in the operation of the hardware of a computer. (*See also* Error.)

Mark sense The procedure of marking a punched card with a special pencil in such a way that the marks can later be translated into punched holes by a special device on a punched card accounting machine.

Mask *See* Extract, Extract pattern.

Master file A file of semipermanent information, which is usually updated periodically.

Match *See* Collate.

Memory *See* Storage.

> **Memory access time** *See* Access.

Memory Dump A listing of the contents of a storage device or selected parts of it.
> **Differential** A dump of only those words or characters of memory which have been changed during execution of a routine as determined by a diagnostic routine which rereads the original contents from auxiliary storage and compares them with the present contents.

> **Dynamic** A dump of certain sections of memory under program control as a main routine is being executed.

Memory guard Provision for inhibiting access to prescribed sections of storage devices especially main memory of the central processor.

Merge To produce a single sequence of items, ordered according to some rule (i.e., arranged in some orderly sequence) from two or more sequences previously ordered according to the same rule, without changing the items in size, structure, or total number. Merging is a special case of collation.

> **Merge Pattern** A set of runs for accomplishing merging of multiple files in several levels.

> **Multilevel merge.** A merge program requiring several levels to combine all of the input files.

Message. A group of characters or words, variable in length, transported as a unit. (*See also* Item.)

Microsecond A millionth of a second.

Millisecond A thousandth part of a second.

Mistake A human blunder which results in an incorrect instruction in a program or in coding, an incorrect element of information, or an incorrect manual operation. (*See also* Error.)

Mnemonic Assisting or intended to assist memory; of or pertaining to memory; mnemonics is the art of improving the efficiency of the human memory in relating symbolic representations to the operations and operands for which they stand.

Mnemonic operation codes Operation codes written using a symbolic notation which is easier for human beings to remember than the operation codes actually in the hardware of the machine. The mnemonic codes need to be converted to actual operation codes before execution by the computer, which may be done clerically or by computer.

Modify (1) To alter in an instruction the address of the operand; (2) to alter a subroutine according to a defined parameter. (*See also* **Indexed addressing, Indirect addressing.**)

Modulo n check. A form of check digits, such that the number of ones in each number A operated with is compared with a check number B carried along with A equal to the remainder of A when divided by n. For example, in a "modulo 4 check" the check numbers will be 0, 1, 2, or 3, and the remainder of A when divided by 4 must equal the reported check number, B, or else an error has occurred. This method of verification derives from the topic known as linear congruences in the branch of mathematics known as the theory of numbers. Another example of this kind of check (a "modulo 9 check") is "casting out nines" for checking arithmetical multiplication.

Multiple precision Multiword operations or results generated as multiple word operands. (*See also* **Double precision.**)

Multiprocessing Loadsharing on one or more independent problems by more than one central processing unit.

Multiprocessor Computer with multiple arithmetic and logical units for simultaneous use.

Multiprogramming The programming of a central processing unit so as to permit more than one more or less independent tasks to share use of its facilities on a time-shared basis with overlap or intimate interlacing of the time slots allotted to portions of each task, rather than time-sharing sequentially by task. (*See also* **Concurrent processing.**)

Non-numeric character Any allowable character except a numeric digit.

Normalize To adjust the exponent and mantissa of a floating-point result so that the mantissa lies in the prescribed standard (normal) range usually implying left-hand justification of mantissa also; standardize.

Notation, Positional notation, Number system A systematic method for representing numerical quantities in which any quantity is represented approximately by the factors needed to equate it to a sum of multiples of powers of some chosen base n. That is, a number x

$$= a_q n^q + a_{q-1} n^{q-1} + \ldots + a_1 n + a_0 + a_{-1} n^{-1} + \ldots + a_{-p} n^{-p} = \sum_{i=-p}^{q} a_i n^i, \text{ with } n >$$

$a_i \geq 0$ for all i, is represented by $a_q a_{q-1} \ldots a_1 a_0 a_{-1} \ldots a_{-p}$, with a point to the right of a_0 to identify it. For example, in decimal notation familiar to all, in which n equals 10, $x = 371.426$ represents $3 \cdot 10^2 + 7 \cdot 10 + 1 + 4 \cdot 10^{-1} + 2 \cdot 10^{-2} + 6 \cdot 10^{-3}$. Similarly, in binary notation, in which n equals 2, $x = 1101.01$ represents $1 \cdot 2^3 + 1 \cdot 2^2 + 0 \cdot 2 + 1 + 0 \cdot 2^{-1} + 1 \cdot 2^{-2}$, which equals 13.75 in decimal notation. In writing numbers, the base is sometimes indicated as a subscript (itself always in decimal notation) whenever there is any doubt about what base is being employed (e.g., $1101.11_2 = 13.75_{10}$).

Binary, Ternary, Quaternary, Quinary, Octal (Octonary), Decimal, Duodecimal, Sexadecimal (Hexadecimal), or Duotricenary notation Notation using the base 2, 3, 4, 5, 8, 10, 12, 16, or 32, respectively.

Biquinary notation One of any number of mixed-base notations in which the term n^i in the definition above is replaced by the product $\prod_{j=0}^{i-1} m_j$. In the biquinary system, m_j is 2 for j odd; 5 for j even.

Coded decimal notation (Binary-coded decimal) Decimal notation in which the individual decimal digits are represented by some binary code.

Object language Machine language, programming language directly comprehensible to the computer without being subjected to interpreters, assemblers, compilers, or other automatic programming systems; more generally, the result of transforming any *source* language by any means. (*See also* Source language.)

Octal Pertaining to the number base of eight, e.g. in octal notation, octal 214 is 2 times 64 plus 1 times 8 plus 4 times 1 equals decimal 140; octal 214 is binary 010, 001, 100.

Odd-even check Use of a digit carried along as a check which is 1 if the total number of ones in the machine word is even, and which is 0 if the total number of ones in the machine word is odd, or vice versa. Words are said to be even parity with check bit or odd parity depending on the number of ones permissible.

Off-Line Not requiring the use of the central control, memory, arithmetic, and logical unit. Used especially in connection with operation of input/output devices.

On-line (adjective) Operation of an input/output device as a component of the computer, under central computer programmed control.

On-line processing Operations performed by auxiliary computer equipment while it is connected to and a part of the computer such as magnetic tape units feeding data directly to the main frame.

On-line, Real-time operation A type of system application in which the input data to the system is fed directly from the measuring devices and the computer results obtained during the progress of the event, e.g. a computer receives data from wind tunnel measurements during a run, and the computations of dependent variables are performed during the run enabling a change in the conditions so as to produce particularly desirable results.

Operand Any one of the quantities entering or arising in an operation. An operand may be an argument, a result, a parameter, or an indication of the location of the next instruction.

Operation (1) A defined action; (2) the action specified by a single computer instruction or pseudo instruction; (3) an arithmetical, logical, or transferral unit of a problem, usually executed under the direction of a subroutine.

Arithmetical operations Operations in which numerical quantities form the elements of the calculation (e.g., addition, subtraction, multiplication, division).

Complete operation An operation which includes (a) obtaining all operands from storage; (b) performing the operation; (c) returning resulting operands to storage; and (d) obtaining the next instruction.

Computer operation The electronic operation of hardware resulting from an instruction.

Logical operations Operations in which logical (yes-or-no) quantities form the elements being operated on (e.g., comparison, extraction). A usual requirement is that the value appearing in a given column of the results shall not depend on the values appearing in more than one given column of each of the arguments.

Red-tape operations Operations which do not directly contribute to the result, i.e., arithmetical, logical, and transfer operations used in modifying the address section of other instructions, in counting cycles, in rearranging data, etc.

Transfer operations (Storage operations) Operations which move information from one storage location or one storage medium to another (e.g., read, record, copy, transmit, exchange). Transfer is sometimes taken to refer specifically to movement between different media; storage to movement within the same medium.

Although many operations fit the above definitions of two or more of the terms arithmetical, logical, transfer, and red-tape, these terms are frequently used loosely to divide the operations of a given routine or of a given instruction code into four mutually distinct classes depending on the primary function intended for the given operation in the case at hand.

Operation code That part of an instruction which designates the operation to be performed.

Operator The person who actually manipulates the computer controls, places information media into the input devices, removes the output, presses the start button, etc.; a mathematical symbol which represents a mathematical process to be performed on an associated element.

Order *See* **Instruction.**

Output (1) Information transferred from the internal storage of a computer to secondary or external storage; (2) information transferred to any device exterior to the computer.

Output block A segment of the internal computer storage reserved for receiving data to be transferred out.

Output equipment The equipment used for transferring information out of a computer.

Output limited The characteristic of a program that the central processor produces output data ready for transfer to output equipment more frequently than the output unit can accept them so that the central processor is obliged to wait. (*See also* **Input limited.**)

Overflow In a counter or register, the production of a number which is beyond the capacity of the counter. For example, adding two numbers, each within the capacity of the registers holding them, may result in a sum beyond the capacity of the register that is to hold the sum: overflow.

Overlay   Use of a portion of internal storage alternatively for two sets of data or instructions which are needed at different times.

Pack   To combine several different "short" elements of information into one word—e.g., storing one man's pay number, pay rate, tax exemptions, etc., in different sets of digit columns in one word, or storing several different payments in one word.

Packing density   The relative number of units of desired information contained within certain dimensions; for example, the number of binary digits of polarized spots stored on magnetic tape per linear inch of length of magnetic tape.

Parallel   Handled simultaneously in separate facilities.

Parallel operation   The flow of information through the computer or any part of it using two or more lines or channels simultaneously.

Parallel processing   *See* **Concurrent processing, Multiprocessing, Multiprogramming.**

Parallel running   Testing of a newly developed system by running it comparatively in conjunction with a previously existing system.

Parameter   (1) In a subroutine, a quantity which may be given different values when the subroutine is used in different main routines or in different parts of one main routine, but which usually remains unchanged throughout any one such use; (2) in a generator, a quantity used to specify input-output devices, to designate subroutines to be included, or otherwise to describe the desired routine to be generated.

> **Present parameter**   A parameter incorporated into a subroutine during input.
>
> **Program parameter**   A parameter incorporated into a subroutine during computation. A program parameter frequently comprises a word stored relative to either the subroutine or the entry point and dealt with by the subroutine during each reference. It may be altered by the routine and/or may vary from one point of entry to another.

Parity check   A verification of the accuracy of binary coded data through the testing of an additional (parity check) bit not used in the code. (*See also* **Odd-even check.**)

Pass   A single running of a reel of tape through the computer; a single running of a related group of tapes.

Patch   A section of coding inserted into a routine (usually by explicitly transferring control from the routine to the patch and back again) to correct a mistake or alter the routine.

Peripheral equipment   Units which work in conjunction with the computer but are not part of the computer itself; e.g., tape reader, analog-to-digital converter, typewriter, etc. (*See also* **Input equipment, Output equipment.**)

Plug-board   A removable panel containing an ordered array of terminals which may be interconnected by short electrical leads according to a prescribed pattern and hence designating a specific program. The entire panel, prewired, may be inserted for different programs.

Point   The dot that marks the separation between the integral and fractional parts of a quantity; i.e., between the coefficients of the zero and the minus one powers of the number base. It is usually called, for a number system using base two, a *binary point;* for base ten, a *decimal point,* etc.; base point; radix.

Precision The number of levels of quantization or the degree of exactness with which a quantity is stated; a relative term often based on the number of significant digits in a measurement.

Presort The first part of a sort, in which records are arranged into strings which equal or exceed some minimum length.

Printer An output mechanism which prints or typewrites characters, such as line printer (off-line, on-line) and console printer (typewriter).

Process chart In general, a set of symbols designed to represent various operations connected together by arrows to indicate the sequence of operations. Specifically, the use of symbols to represent computer operations. The process chart is the master plan of the system and is a graphic representation of the flow of data through it.

Program (noun) A plan for the solution of a problem, a sequence of instructions. (*See also* **Routine.**)

Program (verb) To plan a computation or process, to develop a sequence of instructions. (*See also* **Code.**)

> **Automatic programming** Any technique in which the computer is used to help plan as well as to help code a problem. (*See also* **Coding.**)
>
> **Optimum programming** Improper terminology for minimal latency coding—for producing a minimal latency routine. (*See also* **Routine.**)

Program step A step in a program, usually one instruction.

Programmed checking A system of checking whereby (1) before running any problem P a sample problem of the same type with known answer is run, and (2) mathematical or logical checks of operations, such as comparing $A \times B$ with $B \times A$, are included in the program for P, and (3) reliance is placed on a very high probability of correctness rather than built-in error-detection circuits.

Programmer A person who prepares sequences of instructions for a computer, without necessarily converting them into the detailed codes.

Proof listing (Programming) A report prepared by a processor which shows the coding as originally written, any comments that may have been written, and the machine language instructions produced; (General Accounting) an item by item list of transactions and their detail accompanied by control totals, sequence checks, or other data for "proofing," an "audit trail."

Pseudo-code An arbitrary code, relatively independent of the hardware of a computer, which must be translated into computer code.

Pulse A change in the intensity or level of some signal medium, usually over a relatively short period of time, e.g. a shift in electric potential of a point for a short period of time compared to the time period, i.e., if the voltage level of a point shifts from -10 to $+20$ volts with respect to ground for a period of 2 microseconds, one says that the point received a 30-volt, 2-microsecond pulse.

Pulse-code Sets of pulses to which particular meanings have been assigned; the binary representations of characters.

Punch, calculating, electronic A card handling machine which reads a punched card, performs a number of sequential operations, and punches the result on a card.

Punch, card A device which perforates holes in cards in specific locations designated by a program.

Punched card A piece of lightweight cardboard on which information is represented by holes punched in specific positions.

Punched card duplicating Automatic punching of repetitive information from a master card into a group of succeeding detail cards. This is normally performed as part of the card-punching function. Instead of depressing keys repetitively for common information (such as entry date, which is punched in every card) the operator punches the common information only once in the first card of each group, and it is automatically punched into all remaining cards of the group.

Punched tape Paper tape punched in a pattern of holes so as to convey information. Mylar and other plastic tapes may be found used in lieu of paper tapes for more permanent purposes, such as in case of frequent reuse of a tape.

Punch position The location of the row in a columnarized card, e.g., in an 80-column card the rows or "punch position" may be 0 to 9 and X and Y corresponding to position 11 and 12.

Punch, summary A card handling machine which may be electrically connected to another machine, e.g. tabulator and which will punch out on a card the information produced, calculated or summarized by the other machine.

Punch, tape *See* **tape.**

Quantity A positive or negative real number in the mathematical sense. Note: The term "quantity" is preferred by some computer people for referring to numeric data; the term "number" is preferred in the sense of integer or natural number, as in "the number of digits."

Radix The base of a numbering system. It is the total number of distinct marks or symbols used in the numbering system. For example, the decimal numbering system uses 10 symbols (0, 1, 2, 3, 4, 5, 6, 7, 8, 9). The radix here is 10. We obtain decimal numbers by using various powers of 10. In the binary numbering system there are only 2 marks or symbols (0, 1). The radix is 2, and we obtain binary numbers by using various powers of 2.

Random access Access to storage under conditions in which the next position from which information is to be obtained is in no way dependent on the previous one.

Random access storage A storage technique in which the time required to obtain information is independent of the location o fthe information most recently obtained. This strict definition must be qualified by the observation that we usually mean relatively random. Thus, magnetic drums are relatively nonrandom access when compared to magnetic cores for main memory, but relatively random access when compared to magnetic tapes for file storage.

Random number A number formed by a set of digits selected from a random sequence of digits. A sequence of digits is random when it is constructed by a process under which each successive digit is equally likely to be any of the n digits to the base n.

Range The set of values over which a quantity may vary.

Raw data Data which has not been processed; may or may not be in machine-sensible form.

Read To sense the presence of information on a recording medium, such as magnetic tape or punched cards; to copy, usually from one form of storage to another, particularly from external or secondary storage to internal storage; to sense the meaning of arrangements of hardware.

Reader, card A mechanism that permits the sensing of information punched or recorded on cards by means of wire brushes, metal feelers, optically, magnetically, or by other means. Also, a device for sensing marks on mark-sensed cards.

Reader, tape, magnetic A device capable of restoring to a train or sequence of electrical pulses, information recorded on a magnetic tape in the form of a series of magnetized spots, usually for the purpose of transferring the information to some other storage medium.

Reader, tape, paper A device capable of restoring to a train or sequence of electrical pulses, information punched on a paper tape in the form of a series of holes.

Real time In solving a problem, a speed sufficient to give an answer in the actual time during which the problem must be solved. For example, in the case of a human being driving a motor car, at 30 miles an hour, he can regularly solve nearly all his problems in real time; at 100 miles an hour, he will regularly fail to solve some of his problems in real time.

Real-time operations; On-line operations; Simulation Deriving data from a physical process and processing this data in synchronism with the physical process in such a fashion that the results of the data processing are immediately useful to the control of the physical operations.

Record A group of related words or fields. (*See also* **Item**.)

> **Record (Reference record)** (1) A listing of information, usually in printed or printable form; (2) one output of a compiler consisting of a list of the operations and their positions in the final specific routine and containing information describing the segmentation and storage allocation of the routine. **Record (verb)** (1) To copy or set down in reusable form for future reference; (2) to produce a reference record.

Records management A program designed to provide economy and efficiency in the creation, organization, maintenance, use, and disposition of records, assuring that needless records will not be created or kept and that valuable records will be preserved.

Reel A spool of tape, generally magnetic tape. Sometimes, a spool of photographic film.

Register A device capable of both storage and arithmetic processes within a data processing machine, a storage location for one or more computer words.

Relative address A label used to identify the position of a memory location with respect to some reference or base address in a routine or subroutine. Relative addresses are translated into absolute addresses by adding some specific "reference" address, usually the address at which the first word of the routine is stored.

For example, if a relative address instruction specifies an address *n* and the address of the first word of the routine is *k*, then the absolute address of the memory location is $n + k$.

Relative coding Coding in which all addresses refer to an arbrirarily selected position.

Reperforator Device for punching copies of punched paper type in whole or selectively.

Report An output document prepared by a data processing system.

Report generator An automatic programming system for producing a complete report given only a description of the desired content and format of the output, and certain information concerning the input file and hardware available.

Reproducer A punch card machine that punches cards to agree as may be specified with other cards. Reproduction may be selective, i.e. call for extraction of specified columns for reproduction. Sometimes, a paper tape reperforator.

Reproducing From one card to another is copying from one record to another. Information from one set of punched source cards is automatically punched into another set of cards. The two sets of cards are fed through the machine synchronously.

Rerun (noun, verb) Use of a rerun routine; to make use of a rerun routine. (*See also* **Routine**.)

Rerun-point That stage of a computer run at which all information pertinent to the running of the routine is available either to the routine itself or to a rerun routine in order that a run may be reconstituted.

Rerun routine A routine designed to be used in the wake of a malfunction or a mistake to reconstitute a routine from the last previous rerun point.

Reset To return a register to zero or to a specified initial condition, to restore a device to a prescribed status.

Retention period The period of time during which records must be kept before they may be disposed of, usually stated in terms of months or years, but sometimes expressed as contingent upon the occurrence of an event.

Rewind To return a magnetic or paper tape to its beginning.

Right-hand justified A number (decimal, binary, etc.) which exists in a memory cell, location or register possessing no right-hand zeros; i.e., | 0 | 0 | 0 | 1 | 2 | 3 | | 4 | 5 | 6 | 7 |, is considered to be right-hand justified. (*See also* **Justify**.)

Round-off To change a more precise quantity to a less precise one, according to some rule.

Routine A set of coded instructions arranged in proper sequence to direct the computer to perform a desired operation or series of operations. (*See also* **Subroutine**.)

> **Bootstrap** The special coded instructions at the beginning of an input tape, together with one or two instructions inserted by switches or buttons into the computer.

> **Compiler (compiling routine)** An executive routine which, before the desired computation is started, translates a program expressed in pseudo code into

machine code (or into another pseudo code for further translation by an interpreter). In accomplishing the translation, the compiler may be required to:

Allocate To assign tape and other facilities and storage locations to the main routines and subroutines, thereby fixing the absolute values of any symbolic addresses. In some cases, allocation may require segmentation. (*See also* **Segment.**)

Assemble To integrate the subroutines (supplied, selected, or generated) into the main routine—to

Adapt To specialize to the tasks at hand by means of preset parameters.

Incorporate Place in storage.

Orient To change relative and symbolic addresses to absolute form.

Convert To change numerical information from one number base to another (e.g., decimal to binary) and/or from some form of fixed point to some form of floating-point representation, or vice versa.

Decode To ascertain the intended meaning of the individual characters or groups of characters in the pseudo-coded program.

Generate To produce a needed subroutine from parameters and skeletal coding.

Select To choose a needed subroutine from a file of subroutines.

Diagnostic routine A specific routine designed to locate either a malfunction in the computer or a mistake in coding.

Executive routine (Master routine) A routine designed to process and control other routines. A routine used in realizing "automatic coding."

Flip-flop routine A routine which alternates addresses.

General routine A routine expressed in computer coding designed to solve a class of problems, specializing to a specific problem when appropriate parametric values are supplied.

Interpreter (Interpretive routine) An executive routine which as the computation progresses, translates a stored program expressed in some machine-like pseudo code into machine code and performs the indicated operations, by means of subroutines, as they are translated. An interpretative routine is essentially a closed subroutine which operates successively on an indefinitely long sequence of program parameters (the pseudo instructions and operands). It may usually be entered as a closed subroutine and excited by a pseudo-code exit instruction.

Minimal latency routine (optimum routine) Especially in reference to serial storage systems, a routine so coded, by judicious arrangement of data and instructions in storage, that the actual latency is appreciably less than the expected random-access latency.

Rerun routine (rollback or return routine) A routine designed to be used in the wake of a computer malfunction or a coding or operating mistake to reconstitute a routine from the last previous rerun point.

Rerun point That stage of a computer run at which all information pertinent to the running of the routine is available either to the routine itself or to a rerun routine in order that a run may be reconstituted.

Sequence-checking routine A routine which checks every instruction executed, printing certain data. (*See also* **Sequence checks.**)

Service routine A routine designed to assist in the actual operation of the computer. Tape comparison, block location, certain post mortems, and correction routines fall in this class.

Simulating routine A routine which represents the operation of one computer in the code of another.

Specific routine A routine expressed in specific computer coding designed to solve a particular mathematical, logical, or data-handling problem.

Test routine A routine designed to show that a computer is functioning properly.

Tracing routine A routine which causes a computer to proceed through all possible logical paths of another routine and to print out these paths.

Run (noun) One performance of a program on a computer; performance of one routine, or several routines automatically linked so that they form an operating unit, during which manual manipulations are not required of the computer operator.

Run book All materials needed to document a computer application, including problem statement, flow charts, coding, and operating instructions.

Satellite computer A small computer associated with a tape-oriented computer usually of larger scale, the smaller computer is generally specialized to provide all peripheral operations and conversion for the larger computer.

Scale (verb) To change the scale (that is, the units) in which a variable is expressed so as to bring it within the capacity of the machine or program at hand. (*See also* **Normalize.**)

Segment (noun) In a routine too long to fit into internal storage, a part short enough to be stored entirely in the internal storage and containing the coding necessary to call in and jump automatically to other segments. Routines which exceed internal storage capacity may be automatically divided into segments by a compiler.

Segment (verb) To divide a routine in parts each consisting of an integral number of subroutines, each part capable of being completely stored in the internal storage and containing the necessary instructions to jump to other segments.

Select A data processing operation in which certain items or fields are chosen from a larger set of input items for further processing, the choice being made according to some rule.

Self-checking number One in which extra checking digits are carried along with the information digits. *See also* **Check digit.**)

Sense (1) To examine, particularly relative to a criterion; (2) to determine the present arrangement of some element of hardware, especially a manually set switch; (3) to read holes punched in paper or cards; (4) to detect signals.

Sentinel A symbol marking the beginning or the end of some element of information, such as a field, item, block, tape, etc; a tag.

Sequence check A data processing operation designed to check the sequence of the items in a file that purports to be already in sequence.

Serial Handle one after the other in a single facility, such as transfer or store in a digit by digit time sequence.

Service routine A routine designed to assist in the actual operation of the computer. Tape comparison, block location, certain post mortems, and correction routines fall in this class.

Set up To prepare a piece of equipment for operation. For example, to put paper in a printer and to adjust the paper feed properly for a particular printing operation is to "set up" the printer.

Set-up time The time required to set up a piece of equipment.

Shift To move the characters of a unit of information column-wise right or left. For a number, this is equivalent to multiplying or dividing by a power of the base of notation.

Sight check To determine visually whether a particular punch is present in all cards of a deck; to validate keypunching by reading corresponding tabulating.

Sign The symbol which distinguishes positive from negative numbers.

Sign digit The character position in which the indication of sign is normally placed within the computer word.

Significance, significant digits The arbitrary rank, priority, or order of relative magnitude assigned to a given position or column in a number; the significant digits of a number are a set of digits, usually from consecutive columns beginning with the most significant digit different from zero and ending with the least significant digit whose value is known are assumed relevant, e.g., 2300.0 has five significant digits, whereas 2300 probably has two significant digits.

Simulation The representation of physical systems and phenomena by computers, models, or other equipment.

Snapshot Dynamic printout of selected data in storage at programmed checkpoints (*See also* **Memory dump.**)

Software Programming systems, libraries, and other programming and non-hardware operating aids; sometimes extended to include all sales support provided by a computer manufacturer—training, reference material, installation planning, etc.

Sort To arrange items of information according to rules dependent upon a key or field contained by the items.

> **Multicycle sort** A sort program which requires several cycles because of a large volume of input.

Sorter Punch Card Machines. A machine which sorts cards according to the punches in specified columns of the card.

Source language The original form in which a program is prepared. It is usually an advanced programming language prior to processing by an interpreter, assembler, compiler, or other automatic programming system. In this sense, it is opposed to machine language coding, called *object* language.

Special purpose computer An electronic data processing machine designed to perform a fixed function or group of functions. The instructions to these machines are usually built into the equipment by the manufacturer and they require little or no additional programming.

Spot carbon Carbon paper carbonized on some areas only so that certain entries will not be reproduced on the copy.

Stacker, card A mechanism that accumulates cards in a bin after they have passed through a machine operation; a hopper.

Standardize (1) To adjust the exponent and mantissa of a floating-point result so that the mantissa lies in the prescribed normal range; normalize; (2) to adjust various sets of procedures to conform to a single set; (3) to restrict choice of data medium to one of a set of acceptable forms and formats. (*See also* **Floating-point representation.**)

Standby equipment Automatic data processing equipment which is not in use and which is available in emergencies such as machine breakdowns or cases of overload.

Storage (1) The unit which holds or retains items of information. (2) Any device into which information can be introduced, held, and then extracted at a later time. The mechanism or medium in which the information is stored need not form an integral part of a computer. Synonyms: memory, store (in English usage).

Store (verb) The operation of placing data in storage.

Store (noun) Storage (English usage).

Stored program computer A computer in which the instructions which specify the operations to be performed are stored in the form of coded information in main memory, along with the data currently being operated upon, making possible simple repetition of operations and the modification by the computer of its own instructions.

String A set of records arranged in ascending (descending) sequence according to increasing (decreasing) magnitude of their keys.

String break The point at which a sort can find no more records with sufficiently high control keys to fit on the current output string.

String length The number of records in a string.

Subroutine The set of instructions necessary to direct the computer to carry out a well-defined mathematical or logical operation; a subunit of a routine. A subroutine is often written in relative or symbolic coding even when the routine to which it belongs is not.

> **Closed subroutine** A subroutine not stored in its proper place in the linear operational sequence, but stored away from the routine which refers to it. Such a subroutine is entered by a jump, and provision is made to return—to jump back to the proper point in the main routine at the end of the subroutine.

> **Dynamic subroutine** A subroutine which involves parameters, such as decimal-point position or item size, from which a relatively coded subroutine

is derived. The computer itself is expected to adjust or generate the subroutine according to the parametric values chosen.

Library subroutine (Standard subroutine) A member of a subroutine library.

Open subroutine A subroutine inserted directly into the linear operational sequence, not entered by a jump. Such a subroutine must be recopied at each point where it is needed in a routine.

Static subroutine A subroutine which involves no parameters other than the addresses of the operands.

Substitute To replace an element of information by some other element of information.

Summarize To present briefly, especially replacement of a list of detail items by totals of the items or other summary information.

Summary punch Punch Card Machines. A punch card machine which may be attached by a many-wire cable to another machine (for example, a tabulator), and which will punch out on a card the information produced or calculated or summarized by the other machine.

Summary Punching The automatic conversion into punched-hole form of information developed by the accounting machine.

Supervisory system One or more executive routines or a system of such routines for facilitating operating, scheduling, and monitoring of a computer center.

Swap (tape, servo) When a tape file contains enough information to require more than one tape on which to record the information, it is often the practice to allocate two tape handlers, rather than one, to the file. The first tape in the file is mounted on one handler; the second, on the other. Then, when the first tape is completely used, the computer can immediately start using the second tape on the other handler while the handler first used is rewinding the first tape and subsequently having this rewound tape dismounted and the third tape in the file mounted. When the second tape is completed, the computer reverts to using the first handler while the second is being rewound and serviced. And so on until all tapes in the file have been used. This process is known as a tape swap, also as servo (Sperry Rand users) swap.

Switch An instruction set to more than one state by the program.

Symbolic address A label chosen for the convenience of the programmer to identify a particular word, function or other information in a routine, independent of the location of the information, within the routine. Also called "floating address."

Symbolic coding Broadly, any coding system in which symbols other than machine addresses are used. The term is used, unfortunately perhaps, to refer to two rather different types of coding: (1) a relative coding system in which machine instruction are written, but in a much freer form than actual instructions. (2) A method of coding in which addresses are represented by arbitrary symbols which bear no absolute or relative relationship to actual memory locations; in fact, the coding itself may bear little resemblance to machine language.

System (1) An assembly of components united by some form of regulated interaction to form an organized whole. (2) A collection of operations and procedures, men and machines, by which business activity is carried on. (3) Any purposeful organization of resources or elements.

System analysis The analysis of a business activity to determine precisely what must be accomplished and how. (*See also* **System.**)

Systems test The running of the whole system of runs making up a data processing application against test data; actually, a complete simulation of the actual running system for purposes of testing out the adequacy of the system.

Table look-up The process of extracting from a table the additional information associated with a particular field in the table.

Tabulate The accumulation of a family of separate totals simultaneously. Each total is usually controlled by a different key. Whenever the key changes (a total break) the completed total is usually printed and also added into the next higher level of totals. The completed total packet is then reset to zero for the accumulation on the next key value.

Tabulator A machine which reads information from one medium, e.g., cards, paper tape, magnetic tape, etc., and produces lists, tables, and totals on separate forms or continuous paper.

Tag (also Tab) A unit of information, whose composition differs from that of other members of the set so that it can be used as a marker or label; a sentinel.

Takedown Those actions performed at the end of an equipment operating cycle to prepare the equipment for the next setup. For example, to remove the tapes from the tape handlers at the end of a computer run is a "takedown" procedure.

Takedown time The time required to take down a piece of equipment.

Tape Magnetic tape or punched paper tape, sometimes other kinds of tape such as adding machine tape or paper loops used to control vertical formatting of printers or plastic tapes used to control automatic typewriters.

Tape feed A mechanism which will feed tape to be read or sensed by the machine.

Tape file A sequential set of tape records.

Tape limited A computer application or run in which the time for tape reading and writing exceeds the calculating time. This definition has significance only for computers which permit overlap or simultaneity of tape operations with computation. (*See also* **Input limited, Output limited.**)

Tape swap *See* **Swap.**

Temporary storage Internal storage locations reserved for intermediate and partial results.

Test data Data developed specifically to test the adequacy of a computer run or system. The data may be fabricated from scratch, or it may be actual data that has been taken from previous company operation and edited to make it more useful for its purpose.

Time, idle Time in which machine is believed to be in good operating condition and attended by service engineers but not in use on problems. To verify that the machine is in good operating condition, machine tests of the diagnostic variety may be run.

Time, production Good computing time, including occasional duplication of one case for a check or rerunning of the test run. Also, duplication requested by the sponsor; any reruns caused by misinformation or bad data supplied by sponsor. Error studies using different intervals, convergence criteria, etc.

Track In a serial magnetic storage element, a single path containing a set of pulses.

Trailer Record which follows a header. (*See also* **Header.**)

Transaction Record of an event or entity.

Transaction file A file containing current information relating to a data processing activity; usually used to update a master file.

Transcribe To copy, with or without translating, from one storage medium to another.

Transfer To copy, exchange, read, record, store, transmit, transport, or write data; to change control; to jump to another location.

Transform To change information in structure or composition without altering the meaning or value; to normalize, edit, or substitute.

Translate To change information (e.g., problem statements in pseudocode, data, or coding) from one language to another without significantly affecting the meaning.

Transmit To send data from one place to another.

Troubleshoot To debug.

Truncate To drop digits of a number of terms of a series thus lessening precision, e.g., the number 3.14159265 is truncated to five figures in 3.1415, whereas one may round off to 3.1416.

Unpack To decompose packed information into a sequence of separate words of elements. (*See also* **Pack.**)

Update To apply all current changes, addition, and deletions to a file.

Utility routine A standard routine, especially service routine. (*See also* **Routine.**)

Validate Establish validity.

Validity Correctness; especially, the degree of the closeness by which iterated results approach the desired correct result. Also, approval of data by responsible accounting or other management authority.

Verifier A device on which a manual transcription can be verified by comparing a retranscription with it character by character as it is being retranscribed.

Verify To check a data transfer or transcription, especially those involving manual processes.

Visible file The systematic arrangement of a group of forms or cards so that the data placed on the margin serve as an index which the user can see without thumbing through the file.

Volume statistics Pertinent facts concerning the nature and level of operations of an area under consideration expressed in numbers, e.g., number of vendors, number of purchase orders placed, number of different items, orders, etc., plus subclassifications of these data to obtain a clearer insight into the pattern of the operations.

Word A set of characters which occupies one storage location and is treated by the computer circuits as a unit and transported as such. Ordinarily a word is treated by the control unit as an instruction, and by the arithmetic unit as a quantity. Word lengths are fixed or variable depending on the particular computer.

Word time Especially in reference to words stored serially, the time required to transport one word from one storage device to another. (*See also* **Access time**.)

Work cycle A series or sequence of elements which are required to perform a task or yield a unit of production and which recur in like order for each task or unit of production. Upon completion of the last element of the task, the first of the series is started again for the succeeding task or unit of production.

Work distribution chart An inventory of duties and personnel in the area under survey, showing the relationship of each duty performed by each individual to the appropriate activity (function) together with a brief indication of volume of occurrences and estimated time to perform each duty.

Working storage A portion of the internal storage reserved for data upon which operations are currently being performed, and for intermediate and partial results, like a work sheet in pencil and paper calculation.

Work load The assigned amount of work to be performed in a given period.

Write (1) To transfer information to an output medium; (2) to copy, usually from internal storage to external storage; (3) to record information in a register, location, or other storage device or medium.

Write To copy usually from internal storage to buffer storage or to an output device or auxiliary storage, or from buffer storage to an output device or auxiliary storage. (*See also* **Read**.)

Zero suppression The elimination of nonsignificant zeros to the left of the integral part of a quantity before printing operations are initiated; a part of editing.

Zone (1) Punch Cards. Any of the three top positions 12, 11, and 0. In these zone positions a second punch can be inserted, so that with punches in the remaining positions 1 to 9, enough two-punch combinations are obtained to represent alphabetic characters. (2) That portion of a character code which is used with the numeric coding to represent non-numeric information. (3) A portion of internal storage allocated for a particular purpose.

BIBLIOGRAPHY

Alexander, L. T., and A. Cooperband, "A Laboratory Model for Systems Research: A Terminal Air Traffic Control System," Western Management Sciences Institute, University of California at Los Angeles, Report TM-639 (September 5, 1961), 16 pp.

Alt, F. L., *Electronic Digital Computers,* Academic Press, New York, 1958, x + 336 pp.

Baer, R. M., and P. Brock, "Natural Sorting," *Journal SIAM,* Vol. 10, No. 2, 284–304 (June 1962).

Betz, B. K., and W. C. Carter, "New Merge Sorting Techniques," *Proceedings ACM Conference* (September 1959).

Blair, C. R., "A Program for Correcting Spelling Errors," *Information and Control* Vol. 3, 60–67 (March 1960).

Blumenthal, S., "A Dual Master File System for a Tape Processing Computer," *Journal, ACM,* Vol. 5, No. 4, 319–327 (October 1958).

Boardman, L., "The Effect of Electronic Data Processing on Audit Procedures," *System and Procedures Magazine* (January–February 1961).

Boyd, A. G., "A General Approach to Information Systems Design," *Control Engineering,* 100–104 (August 1962).

Brillouin, L., *Science and Information Theory,* second edition, Academic Press, New York, January 1962, 351 pp.

Brown, D. T., "Error Detecting and Correcting Binary Codes for Arithmetic Operations," *IRE Transactions on Electronic Computers,* Vol. EC-9, 333–337 (September 1960).

Brouse, R. A., "The Data Sequenced Computer," Western Management Science Institute, University of California at Los Angeles, Research Paper TM-562 (December 1960), 26 pp.

Casey, R. S., and J. W. Perry, *Punched Cards: Their Application to Science and Industry,* Reinhold Publishing Publishing Co., New York, 1951.

Chapin, N., *Programming Computers for Business Applications,* McGraw-Hill Book Co., New York, 1961, 275 pp.

Conway, B., *Programming Electronic Computers,* Controllers Institute Foundation, 1959.

Davidson, J. F., *Programming for Digital Computers,* Gordon and Breach, Science Publishers Inc., New York, 1961, 186 pp.

De Jong, J. H., "COBOL, Computer Language of the Future," *Data Processing,* Vol. 2, No. 9, 9–12 (October 1960).

de Paula, F. C., "Problems of Auditing Computing Data," *Computer Journal,* Vol. 3, 11–14 (April 1960).

Dickey, E. R., "Put Integrity into Business Data," *Systems and Procedures Journal,* 32–37 (July–August 1962).

Donegan, A. J., "Programming Real-Time Process Control Computers," *I.S.A. Journal,* Vol. 8, 46–49 (November 1961).

Dunleavy, J. F., "Management's Intelligence System," *Systems Magazine,* 9 (December 1952).

Evans, O. Y., "Advanced Analysis Method for Integrated Electronic Data Processing," IBM form F20-8047, IBM Corporation, 1960, 30 pp.

Gilstad, R. L., "Polyphase Merge Sorting, an Advanced Technique," *Proceedings, EJCC,* New York (December 1960).

Goldsmith, L. D., "Nonbanking Applications of Character Sensing," NMAA Data Processing, *1960 Proceedings,* 177–180.

Gottleib, C., "General Purpose Programming for Business Applications," in *Advances in Computers,* Vol. 1, Academic Press, New York, 1960, 316 pp.

Gottleib, C., and J. N. Hume, *High Speed Data Processing,* McGraw-Hill Book Co., New York 1958, xi + 338 pp.

Grabbe, E. M., "Handbook of Automation, Computation, and Control: Computers and Data Processing (Volume 2)," John Wiley and Sons, New York, 1959, 1,020 pp.

Graese, C. E., "Auditing Electronically Processed Data," *Management Controls,* Marwick, & Mitchell Co. (June 1962).

Graham, J. W., and D. W. Sprott, "Processing Magnetic Tape Files with Variable Blocks," *Communications ACM,* Vol. 4, 555–557 (December 1961).

Gregory, R. H., "Computers and Accounting Systems; a Bibliography," *Accounting Review,* Vol. 31, No. 2, 278–285 (April 1956).

Gregory, R. H., and R. L. Van Horn, *Automatic Data Processing: Principles and Procedures,* Wadsworth Publishing Co., San Francisco, 1960, 705 pp.

Grems, M., "A Card Format for Reference Files in Information Processing," *Communications ACM,* Vol. 4, No. 2, 90-98 (February 1961).

Grody, C. E., *The Auditor Encounters Computers,* New York Life Insurance Co., New York, 1957, 28 pp.

Gruenberger, F., *Diagrams in Punched Card Computing,* University of Wisconsin Press, Madison, 1954.

Hein, L. W., *An Introduction to Electronic Data Processing for Business,* D. Van Nostrand, Princeton, New Jersey, 1961, 300 pp.

Homer, E. D., "A Generalized Model for Analyzing Management Information Systems," *Management Science,* Vol. 8, No. 4, 500–515 (July 1962).

IBM Corporation, "Data Processing Bibliography (Second Revision)," IBM form J20-8014-2 (March 1961), IBM Data Processing Division, White Plains, New York.

——, "Glossary for Information Processing," IBM form C20-8089, 1962, IBM Data Processing Division, White Plains, New York.

——, "Flow Charting and Block Diagramming Techniques," IBM form C20-8008, 1959.

——, "The COBOL Translator," October 1960.

——, "Accounting and Cost Finding for the Printing Industry," IBM form E20-8024, 1960.

Isaac, E. J., and R. C. Singleton, "Sorting by Address Calculation," Stanford Research Institute Report, Stanford, California (September 1955).

Jeenel, J., *Programming for Digital Computers*, McGraw-Hill Book Co., Inc., New York, 1959, xi + 517 pp.

Johnson, E. A., *Accounting Systems in Modern Business*, McGraw-Hill Book Co., Inc., New York, 1959, 453 pp.

Kaufman, F., *Electronic Data Processing and Auditing*, Ronald Press, New York, 1961, viii + 180 pp.

Kellogg, M. G., "Preparing the Office Manual," *American Management Association Research Study No. 36*, New York, 1959, 72 pp.

Kushner, A., "Simplified Flow Charting," *Business Automation*, 16–23 (August 1962).

Laden, H. N., "Making a Computer Pay," *Paperwork Simplification*, Standard Register Co., Dayton, Ohio, No. 42, 12–17 (June 1956).

———, "Getting Acceptance of Computer Processed Results," *Journal National Machine Accountants Association*, Vol. 8, No. 4, 10–11, 33 (April 1957).

———, "Experience Points the Way," *Systems Magazine*, Vol. 21, No. 5, 17–18 (September 1957).

———, "Automatic Programming—Fact or Fancy," *Management and Business Automation*, 29–35, 45 (February 1959).

———, "Total Systems Concept," *Ideas for Management 1961*, Vol. 2, 22–27, Systems and Procedures Association.

Lazzaro, V., *Systems and Procedures: A Handbook for Business and Industry*, Prentice-Hall Inc., Englewood Cliffs, New Jersey, 1959, 464 pp.

Ledley, R. S., *Programming and Utilizing Digital Computers*, McGraw-Hill Book Co., Inc., New York, 1962, 592 pp.

Lee, T., D. McCracken, and H. Weiss, *Programming Business Computers*, John Wiley and Sons, New York, 1959, xvii + 510 pp.

Lum, M. D., "A Comparison of an Error-Correcting Eight-Unit Code with Other Teleprinter Codes for Binary Transmission and Ternary Reception," Aeronautical Research Laboratory, Wright-Patterson Air Force Base, Dayton, Ohio (January 1959) 45 pp; Order PB 151659 from Office of Technical Services, Washington 25, D.C.

Marien, R., "Forms Design for the IBM 1403," *Data Processing*, 24 (June 1962).

McCracken, D. D., "Object Program Efficiency," *Datamation*, 32 (June 1962).

McKenney, J. L., "Simultaneous Multiprogramming of Electronic Computers," Doctoral dissertation, UCLA Department of Business Administration (1960). Also Management Sciences Research Project Report 69.

Mittman, B., and A. Ungar, *Computer Applications, Proceedings of the 1960 Computer Applications Symposium, Armour Research Foundation, Illinois Institute of Technology*, Macmillan Co., New York.

Optner, S. L., *Systems Analysis for Business Management*, Prentice-Hall Inc., Englewood Cliffs, New Jersey, xii + 276 pp.

OEEC, "Integrated Data Processing and Computers," Organization for European Economic Cooperation, European Productivity Agency, EPA Project 6/02B, (November 1960), 78 pp.

Price Waterhouse & Co., "The Auditor Encounters Electronic Data Processing," IBM Corporation, New York, IBM form F20-8057, 24 pp.

———, "In-Line Electronic Accounting, Internal Control and Audit Trail," IBM Corporation, New York, IBM form F20-2019, 9 pp.

Sperry Rand Corporation, "Electronic Data Processing for the Line Official," Univac Publication UT-2448, 1960, iv + 86 pp., Univac Division, New York.

Sperry Rand Corporation, "COBOL Programmer's Guide, *Univac III Technical Bulletin U-3389* (April 1962) Univac Division, New York.

Sprague, R. E., *Electronic Business Systems.* Ronald Press, New York, 1962, 190 pp.

Statland, N., and G. Webster, "Instant Data Processing," *Business Automation,* 34–38 (June 1962).

Statland, N., and G. Webster, "Instant Data Processing," *Business Automation,* 61–65 (August 1962).

Thompson, T. R., "Problems of Auditing Computing Data," *Computer Journal,* Vol. 3, 10–11 (April 1960).

Thornley, J. M., "Good Times on Computers," *Automatic Data Processing,* 26–28 (September 1960).

Trombly, R. N., "Auditing through EDP Equipment," *NAA Bulletin,* 67–72 (May 1961).

United Nations, *Handbook on Data Processing Methods,* Food and Agriculture Organization, United Nations, Rome, 1951, vi + 111 pp.

Williams, R. P., "File Arrangement," *Proceedings, Univac Users Conference* (February 25–26, 1960); available from Sperry Rand Corp., Univac Division, New York

——, "Automatic Data Processing Seminar for Federal Executives," Graduate School, U.S. Department of Agriculture, Washington 25, D.C., 262 pp.

——, "Bibliography for the Management Analyst," *NAVSANDA Publication 405,* Library, Bureau of Supplies and Accounts, Navy Department, Washington 25, D.C. (September 1961), ii + 144 pp.

——, "Classification and Coding Techniques to Facilitate Accounting Operations," Research Series No. 3, National Association of Accountants, New York, 1959, 52 pp.

——, "Forms Considerations in SDA (Source Data Automation)," *Navy Management Review* 8–10 (March 1960).

—— "Guide for Auditing Automatic Data Processing Systems," Department of the Air Force Comptroller, Washington 25, D.C. (1961).

——, "How to Beat the Forms Problem in High Speed Printers," Office Equipment and Methods, 23–25 (March 1959)

——, "NOMA Glossary of Automation Terms," National Office Management Association, Willow Grove, Pennsylvania (1958).

——, "Random Access vs. Sequenced Processing," *Navy Management Review,* 4–8 (February 1959).

——, "Random Access vs. Serial Access," *Automatic Data Processing,* 20–24, 56–57 (October 1961).

——, "Source Data Automation Equipment Guide," NAVEXOS P-2318, Navy Management Office, Data Processing Systems Division, Department of the Navy, Washington 25, D.C. (March 1961).

——, "Data Communications Terminal Equipment Guide," NAVEXOS P-2414, Navy Management Office, Data Processing Systems Division, Department of the Navy, Washington 25, D.C. (June 1962).

INDEX